James in the Suburbs

A Disorderly Parable of the Epistle of James

APRIL LOVE-FORDHAM

With a foreword by
STEPHEN A. HAYNER

RESOURCE *Publications* · Eugene, Oregon

Resource Publications
An Imprint of Wipf and Stock Publishers
199 W. 8th Ave., Suite 3
Eugene, OR 97401

www.wipfandstock.com

ISBN 13: 978-1-62564-677-4

Manufactured in the U.S.A.   08/01/2014

Unless otherwise noted, all biblical quotations are taken from the Holy Bible, New Revised Standard Version (NRSV), copyright © 1991, 1994 Oxford University Press, Inc.

To Steve, who says I am perfect,
To Brent, who says I am random and spontaneous,
To Kit, who says my brain is *this* big, and
To Sophie, who knows the truth.
You are my heroes and best friends. I love you.

Almighty God, the fountain of all wisdom:

Enlighten by your Holy Spirit those who teach and those who learn,

That, rejoicing in the knowledge of your truth,

They may worship you and serve you from generation to generation;

Through Jesus Christ our Lord,

Who lives and reigns with you and the Holy Spirit, one God,

Forever and ever. Amen.

—*THE BOOK OF COMMON PRAYER*, P. 261

Contents

Foreword

For years I had a cartoon pinned to the bulletin board over my desk with the caption, "It's not the parts of the Bible that are unclear that bother me, it's the parts that are just a little too clear!" Studying the Bible frequently has this sort of effect. It can jolt us to attention, call our focus back to the truth, and reorient our lives. Many have discovered that studying the Bible can be a dangerous thing—that is if you are one who prefers to live life without the meddling inconvenience of God's light being shined in the corners.

If you do decide to take the risk of exploring what the Bible might have to say, two important steps must be followed.

The first is that it you must actually take the time to study it. Studying the Bible requires some work, because these are ancient texts after all. While it is often surprising how contemporary the scriptures seem to be—describing human interactions and emotions that are all too familiar to us—this is still literature that originated in another time, place, and culture. There is plenty in the Bible that feels strange to us when read through the lens of modern culture and contemporary experience. To understand the Bible requires a certain breadth of knowledge concerning cultural background, historical setting, and linguistic peculiarities. It also requires a feel for the context of the whole Bible and for how the Church has come to interpret it over the centuries.

Many casual readers soon give up, or they defer to those whom they see as experts. My library shelves are crammed with books, which claim to interpret accurately what the Bible says. Over the years, I have learned a great deal from both Bible teachers and preachers and from books about the Bible. But that isn't the end to what the Bible might want to teach.

Because the Holy Spirit is also at work in the teaching process, it is important to study the Bible directly. This can be done as individuals or in groups. When we study the Bible alone, we are given the opportunity to focus on those particulars to which we are personally drawn, and even to follow what at first may seem like rabbit trails of interest and application. When we study the Bible with a group, we have that rare opportunity of seeing through the eyes and experiences of others, often discovering things that we wouldn't have discovered alone. Our own experiences can open the doors to insight, but also blind us to seeing what can only be seen through the lens of a different experience or culture.

The Apostle Paul reminds his young protégé, Timothy, "All scripture is inspired by God and is useful for teaching, for reproof, for correction, and for training in righteousness, so that everyone who belongs to God may be proficient, equipped for every good work."[1] And he encourages him by saying: "Do your best to present yourself to God as one approved by him, a worker who has no need to be ashamed, rightly explaining the word of truth."[2]

So making it a discipline to study the Bible diligently is the first step. The second step if we truly want to be transformed by the Scriptures and the Holy Spirit is to take steps to apply what we discover to our attitudes and behaviors. This is actually the harder part of the process. It is, in fact, easily and often avoided.

But the scriptures are clear. Jesus says at the end of the Sermon on the Mount, "Everyone then who hears these words of mine and acts on them will be like a wise man who built his house on rock."[3] Note that it is not merely hearing God's word or even understanding it that is the foundation for a well-grounded life. Rather, Jesus says that the wise person takes steps to align his or her life with the truth that is being learned. And on his last night with the disciples before Jesus went to the cross, Jesus told his follow- ers, "If you know these things, you are blessed if you do them."[4]

Christians over the centuries have been better at knowing than at do- ing. Many churches aren't very helpful at this point, because leaders assume that if they just teach people something that they will immediately under- stand what they are to do, and will want to be obedient. But this "know it—do it" pattern often does little more than leave people smarter but not very transformed.

It is this concern for transformation that is at the heart of Dr. April Love-Fordham's book. You are about to enter into a journey which com- bines biblical commentary on the Letter of James with parable—the account of an intriguing group of suburban Christians who agree to do a Bible study

1. 2 Tim 3:16–17.
2. 2 Tim 2:15.
3. Matt 7:24.
4. John 13:17.

together. This is the story of how the Holy Spirit can use a study to change people and to help them to take new steps of self-discovery and faith. It is a journey of wonder and sometimes discomfort, not only into what James has to say, but into how his words can transform human lives when we take the time to listen deeply both to the text and to one another. Get ready to dive into the book of James, but also to learn how Bible study can transform your life!

Dr. Stephen A. Hayner
President of Columbia Theological Seminary
Teaching Elder in the Presbyterian Church (USA)
Former President of InterVarsity

Preface

Jesus used parables—stories of everyday people—to illustrate spiritual truths. This book is a story of everyday people that illustrates the spiritual truths found the Epistle of James. If you read this book, you will walk away with both a story that will challenge you, and a thorough understanding of the Epistle of James. There is a study guide in chapter 29 designed both for groups who read the book together and for individuals.

This parable is a true story in the sense that it is a combination of embellished facts. All names, dates, places, events, and details have been changed, invented, and altered for literary effect. The reader should not consider this parable to be about any particular part of my life or any particular community of people. It is a work of literature.

The idea of writing this book came to me as I completed a commentary on the Epistle of James. Quite frankly, afterward, I found it boring to read facts and theories about the epistle—even if they were of my own scholarly effort. I wanted my commentary to grab the readers, immediately relate to their lives, and open the door for the teachings of James to transform them. Having written my doctoral thesis on using biblical storytelling to initiate spiritual transformation, I decided to employ what I had learned to write a unique parable/commentary.[1] My prayer is that the Holy Spirit will use this book to transform not only the life of the suburban church, but churches everywhere.

---

1. Love-Fordham, "Using Biblical Storytelling in Pastoral Care," 110–13.

Acknowledgments

I would gratefully like to acknowledge the following people who have played significant roles in the writing of this book:

Steve Fordham, who loved me, encouraged me, and cheerfully bank-rolled our lives the months I spent writing this book. Moreover, who took me hiking in Italy, biking in France, and mountain climbing in the Alps when I needed a break. He is simply the best husband ever.

Brent Fordham, who spent mornings in the park with me during his summer break from seminary, researching, editing, and giving me invaluable advice for this book. His name really should be on the cover as a co-author. However, it turns out that co-authoring a book with your mother isn't as cool as it might sound.

Kit Fordham, who made practical for me the lessons of James by living them out better than anyone I know and by giving me outstanding practical advice. This book would not be as relevant to our culture without him. He also did a great thing in bringing the wonderful Chanelle Gallagher into our lives.

Sharon Fordham, who faithfully made thoughtful and insightful suggestions. She has been tireless in reading the manuscript through several iterations while faithfully living out the teachings of Jesus in the suburbs.

Becky Mathews Beal, for being an editor, advisor, and mentor. She has worked so hard and has been such an enormous blessing to me both working on this book together, but also every Thursday night tutoring high-risk boys and girls together. She is a shining example to me!

The congregations of the churches I pastored. To Calvary Presbyterian, where we explored James together in a racially and economically diverse setting; to Oak Mountain Presbyterian, where I first understood how the teachings of James could dramatically upset the status quo; and to the women of North Avenue Presbyterian, who encouraged my writing and teaching ministry, especially Diane Summers Baier, Carolyn Christ, Wrenda Crain, Maureen Hill, Sara Anne Johnson, and Keziah Kamau.

The parishioners, clergy, and staff at Saint David's Episcopal Church, who generously and cheerfully serve God and others. Father Ken Swanson, who not only taught me how to pray, but *to* pray. I have never met a group of people who live in a greater expectation of God showing up.

Bishop Malcolm Smith, whose excellent teachings first made me interested in studying Scripture.

Dr. Steve Hayner, who walked with me through seminary, preached at my installation, told me I could write, and wrote the foreword for this book. Most importantly, he lives out the love of Christ in all that he does.

The wonderful faculty of Columbia Theological Seminary, who practiced great patience as I hammered them with my unending questions, especially Dr. Rodger Nishioka and then-visiting professor Dr. Bill Campbell.

Dr. Haddon Robinson, Dr. David Currie, and Dr. Kenneth Swetland, who taught me how to preach and write a dissertation, then granted me a doctorate.

The fabulous team at Wipf and Stock Publishers—especially Matthew Wimer—for taking a chance on an inexperienced writer and bringing this work into print.

To my heroes whose actions prove that the life James describes is possible: Jimmy Carter, Shane Claiborne, Katie Davis, Johnathan Daniels, Clarence Jordan, Martin Luther King Jr., Sara Miles, Frances Perkins, Becca Stevens, William Stringfellow, Mother Teresa, Richard Twiss, and Jonathan Wilson-Hargrove. For those of you still living, please keep on being the hands and feet of Jesus. Do not let me down!

My parents, whose greatest gift to me is that they have prayed for me every day of my life.

And finally, to Sophie, my enormous black and white spotted Great Dane, who sat by my desk day after day watching me write, who would stand nose to nose with me begging for a walk as I sat at my keyboard, and who would nuzzle her nose between my keyboard and hands when I ignored her. You have been a good friend.

1

You've Been Warned

What follows is just one of the finales of a disorderly parable of the Holy Spirit breathing life into the dead faith of the men and women of a suburban church. The parable meanders through the teachings of the Epistle of James meddling endlessly in the culture of the wealthy and middle class churchgoer. The men and women whose lives unfold in it are forever changed. Therefore, consider this a warning: I guarantee the Holy Spirit wants to meddle in your life too.

Be prepared.

My cell phone erupted into the serene silence of the sanctuary echoing from the ceiling to the crucifix and right back at me. The bubblegum-country ringtone, "This One Is for the Girls," made me smile. It was a fitting tribute to girls everywhere and an encouragement for them to dream big. Isabella Perez, the teenage all-American Latina beauty, had installed the ringtone on my smart phone just the week before. Bubblegum-country might not be the trending sound most Latina girls her age were attracted to, but it had become the official theme song for *Sueños*, the afterschool club for Latina girls now going on its fifth year at our church. *Sueños* meant dreams—and these girls had dreams in spades! The song had permanently attached itself to us when Helen, one of the founders of *Sueños*, in her usual bebopping way, had sung it to the girls one afternoon while dancing her way through clean up. The song had stuck and each class of girls at *Sueños* taught it to the next class. The girls had even choreographed an official *Sueños* line dance to which my husband and I had danced, along with parents and others, at multiple celebrations over the years. So when Isabella asked for my phone to install it, how could I say no?

Sueños's goal was to equip and support the physical, spiritual, and educational needs of Latina girls from preteen into womanhood. It was the brainchild of Olivia and Helen, two very unlikely candidates to lead such a ministry. In fact, they were the most unlikely candidates to lead any ministry. Both, in their own way, had been living the suburban dream with accomplished high-paying careers and children in tow. Until, during a study of the Epistle of James, the Holy Spirit took hold of their lives—and the lives of the other men and women in their study group—and turned them all inside out.

My thoughts jumped to the very first meeting of *Sueños*. Isabella had been only twelve then, and shy. She and her equally beautiful *mamá* had immigrated here illegally just a month before her birth, seventeen years ago. Her mother, who cleaned hotel rooms at the Hyatt in order to afford their tiny one-bedroom apartment in a good school district, had made sure Isabella didn't miss the first meeting. Little did Isabella and the four other young attendees know, Olivia and Helen were more anxious than the girls. Nevertheless, Olivia and Helen put on a great welcome. In truth, all they had to face the girls with was love and the unfailing faith that connecting with these girls was their destiny. They knew nothing about being a Latina pre-teenager growing up in America—nor would they pretend to. They were depending on the girls to teach them. Their Spanish was pathetic at best. Yet, this was no accident and no whim. The two of them knew they were called there to be the humble hands and feet of Jesus to these precious girls at high risk of experiencing violence, abuse, teenage pregnancy, and the ever-spinning cycle of poverty. Convinced that they were on God's mission, what more did they need than love?

I looked down at my phone to see who was calling me. It was Olivia.

"*Hola amiga*," I answered cheerfully.

My words echoed. I was alone in the sanctuary. I went there every Monday morning on the weeks when I would be preaching the following Sunday. I would read the lectionary Scripture and pray for the Holy Spirit to illuminate my sermon preparation that week. Then I would stay a little while meditating in the sunlight that filled the church.

"And to you!" I responded to Olivia's "*Buen día*." My Spanish was still not good and completely unnecessary for this phone call anyway. Olivia and I were as white bread as they came. No response followed, but I could tell the call was still active.

"Are you there?" I asked, confused.

No answer.

"Olivia?" I heard a catch in her breath. "Olivia, is everything okay?"

She could barely get out "Yes."

"Are you crying?" This was baffling, because professionally polished, cool-as-a-cucumber Olivia never ever cried.

"No," she claimed. We both knew she was lying. She followed her "No" quickly with a laugh. A really good laugh. The unearthly kind. The kind filled with overwhelming joy that can't be expressed in any other way. "I better call you back when I can get my words out," she half-whispered, half-choked into the phone.

Standing now and beginning to pace, I laughed, saying, "No way. Do not hang up. Breathe deep!"

She said okay and told me she was going to put me on mute for a second. I was amused to be able to hear her still. She was breathing in deeply and talking to herself at the same time. Then she would exhale with a high-pitched voice in rapid staccato syllables, "Be calm! Be calm! Be calm!" This was a priceless and humorous insight into the mind of Olivia. While I waited, I wandered from the pew down the aisle toward the crucifix, looking up at it and smiling. I asked God out loud, "What have you done now?"

Finally she spoke. "I had a phone call from the recruiter at Georgia Tech. Both Isabella and Luciana have been sent acceptance letters. And . . . are you ready for this . . . they are getting a combination of merit and need based scholarships!"

Looking back at the crucifix, I mouthed the words, "Thank you!"

It was happening. The dreams of these remarkable young women and their families were coming true. Furthermore, these girls were just the first-fruits. There were now more than a hundred girls and fifty volunteers at three churches across the city, with plans to expand to even more churches. The Holy Spirit's wisdom and power, as promised, had shown up time and time again. And it was obvious that God had no plans to stop.

Now, let's start at the beginning. The journey is important.

PART 1

The Journey to Servanthood

The Parable of the Good Samaritan—Dissecting the Priest

One morning, I ran into my pastor who said, "There was a man who was going down from the city to the suburbs, and fell into the hands of robbers, who stripped him, beat him, and went away, leaving him half dead. Now by coincidence, I was driving down that road; and when I saw him, I passed by on the other side."

I asked, "Why did you pass by on the other side without helping him?"

My pastor replied, "I could see the man needed healing, but I don't know how to heal."

—ADAPTED FROM LUKE 10:30–37

2

The Church in the Suburbs

All I longed to do was to open one of the old painted-shut office windows and let in some fresh air, but the windows would not budge. I pushed, pulled, and jiggled them side to side. I even took off one of my high-heeled shoes and thumped around their edges. Nothing. These shoes were worthless! I had not bought them because they felt good. They gave me blisters. I bought them because my ankles and feet were the only part of me exposed under my clerical robes. I wanted some part of me—even if it was just my feet—to look stylish and feminine. I stared at the shoes wondering if they were indeed inappropriate. The heels were awfully high.

But before I could decide, I hit the window with them one more time. Nothing. I gave up and stood near the window trying to satisfy myself with a draft of slightly cooler air, which I hoped would seep into my office from around the panes, if the wind would just kick up. Again, nothing—not even a bit of wind. Standing there, I could see below into the shadow-filled courtyard of the adjoining white clapboard church. The gloomy view seemed to confirm that the approaching holidays would be anything but cheery. Congregant after congregant had made appointments to see me that past week. Their grief, loneliness, and anxiety filled my tiny stuffy office. For some reason the week before Thanksgiving—like the week before Christmas—made their problems bigger and their burdens so much heavier than usual. I longed to be cheery, but these people had depressed me more and more as the week had gone on. If I was honest about this, and it should be noted that I didn't want to be honest about this, it wasn't really my congregants who had depressed me, it was my inability to cure their problems that I found so depressing. Somehow, I must have missed class the day they taught us how to do miracles in seminary.

We were having a heat wave. The leaves had turned, but the temperature hadn't dipped as much as it should. It was unseasonably warm in Atlanta and extra stuffy inside the church. Nevertheless, the heat wave hadn't stopped those of us in the suburbs from decorating with all the lights and glitter needed to make a spectacular showing of the holiday festivities. Typical of many of the suburbs surrounding Atlanta, the old center of town, usually designated "Main Street," had been restored with artsy boutiques and unique restaurants. The Church in the Suburbs sat on the corner of Church Street and Main. From the church office hallway, I could see across Main Street to the doors of flourishing establishments. There was a trio of singers dressed in black gabardine pants and tapestry jackets embellished with embroidered fall leaves. They stood in an open restaurant door loudly singing out the traditional Thanksgiving hymn "Come, Ye Thankful People, Come." Their music poured into the streets, beckoning "come inside" to those walking to lunch from the office park a few blocks away. I had to admit that the song was appealing, for it promised that all of our wants would be fulfilled. It promised a life of abundance and happiness that I could not conjure up for my hurting congregants. Smells of fresh baked Christmas cookies and hot chocolate from the bakery next door filled the air. I knew, because I caught a whiff every time the church doors opened.

As I walked closer to the window in the hall, my mood began to lighten as I glimpsed another angle of this suburban wonderland. The streets of suburbia on that Friday afternoon were nothing short of idyllic. Expensive late-model sports cars, SUVs, and well-dressed lunch goers littered the street. Even though the air didn't have the nip of the approaching winter, I had no problem pretending that snow was just about to cover the ground, making way in the coming weeks for Santa's sleigh to land with some delightful Christmas presents wrapped up in bows and shiny paper. I wondered how long it would take someone to notice if I were to disappear from my office. A moment strolling down Main Street—just a few precious moments of escape—would have made me feel like a new person.

Before I could run from the dreary church building into the cheerful Friday afternoon, Joe Norman walked into my office without speaking a word. I hadn't expected him, but he wasn't the type who would ever make an appointment. Scheduling an appointment would be admitting that he needed to talk with someone. Joe was a self-made man who had proudly pulled himself up by his own bootstraps. He wasn't going to start being needy now. So instead of making an appointment, he dropped by between the many appointments of his own and entered my office as if he worked in the room next door and was just passing by on his way to the water cooler.

Joe always made me feel uneasy. I think it was the egocentricity that permeated him that bothered me the most. Seeing me in the hallway, he held out a lanky arm to shake my hand. Taking his hand, I looked up into his eyes. He looked away. Today he looked even older than his seventy years. His six-foot-four inch frame, deeply receding hairline, and his tanned face covered with the appropriate wrinkles served to solidify the fact that he was a man of great accomplishments—a man who demanded that you see him as important and stately. Anyone who failed to comply did so at his or her own peril.

For more than three decades, he had been an entrepreneur, building a worldwide engineering company headquartered in the business park a few blocks away from The Church in the Suburbs. He was a mover and shaker not just in Atlanta, but also around the world. He knew it—to the point of being narcissistic. The newly formed deep circles under his eyes made me suspect that he was struggling with memories of his wife, Annie. Annie had suddenly found out she had cancer two years ago and within a month was gone. I think she may have been the only person in the world for whom Joe could feel empathy and compassion. His reputation for having nothing but contempt for others and readily taking advantage of them was widely known. Although Joe could be charming, it was shallow and superficial. One would think that as uncomfortable as he made me feel, I would have hidden from him, but instead, I found him curious. I actually enjoyed observing him. It was a challenge to try and understand how someone could be so successful in business, yet be so antisocial.

Joe sat down on my small yellow couch, still not looking at me, and stared out the window behind me. He wouldn't normally confide in anyone, and especially not a woman. Moreover, he wasn't going to confide in me now. However, I had been friends with his wife. By talking with me—even small talk—it somehow kept her memory alive a little longer and eased the pain for him. I could tell that his sorrow and loneliness were fresher than the day she had died. Asking how Joe was doing would be an intrusion, so after sitting for a moment in silence, I motioned toward the tie he was wearing and said, "I remember when Annie bought that tie for you. We had gone to lunch at the mall and she saw it in the window of one of the stores."

It was a hideous tie. Cheap and covered with machine embroidered golden retrievers wagging their tails and fetching red balls. It was hardly a tie that a corporate giant would wear. Annie knew this and so did I, which made watching Annie buy it for Joe all the more fun. Annie had it wrapped in serious gift-wrap and gave it to him, swearing me to secrecy that the gift was a joke. We both knew he'd hate it, but wear it anyway because Annie was the one person in this world he adored. It was his way of showing her he loved her. Sure enough, he had shown up the next Sunday morning for church with Annie by his side. Annie was smiling mischievously when I caught her eye. Then with one hand hiding the other from Joe, she pointed at the tie quickly looking away from me while stifling a giggle.

At my mention of the tie, Joe looked up at me for the first time and smiled, finishing my thoughts with his version of the story. He told me how the golden retrievers embroidered on it looked like the dog Annie had given him for his sixty-fifth birthday. He loved that dog. In fact, now that Annie was gone, the dog may have been his only trusted friend. He went on to say the dog had treed a cat in the backyard the evening before. Our chitchat wandered around in this way, meandering through memories, until some unknown thing prompted Joe to leave. As he departed, he turned back to look at me and mumbled something that I couldn't make out. Then he lumbered down the hall to the water fountain and back to his office several blocks away.

3

Dream Catcher

My next appointment was waiting unobtrusively for me in the grimly lit jewel-toned reception area. Her wide-eyed glow looked completely out of place. It was Helen Callil, dressed in what I could only describe as classy boho attire. Her edgy short umbra red and black baby doll dress was meant for a teenager—as were her ankle high black boots. However, they suited Helen even though she was nearing thirty. Her shoulder-length brown hair and bright brown eyes were accented by triangle-shaped earrings dangling from her ears. The earrings bounced as she walked side by side with me back to my office. Helen loved to smile. Laughing at things you and I might consider mundane came very easy to her. Even so, the ease of her laughter shouldn't be confused with lack of intelligence. She was unassuming, that was for sure, but not dumb.

She had come to Atlanta from a small town in South Georgia right after high school to attend Agnes Scott, an exclusive all-girls school in Decatur. One fall day during her freshman year, after walking the few blocks from her dorm into quaint downtown Decatur, she had come across a natural foods store. She had been looking for something to combat her newly acquired Atlanta hay fever. The Lebanese man, about a decade older than her, who waited on her not only cured her hay fever, but over the months that followed romanced her into accepting a proposal to become his wife. Much to her racist parents' disappointment, she had left school and married him. She found his Lebanese heritage, his interest in the sometimes mystical alternative medicines, and his gregarious nature mesmerizing. He made up for her slight hint of shyness.

Together, over the next decade, they had built his one store business into twenty-some stores up and down the East Coast. A few years back, they had moved the store's headquarters and their home from downtown Decatur into the wealthy suburbs in an effort to help their twin toddlers escape from the perils of inner-city living within I-285, the interstate highway circling the perimeter of Atlanta. Building their company together had been fun, especially in the early days when Helen was essential to the expanding business. After the twins were born, she had left running the business to her husband. He was not only a good businessman, but he also tried to be a good husband and father—and most of the time succeeded. She had been a full-time stay-at-home mom for the last five years.

I relaxed at seeing her, thinking this might be a bright point in my day. However, as soon as my door was closed, her happy mask came off and tears began to flow. Helen was going through a bout of misery. Her twin daughters had started all-day kindergarten in the fall. Not only had their school attendance left time on her hands, but people, including her husband, kept asking her when she would be back at work. It wasn't that she did not like the business and it wasn't that she hadn't enjoyed helping her husband run it; it was simply that she wanted to concentrate on her kids.

To complicate things, she felt embarrassed. She was sure that her friends from the Atlanta Business Women's Association were talking about her at their power luncheons. They were probably looking down their noses at what they perceived as her inability to juggle both career and home. The fact of the matter was that she did have extra time on her hands while the kids were at school, and she wanted to fill her free time with something purposeful. She didn't want to be a tennis wife or spend her life at the clubhouse or attend art and fashion events. At the same time, she didn't know what she could do that would make a difference in the world. Her question to me was how she could have, in her words, "a ministry of her own" while the girls were in school.

As we talked, she alternated between pulling on her earrings and twisting an unusually large tourmaline ring around and around her finger. These nervous habits seemed to help her be brave enough to confide in me and ask me for some help. She had some definite ideas about what kind of ministry she was willing to do for God. Actually, it was more about what she wasn't willing to do for God than what she was willing to do. She didn't want to wade into anything too messy like visiting sick people or the elderly unless they were already friends of hers. She liked the idea of doing something with other mothers. She went on with a list of possibilities intermingled with a list of things too outside her comfort zone to take on. After listening for a while, I summarized with an affectionate laugh and said, "Simply put, you'd like to have a ministry where you could be nice to the nice." My summary was meant to playfully challenge her, not comfort her. To my surprise, it had the opposite effect.

She immediately quipped, "Exactly! I knew you would understand."

Her eyes suddenly dried up and began to sparkle again. She thought I had understood. She had no clue I was being facetious. I was hoping that her vision for a ministry, when put the way I had just framed it, would seem a little on the shallow side to her and start her thinking. However, she was giddy with anticipation that by the next time we talked I would have discovered a perfect ministry for her. While I wanted to help, I could tell there was more going on inside Helen than even Helen was aware.

I began to correct Helen's misconception of how I was going to help when half of Olivia Johnson's face peered in through the narrow but long rectangular window cut into my office door above the door handle. Upon seeing Helen sitting on my couch, Olivia cleared her throat in order to be noticed. Olivia was the brilliant and aggressive thirty-five-year-old Senior Vice President of Marketing at the engineering company Joe Norman ran. She had recently been given a big promotion and transferred from the Chicago office to the corporate headquarters in Atlanta, where she had promptly joined our church. The Church in the Suburbs was the first church she had ever attended in her life. She was an outsider in more ways than one. She had no idea of the rich Southern history and culture that she disregarded with almost every sentence she uttered. Her Yankee bluntness was not serving her well in the South. It certainly wasn't making her any friends, but I am not sure she wanted any either. Wrongly, I had enjoyed more than one humorous moment at her expense as she stumbled over herself in the presence of women who were graceful Southern belles, yet whose "grace" was somewhat scary even to me. Obviously not all the Southern belles at The Church in the Suburbs were scary, but there was a group of them who made Scarlet O'Hara look kind and gentle.

Selfishly, I was glad that this group of women was focusing their Southern hospitality on Olivia rather than me. Olivia had yet to figure out that when they followed her comments with "Bless your heart, Olivia," they weren't actually offering her a blessing. On the other hand, she didn't show these women the respect they deserved, either. They were mostly her age—mostly stay-at-home moms with successful professional husbands. Even though these women volunteered to teach her children's Sunday school classes and run a Vacation Bible School in the summers, Olivia didn't value their work. For Olivia, volunteer work had no value. It was the paycheck that mattered—and the bigger the paycheck, the better. Money bought you power. And power was important to Olivia.

In turn, the women were stunned at Olivia's sense of entitlement as she wedged herself and her kids into empty spaces on their families' pews on Sunday mornings and into the buffet line at church fellowship dinners on Wednesday nights. In particular, the way Olivia thought that she had a right to speak her mind on how things should be done ruffled more than one Southern belle's feathers. Olivia was looking down her nose at them, but they were looking down their noses at her, too. Probably most offensive was Olivia's attempt to make her way in a man's world. It wasn't that this group of women believed that women were the lesser of the species. It was that they believed women were actually the ruling sex and that men were meant to cater to their every need. Therefore, most of these women could not even begin to fathom what motivated Olivia. In their minds, she should be staying at home spending her husband's money on herself. It didn't help that Olivia was neither genteel nor friendly to any of us.

Yet, there was something deep inside her that I could not help but really like. It was something that I could identify with. Maybe it was simply the struggle to be accepted in a man's world. Or maybe it was the struggle to be heard. She was married to a wealthy lawyer almost twenty years older than herself. He was partly retired, but still spending most of his time in Chicago at his firm. The rumor was that their marriage was on the brink, but the catty rumors that flew through church halls were often questionable. Together Olivia and her husband had two elementary-aged kids who had moved with Olivia and their professionally trained English nanny to Atlanta.

Olivia was not the first of our congregants to be employed by the engineering company Joe Norman ran. What Olivia didn't know, because she was new in town, was that women didn't tend to do so well in the executive offices at Joe Norman's company. Despite his longtime active leadership at our church and within our increasingly progressive denomination, he was old fashioned and intolerant. Plainly put, he was sexist. He had a reputation for pushing women out the door of his company if they got too high on the corporate ladder. In fact, it was a running joke at Pastoral Care Committee Meetings that The Church in the Suburbs should look into forming a support group for the displaced women executives from Joe's company.

Helen heard Olivia clear her throat and turned around to see Olivia at my door. Then, still considering our session a great success, Helen thanked me with a relieved smile and got up to leave. I stood, too, and hurriedly explained that I wanted to give her some homework to do. I'd like her to spend fifteen minutes a day in meditative prayer letting the Holy Spirit work in her free-flowing thoughts and asking God to reveal her next steps to her. Then we would get together to talk again. I told her to write down anything the Holy Spirit revealed to her either while she was praying or as she was going through her day. She enthusiastically shook her head yes.

Even though my office door was not quite wide enough to accommodate both women at the same time, Olivia, in her usual harried manner, somehow managed to squeeze through the doorframe as Helen exited. It wasn't until Helen was in the hall and said, "Hi Olivia," that Olivia said hello back without even looking at Helen.

Olivia had made an appointment to come by my office. So in her high-heeled pumps (whose appropriateness rivaled my own shoes), high-cut pin-striped skirt, and low-cut silk blouse, she took no time with chitchat. Speaking as one with authority, she rapidly spewed out, "As another working female, I want you to be successful. Your success is my success!"

She said it stiffly, as if she had rehearsed it several times in the car on her way over. Her words hung in the air as I tried to make sense of them. She obviously felt awkward, too. She handled it by straightening her skirt, standing up taller, and forcing a smile, while offering, "How can I help you be successful?" It was obvious that she wasn't expecting a lot of conversation. She had something to accomplish with me and wanted to get her point across quickly.

I was tongue-tied. She was trying hard to communicate something to me. I could tell she was offering something she felt should please me, but I was not sure what she was offering. My lips began to curl into a smile as I watched her sit down and grab for a Kleenex from the box on top of my desk. She began peeling chewing gum from the heel of her left pump. As meticulously as she dressed and as rehearsed as she acted, there was always some kind of catch that brought her back down to earth and made her just like the rest of us. Her question, "How can I help you be successful?" hung in the air while I watched her pull the wad of blue bubble gum from her shoe into long strings that eventually stuck to the underside of the sleeve of the silk blouse covering her arm. It was a priceless sight to see; Olivia tangled in blue bubble gum.

I was distracted watching her, but also too confused to respond intelligently to her question. Eventually, she paused and looked at me for an answer. Knowing I needed to say something, I blurted out, "You could pray for my work here"—knowing even as I said it that praying for me was not what she had in mind. As I suspected, there was no doubt from the look of confusion on her face that this was obviously not the answer she had expected. But seeing the need to connect to me in order to accomplish her goal, she dropped the Kleenex into her lap, gave what I had just said a second thought, and then folded her hands together at chest level, closed her eyes and prayed out loud, "Dear God, please bless the Mother's work." She prayed several more sentences before ending with an "Amen." I had no idea what else she might have said in her prayer. She had lost me when she called me "Mother."

Oh my. Wrong on so many levels. First, I was embarrassed that I had made her feel she needed to pray out loud for me at that moment. Second, I was not "Mother."

"Olivia, thank you so much for the prayer. That was beautiful!" I let a few seconds pass and added, "But I am not a 'Mother.' Well, I have two sons, but I am not *that* kind of 'Mother.'"

"No? I thought you were ordained?" quizzed Olivia.

"I am, but I am . . ." before I could finish my sentence, Olivia abruptly finished it for me.

"A priest! You are a priest!" Turning red, but not daunted, she added a cutie-pie, "Ooops! So sorry," as she cocked her head to the side and forced a chuckle. She waved her hand as if to push away the foible and added, "I knew that. Of course. You are a priest!"

Something got the best of me and with a big smile, I blurted out, "Nooooo—I am a priestess!"

"Priestess? Seriously?" She scrunched her nose at me.

"Nooo!" I laughed. "In this denomination, we all just go by pastor or reverend or even just our first name is fine."

She stared at me with her head once again cocked sideways, looking at me out of just one eye. She wasn't used to joking around and didn't know what to think about having just been teased. She regained her composure, sat up straight, and asked the original question again, "So how can I help you be successful?"

The term "successful" was not one that I had heard used very often by pastors in describing their needs. Most of us are underpaid and overworked. We tend to lean toward vows of poverty and long work hours helping people in physical and spiritual need. At least we like to think of ourselves that way. The world would certainly think of success differently than most pastors would. All the same, her offer confused me. It took me some time to realize that she was simply networking with me, trying to establish herself as an important person with my interests in mind. She wanted to establish a relationship where we helped each other. This was to be purely professional though. I could tell she had no real desire to get to know me or for me to get to know her. My friendly questions about her and her family had always been answered with short obligatory answers rather than enthusiasm. She had never asked me anything at all about myself.

Once, when I asked her why she had chosen to join The Church in the Suburbs, she thought for a second before saying that she had wanted her kids to learn about God. It struck me that the answer was only sort of true. I suspected membership seemed more like a good career move rather than a desire to expose her children to Christianity. We have had several people over the years who we suspected joined the church hoping to impress Joe or even make friends with him. A few of his board members were also long-time congregants. Together, they had their own unintentional evangelism program gathering an unwanted entourage whenever word got out that they regularly attended a particular worship service. I thanked her for her vote of support, telling her that I looked forward to supporting her, too.

That did the trick. It was what she had come for. With that task done, she was immediately up out of her chair and headed toward the door. I shook my head and tried not to laugh as I watched her stumble over a loose piece of carpet in the hall. No matter how hard she pursued power and success, she was still just one of us and vulnerable to the same things to which we are all vulnerable—even the loose carpet in this neglected building.

These few appointments were mild considering the nature of some of the appointments that had come, one on top of another, day after day, since the holidays had begun. Some congregants were more grumpy than anything else. They had come complaining that the senior pastor's sermons were empty (often true), that the worship services at The Church in the Suburbs were becoming contemporary (also true), and that most of what was advertised about the good work the church was doing for the community was nothing but propaganda these days (sadly true). The grumpy ones felt stuck at The Church in the Suburbs because it was the only congregation they had ever known. Other congregants came to me for emotional or spiritual help. Help with son-in-laws who they couldn't get along with no matter how hard they tried. Help for depression and loneliness. Help for grief. Most of them had had these same problems for years now, finding temporary relief from time to time, but it never lasted.

Although each congregant was different with different circumstances, basically what they each were seeking from me, whether they realized it or not, was assurance of a God who cared about them and loved them. They wanted to know that God understood their problems, had power to give them peace, and would miraculously fix their situations, or at least make them a promise of a happy ending.

Most of them had heard the story of this God many times before and wanted to hear it again. Some had even made evangelistic work out of telling the story to others. They had felt reassured by this story in the past and it had kept them going. Although, in quiet moments, they wondered why the story didn't seem to stick—why it seemed to lose its ability to keep their spirits up over time. They wanted to recapture how it had first made them feel or how they perceived it had made others feel. They wanted assurance that things would get better—that someday God would come alongside them and take away their problems once and for all. They wanted me, and hence, God, to make them feel good. Moreover, they would have liked those good feelings to last this time. After all, wasn't that what faith was all about—trusting in God to take away our problems? And wasn't it true that if we had enough faith, we would find that peace and joy forever—not just for a few hours or days until we were reminded of our pain once again?

At any rate, their faith hadn't worked that way for them. They wondered why. Because I dearly loved them, this dilemma haunted me, too. I felt inadequate and often like a fake who sold sugar water tonic from a roadside stand, promising it would cure their ills. I tried to think of success cases—congregants who had overcome tragedies and disappointments to go on to live abundant lives. One person in particular came to mind: Liz Black. I jotted down a note to invite her to lunch to pick her brain after Christmas. There were too many counseling appointments and too many Christmas services to plan to do anything earlier.

4

The Group Forms

The Christmas holidays had finally come and gone. To my great relief, I found that the New Year felt invigorating and fresh. The congregation of The Church in the Suburbs had settled down from the stress of Thanksgiving and Christmas and all was well. Even so, I wasn't going to let go of my desire to find a better way to minister to my congregants. The note I had left myself before the holidays said to give Liz Black a call—so I did.

A week later, Liz, a sassy, bright blue-eyed, silver-haired eighty-year-old church elder came and got me for lunch. I admired Liz. She worked tirelessly as an advocate for the homeless. Whether she was backing legislation at the state's general assembly or passing out food in the daily soup lines of the downtown church where she volunteered, Liz was busy doing God's work. She had purpose and joy in her life when so few people did. But Liz had also suffered heartbreak. Liz had lost her husband more than fifty years ago—not to cancer or an accident, but to his secretary. Liz had been left alone to raise a devastated teenage son who was deeply injured by his father's actions. I explained to Liz what was bothering me and asked her how she had gotten over the pain of the divorce.

She said, "Oh honey, I got over it, but it is why I am so mean."

"Mean" was not exactly what I would call Liz. Honest, straightforward, and pulling no punches. Yet she was also lighthearted with a puckish sense of humor and an ability to laugh at herself.

"Are you just being sarcastic?" I asked tentatively, not knowing what she would throw back at me.

"I don't know how much my meanness has to do with it!" she laughed. "But I am pretty much over it, though there are still times when I wake up in a cold sweat wondering if I will die alone. And at eighty years old that really is something to worry about."

Then she reached into her purse and pulled out a small tattered leather book. She handed it to me and said, "Over the years, I have tried all kinds of things to make the pain go away. Everything from wearing crystals to Yoga to even one night stands."

"Liz! No!" I replied with eyes wide open in shock.

"Don't act like you are shocked," she quipped as she straightened the scarf around her neck as if to regain her dignity. Reaching for my hand, she held it, saying, "All kinds of things took my mind off of the divorce for a while, but nothing was permanent." She paused, as if remembering, and then went on. "You knew he was on the church board, a Sunday school teacher, and a respected trial lawyer in partnership with several of the men who still attend The Church in the Suburbs. The ordeal was a scandal that rocked the whole community. My son never got over the shame and embarrassment of it."

Then her attention went to the book. "A friend loaned me this devotional last week. She says it has done great things to ease pain that she was going through, but it is all fluff. I hate fluff."

I paged through it, glancing at several of the entries. On each page, the reader was offered inspiration for their day. The reader was encouraged to have faith—to believe that God's grace and strength would get them through the day. Faith, by the author's definition, was found in believing that God was there for you, had compassion for you, and loved you. It was strongly implied that if you had enough faith, everything would work out okay. I asked Liz why she found the book fluffy.

"It is nothing but Hummel Christianity!" exclaimed Liz.

"*Humble* Christianity?"

"No. It is like those beautiful Hummel figurines that depict a delightful place where everyone gets everything they have always wanted. It isn't a real place. The author never seriously leads her readers toward doing anything hard, making any significant sacrifice, or going out of their way to meet the needs of strangers. It is just a daily dose of sugar that in the end only makes the reader fat and lazy. What helped me get past my disappointments," emphasized Liz, "was when I discovered that I was called to help others. Getting my mind off me and onto others worked. Nothing else lasted."

I had been thinking about Liz and that devotional ever since. I began to wonder if my congregants and I weren't mistaking God for our sugar daddy who treats us to all the goodies that we can't buy for ourselves. And though the story that God loves us and cares for us was absolute truth, what if believing that story alone was not enough for a life of peace and joy? Was

Liz right? Was a life of service the way to overcome life's disappointments and tragedies?

My lunch with Liz made me more observant of the congregants whose problems overwhelmed them. I noticed that the congregants—the ones who struggled the most with their problems, especially problems that never ever seemed to go away—were the same people who attended every Bible study we offered. Moreover, when those studies weren't enough, they would attend a few more Bible studies at other churches. They attended numerous prayer meetings and took classes on spirituality, hoping to find the key to finally feeling good about their lives and their relationships with God. They had counselors and spiritual directors. In worship services, they lifted their hands highest and sang the loudest. During prayer time, either they had a prayer request for themselves or for someone they'd met that week who was suffering in a similar way. They walked labyrinths and sought out spiritual guides from other denominations that were apparently more spiritual than ours were. They followed a strict set of rules that they felt any good Christian should follow. They would tithe their ten percent to the church and pledge some extra. They seemed to be doing all the right things. Yet, they only caught fleeting glimpses of peace and joy. They knew something was wrong with their faith and most would even admit it—even if they didn't know *what* was wrong. Saddest of all, I hadn't really known what was wrong either, but perhaps Liz had provided some clues.

I had been splitting my time between being a pastor and trying my hand at authoring a book. I was working on a book about the Epistle of James. I was just about finished with my research and needed to get busy writing in the coming weeks. On my days at home, my husband and I woke before dawn. He rushed off to his client's offices before the rat race got into full swing, avoiding as much traffic as possible, while I headed into our study where I would work until lunchtime. Our study was a pleasant place at the front of our house where the morning sun shed direct sunlight into its windows. From my desk, as the sun rose, I could catch glimpses of my fellow suburban neighbors heading to work in their expensive cars. I could see school kids catching their big yellow school buses dressed in seventy-dollar Hollister jeans with the denim fashionably "destroyed" in just the right places.

My favorite thing about working in my office was the hummingbird feeder my husband had installed at the exact angle outside the window for me to watch the birds come and go. Of course, the hummingbird feeder was empty this time of year, but a little chipmunk who had made his home in my flowerbeds entertained me by warming himself on the bricks underneath. Sophie, my old black-and-white spotted Great Dane, alternated her time in the mornings between soaking up sunshine through the glass front door and venturing into my office. Although she could see the little chipmunk from the front door, she was uninterested in him, preferring instead to bark at neighbors taking early morning walks. She would bark. They would wave. For her, at the grand old age of thirteen, an almost unheard of life span for a Great Dane, this was heaven.

However, Sophie knew that greeting the neighbors was not her most important duty. She firmly believed that she had been put here on earth to keep me from working too hard. To that end, she insisted on regular breaks together. That morning had been no different as she walked up beside my chair and stood nose to nose next to me as I typed. When I failed to stop typing and pet her, she would kiss my cheek with a big lick of her tongue. Lost in my thoughts, if I still failed to respond, her nose inevitably would find its way under one of my wrists, pushing upward to disengage my hand from the keyboard. She would not be denied. With my sons away at school, Sophie's companionship was particularly treasured.

I decided to take a break to walk her. The sky was clear and the air was dry. In what seemed like a moment of clarity, a thought occurred to me about the Epistle of James. The months of research I had done had been important, but it was not enough to do exegetical and theological research in order to write about the teachings of James. James was a man of action not theology. He wasn't to be understood by the view from my office. The view I needed was at ground level, where real people were taking his teachings and putting them into action. I needed partners who would be willing to study the Epistle of James with me and apply its teaching to our lives together. How would this work?

Suddenly it was there in front of me, taped to my mailbox and waving in the wind—a flyer distributed by a group of neighborhood women. They were inviting all the women of the neighborhood to a Bible study. Then it dawned on me. What if I invited several people to form a study group with the purpose of living out the teachings of James together—a study that wasn't focused on learning facts, but on transforming our lives? By the time I arrived back at the house, I had made a mental list of six people to invite.

The three men on my list were Joe Norman, Rodney Tate, and Carlos Martinez. I wanted as diverse a group as possible. I was not sure Joe would accept the invitation. It wasn't something he would normally do. But I was feeling bold so I decided to take a chance, thinking he just might say yes because it was his late wife's friend asking him. He hesitated, but then agreed. He would be the one to help me apply James to corporate life.

Next, I called Rodney Tate. I knew he would bring an interesting perspective to the study group. He and his wife were medical missionaries home from Malawi on furlough for three years along with their three biological children and five adopted children. They had been home a little over a year, and I knew Rodney had been looking for what he called a "meaningful" Bible study group. When I called he immediately said yes.

I hoped Carlos would join us, too, because of his Cuban heritage. Like most suburban churches, there wasn't a whole lot of diversity in our church even though the pictures on our website made it look like the church was a melting pot of races and ethnic backgrounds. In reality, very few members were not Anglo. However, if I could get Carlos into our study group, his experiences would give us an international perspective. He said he would think about it. Something in his tone made it obvious to me that he was just putting off saying no until he could discover a good reason to say no. Disappointed, I moved on to calling the women.

The three women on my list were Helen Callil, Liz Black, and Sarah Adams. Sarah, another congregant whose picture was featured prominently on the church's web site, was an African American working mother of three and a physician. I knew she would have great insights. Disappointingly, she said no, referring to her relentless schedule. Helen was too nice to say no, especially since I framed it in a way that suggested the study might help to reveal to her this new ministry she was seeking. Liz seemed thrilled to be asked and agreed immediately.

It didn't take Carlos more than an hour to come back with a graceful no. That gave me two males and two females so far. Four might have been a good number, but I really felt I needed six to have a well-rounded group. Trying to find some racial diversity was going nowhere when Pastor Eddie phoned. Pastor Eddie, a senior colleague, was nothing short of incorrigible. No manner of instruction would have ever helped him see his way to being politically correct. He was about fifty with no known family and his "appropriate meter" was completely broken. Therefore, when I saw his name come up on my cell phone on my day at home, I debated whether to answer or let it go to voice mail. Against my better judgment, I answered. Pastor Eddie had run into Carlos at the coffee shop in town and had heard about the study group.

"Uh . . ." began Eddie, "So this group studying the Epistle of James . . . why didn't you run the idea by me first?"

"Eddie, the study group really has nothing to do with The Church in the Suburbs. I am simply asking a few friends to help me do research for my book."

"You didn't ask me," he whined. Pastor Eddie was not a bad looking man—muscular, in shape, and always impeccably groomed—over groomed really. Many a single woman at church had been deluded into thinking he was a catch. That was until they had a conversation with him. He was a man who could find a way to be inappropriate in just about every situation.

"No, I didn't ask you to be in the group, Eddie. I am sorry." I knew exactly where this was going.

"Well, I want to be in it."

Long pause on my end of the phone. This was not going to work. Eddie said all the wrong things, insulted everyone in his wake, and I seriously doubted he would be willing to come prepared each week.

"Eddie, everyone will be encouraged to give their opinions, so you can't insult people."

"When have I ever insulted anyone?"

"Eddie, you insulted a good portion of the women in church last Sunday when you asked that only the young pretty female congregants sing the last verse of the opening hymn."

"What was wrong with that?"

"Women don't want to be judged by whether they are young and pretty or not. It just isn't appropriate. The songs are to lift our hearts to God and it was a distracting and rude request."

"Done! I promise not to insult anyone."

So the men in the study group were finalized: Joe, Rodney, and Eddie. I was terribly disappointed that Eddie was going to join us and I still needed one woman. I picked up the church directory and started thumbing through it. It was not another five minutes before my cell phone rang again. This time it was Olivia. In typical Olivia fashion, without introducing herself or even offering a greeting, she started speaking.

"Can I get in the study group you are starting?"

"Olivia?"

"Yes. This is Olivia. Can I get in the group?"

"How did you find out about the study group?" Word sure traveled fast.

"I wanted to schedule my monthly 'State of Marketing' meeting with Joe Norman on first Thursday afternoons. His secretary told my secretary that he is doing a study group with you on Thursdays and has to go home for dinner beforehand. You got my slot on his calendar. What are we going to be studying?"

Direct. Aggressive. Rude. I guess by joining my study group, she was planning to "make me successful?" More likely, this is how her networking with me before the holidays was now going to bear fruit. All the same, I still honestly liked Olivia. "Olivia, there will be some preparation required each week. It isn't optional. Do you still want to be in the group?" She said she did.

I hung up the phone wondering what Joe's reaction would be to her attendance. He had never tried to conceal the fact that he was disappointed that so many of his employees had joined *his* church. He had told several of us at a church board meeting years ago that he felt stalked by some of the new members. There was something to this. Annie, before her illness, would often go ahead of Joe into the sanctuary to scope out the available seats. She would try to find a place where they could slip out quickly before the service ended. If they didn't leave while people were still singing the last hymn, they would be inundated with people wanting to shake Joe's hand. On several occasions over the years, Joe had been bombarded by a few reporters in the church parking lot eager to learn something about an upcoming product release. It was then that Joe had contributed a sum of money toward hiring security at the church for Sunday mornings. I wondered if I should tell him beforehand that Olivia would take part, but I decided against saying anything. Whatever was going to happen would happen.

In a matter of hours, a study group had been formed. We would begin meeting first Thursdays in February. I have often wondered if Sophie's demand for a walk was a divine intervention sent to free my mind of its cobwebs so such an idea could be breathed into its crevasses. Looking over at her that afternoon, a black-and-white spotted mass lying next to the heat vent snoring, she did seem to have a sort of holy aura about her. Well, if one stared at her long enough and maybe squinted a little.

5

Mystery and Controversy

The Scripture that we would be studying was listed in the table of contents of my Bible as just "James." It was actually a letter that James had written to the first-century church. Often letters of this nature are designated "epistles" because they were written with the intention of teaching the recipients. On this particular morning, I found myself wondering how James's teachings applied to life in the modern suburbs. Life in the suburbs was different from life in the city or life in the country—and especially different from James's life in the first century.

In the sprawling suburbs of Atlanta, life was enveloped in safety and privilege. We had built up walls to keep out anyone who didn't conform to our standards—especially our economic standards. The walls were sometimes as physical as the gated communities that dotted our landscape. Sometimes those walls, although virtual, were just as real as walls of concrete or stone. We had rules about everything; lots had a minimum acceptable size, house exteriors and lawns had to be maintained, cars had to be kept tucked inside garages. Even our garages were far nicer than the average home in many third world countries. When I went to the store to do my grocery shopping, most of the shoppers were Caucasian. The stores were pristine and glamorous. The shoppers, even on the most casual days, were dressed in expensive clothes with expensive jewelry.

It occurred to me that I had never seen a homeless person or someone begging in the suburbs. Though we had problems, they weren't generally issues of survival. Few of us ever worried about where our next meal was coming from or if we would be able to pay the utility bills. We didn't lack for warmth or any number of luxuries. Our most authentic problems were usually those that affected our health (physical or mental), but even then, our wealth allowed us to receive superior medical care. Our life expectancy was actually longer than those just a dozen or so miles away in Atlanta.[1] In contrast, the church James was writing to was under persecution, and some of the congregants lived—or had lived—in serious poverty before the broader church communities had begun to support each other.[2] Here in the suburbs, not only were we not in those conditions, but we couldn't even relate to them. Therefore, I wondered how James's teachings could apply to us. This had not been my concern when I first became interested in James. Then I had been drawn to the mystery and controversy surrounding the epistle over the centuries.

The mystery concerning the Epistle of James surrounded its authorship. Other than knowing the author's name was James, his identity remained a mystery. Many deduced that he was the brother of Jesus, who had stepped up to lead the church in Jerusalem, but there were also two disciples and a father of a disciple, all named James, mentioned in the New Testament. The martyrdom of one of these disciples was recorded in Acts 12:2 not long after Jesus's death. Hence, it was unlikely that he had time to write the epistle before he died. If the author were the brother of Jesus, it would have been written before sixty-two AD when he, too, was martyred.[3] This means the epistle would have likely been written before the gospels, and perhaps before any of the other New Testament documents.

For me, it would have been exciting if the author were Jesus's brother— someone who had grown up with Jesus, watching him grow from childhood into adulthood—someone who knew from personal experience that the words of Jesus were legitimate and that the life of Jesus was not a myth. Moreover, there was some circumstantial evidence that pointed to the author being the brother of Christ. First, it did make logical sense that because the brother of Jesus had become the leader of the church in Jerusalem, he would not have needed to sign his writings with anything other than his first name in order to identify himself.[4] Second, there was both a speech and a piece of correspondence by Jesus's brother recorded in Acts 15. Scholars have analyzed these pieces of communication and some see similarities of style with the Epistle of James.[5]

---

1. Beck, "City vs. Country," para. 5–6.
2. Moo, *James*, 31–34.
3. Mason, *Josephus, Judea, and Christian Origins*, 123.
4. Eusebius, *Church History*, 52–53.
5. Motyer, *Message*, 21.

On the other side of this argument, scholars have also noted that the vocabulary and grammar in the Epistle of James are those of a fairly sophisticated Greek. Yet Jesus and his brother were from the peasant class. Their first language would have been Aramaic. Although it is possible that the brother of Jesus became educated in formal Greek, it wouldn't have been usual given his culture.[6] Two thousand years later, who knows? Perhaps he dictated the epistle to someone who was more educated. Since there was no definitive evidence pointing to the identity of author, the study group would have to continue to live in that mystery.

One thing was certain, the author knew the Jesus of the gospels very well. He understood the message of Jesus. He understood how it applied to the daily lives of Jesus's followers. The epistle demonstrates a distinct closeness, unparalleled by any of the other New Testament documents, to the words of Jesus found in the gospels. In particular, it parallels the lessons of the Sermon on the Mount. Because of this, perhaps we can even go so far as to assume that the author was present to hear Jesus preach this sermon.[7]

While the mystery of the Epistle of James concerned its authorship, the controversy concerned its message. The fact that the epistle was so close to the teachings of Jesus and yet generated heated theological debates was hard for me to fathom. Simply put, James taught what Jesus taught.[8] Sometimes even the language was identical to the words of Jesus as they were recorded in the gospels.[9] Be that as it may, in every generation, there seemed to be at least one significant church leader who had called the epistle "heretical." These leaders most often claimed that because James demanded that the followers of Christ produce good works, he was pushing a works-based salvation instead of salvation by grace alone. In truth, James was not outlining a plan of salvation at all, but teaching those already dedicated to following Christ how to live out their commitment. Hence, I have come to believe that there is more to the controversy than grace versus works theology.

Martin Luther wrote, "James mangles the Scriptures" and "therefore I will not have him in my Bible to be numbered among the true chief books." He even called the epistle "a book of straw."[10] Calvin wrote that James was "sparing in proclaiming the grace of Christ" and judged James's writing not "behooving of an apostle."[11] Many a church leader has tried to kick the

6. Barclay, *Letters of James*, 37–38.

7. Selvaggio, "Hearing the Voice of Jesus," para. 1–12.

8. Nystrom, *James*, 17–19.

9. Stevenson, *Epistle of James*, 4–7.

10. Webster, *Oxford Handbook of Systematic Theology*, 439–40.

11. Calvin, *Commentary on James*, location 3–16.

epistle out of the Bible altogether. In my heart, I had come to believe that James's epistle insulted such leaders because their lives, like mine, lacked the evidence of the servanthood that James demanded of us. I had come to believe the real reason the epistle has been so controversial was that it demanded these leaders—in fact all of us—become the servants of God and others rather than authoritarian theologians and dogmatic rule makers.

Take Luther for example. During the years he spent as a theologian and pastor, the peasants began to revolt against the horrible working and living conditions forced on them by the wealthy landowners in his congregations. Luther, a great theologian, did not stand with the poor by teaching his wealthy congregants the things James teaches us: not to show favoritism to the wealthy, not to hoard resources, not to judge, to speak words of blessings and not curses, to share one's resources with others, etc. Instead, Luther wrote an essay called "Against the Robbing and Murdering Hordes of Peasants," in which he not only encouraged the authorities to kill the peasants, but his words arrogantly damned the peasants to hell for standing up for themselves.[12] At other times, he encouraged violence against Jews and even the Christian reformers who were more radical than he was.[13]

Calvin was not a lot different from Luther in that he failed to demonstrate tolerance and the love of Christ to those with whom he had theological differences. For instance, at Calvin's insistence, Servetus, a Spanish physician passing through Geneva, was burned at the stake. His only crime was to seek face-to-face dialogue with Calvin to discuss their theological differences.[14] My theory was that Luther, Calvin, and many others of us can't help but be offended by the Epistle of James, which calls us into a very different way of being than we are accustomed.

Despite the controversy, the Holy Spirit saw fit to keep the Epistle of James alive. In it, James holds our feet (and faith) to the fire by challenging us with an implied question: "Is our brand of faith in Jesus visible and producing good works or is it merely verbalized and well-intended?"

As anticipated, the first Thursday of February arrived rather quickly. Not wanting looky-loos at the church to interfere with the study, I had invited the group to meet at my home. The day had been cool and crisp without a cloud in the sky. The pansies had exploded into a sea of color on either side of the walkway leading from my driveway down to my house. Olivia was the first to arrive and parked her Jaguar on the street. She finished her hands-free phone call from the car and then exited wearing a red and black

---

12. Luther, "Against the Robbing and Murdering Hordes," 121–24.

13. Luther, *On the Jews and Their Lies*, 111.

14. Rives, *Did Calvin Murder Servetus?*, 457–58.

houndstooth coat and her signature five-inch black pumps. I watched her as she had a choice to make. Her nature was to get to my door as quickly and efficiently as possible and that would mean beelining it down the hill through a pine island and then through my grass. Common sense would tell most people the incline and the five-inch heels weren't a good match. But Olivia had long ago risen above the common sense that grounded the rest of us. She didn't want to walk the extra steps down the driveway to the walkway. So here she came through the pine island over tree roots and the now withered leaves that had fallen since the last fall roundup. I couldn't watch. She was going to fall. I walked away from the window and waited a minute or two for the doorbell to ring. It didn't ring, but Sophie had begun to bark anxiously from the dining room window in Olivia's direction. Curiously, I peeked back toward the pine island. Olivia had apparently decided that the incline was indeed too steep and was wobbling her way back to the street. Relieved that she hadn't fallen, I started to turn away when I noticed a pile of leaves covering her backside telling a story I was glad not to have witnessed. Just as she reached the street, Joe arrived.

In my mind, this was probably the worst of all scenarios, knowing that Joe would not be any more pleased with Olivia's membership in the group than he was with her membership at the church. Olivia, oblivious to Joe's feelings, walked right up to his car, chitchatting away at him as they took the safe route down the driveway to my house. Joe had not said a word back to her the entire way in. When he arrived at my front door, he opened it and rang my doorbell simultaneously. The look on his face was "have mercy and get her away from me."

The others arrived in short order. Helen had with her Valentine-themed organic homemade pop-tarts. They looked like little envelopes with cutout hearts exposing a cherry glaze between the layers. These had been extras left over from one of her children's school parties. When everyone arrived, and after we had indulged in the yummy snack, I began the meeting by sharing my take on the mystery and controversy that surrounded James's epistle. Joe sat alone in a red wingback chair by the glowing stacked stone fireplace. Liz, Helen, and Rodney shared the couch. Olivia and Pastor Eddie had found a place among my collection of rocking chairs. To my great dismay, Sophie took an immediate liking to Eddie. She curled up beside his chair, inviting him to scratch behind her ears. Good grief, my own dog was a traitor. After the meeting, I would ask her not to do this again, but she had made up her mind, Eddie was her kind of guy. From this point forward at every meeting, she would alternate between sitting at his feet and guarding my front door.

When I was done with the introduction to James, I asked everyone to go around the room introducing themselves. Liz, with her silver hair and enthusiastic glow, was going to be the mother figure in the group, doling out equal amounts of unconditional and tough love. Helen didn't say much herself, but smiled as everyone talked—taking great interest in each person. Olivia was clearly there for one reason—to impress Joe. Even so, Joe was unimpressionable and stoic. I couldn't tell if he was mad at me for including Olivia or not. I pretended not to notice his feelings.

As people introduced themselves, Rodney had a look on his normally accepting and friendly face that said he was determining their worth to the human race. I wouldn't say his rugged good looks were exactly diminished by his expression, but his face sure did look judgmental. I doubt many could pass his standards. His open acceptance of me was not extending to the rest of the group. Pastor Eddie was, well, he was just Pastor Eddie, interrupting with inappropriate comments that only he thought were funny.

Pastor Eddie had been doing something new for a few weeks that I had found irritating and odd. He had been asking people to pray for him because he had an "addiction" that he needed to overcome. His choice of the word "addiction" was in his usual dramatic style, but a poor one, in my opinion. Was he addicted to alcohol? To drugs? To porn? Who knew? I certainly didn't want to know and so I hadn't asked. Maybe no one else wanted to know either, because no one else had asked. This request coming from a congregant would have been a very serious request and one that a pastor could not walk away from without seeing if the person needed immediate help of some kind. When Eddie mentioned it again before I closed in prayer that night, I took the bait this time. I asked in front of the group if he wanted to be more specific.

"Chocolate!" he exclaimed.

"What?" I had heard him well enough, but I was befuddled.

"I want you to pray about my addiction to chocolate," he responded. I couldn't help but look around at the faces in the group to see if they thought he was a dolt, too. If they did, no one gave it away, except maybe for Rodney who was shaking his head in disbelief.

"Really?" I said feeling ashamed of myself for being so intolerant of Eddie. "I thought it was something serious."

"It is. My biggest flaw is eating too much chocolate."

Rodney could no longer hold his tongue, "You know Eddie, chocolate is sort of a woman's obsession, don't you think? Do you buy yourself boxes of bonbons?" Rodney was mocking both Pastor Eddie and the women in the group. He winked at Liz to let her know he was kidding. Then he smiled smugly, waiting for someone to react.

Pastor Eddie, however, needing to be taken seriously, began to explain in excruciating detail where he got the chocolate he was overdosing on.

I eventually interrupted Eddie and asked, "You want us to pray that you will stop eating so much chocolate?"

"Yes."

There was more to this exchange than met the eye. As I look back, this exchange summed up what it was about the suburban church that had begun to disturb me. We relaxed in luxury, worried about how many chocolate bars God wanted us to eat, while a homeless man a dozen miles away in downtown Atlanta had feet that were rotting from the sores his ill-fitting shoes had caused. This homeless man had no place to even sit and rest during the day where he wouldn't be scorned. Yet he was out of sight and out of mind from those living in the suburbs. Our faith was dead because it took no action on the things that mattered to God, all the while worrying about chocolate.

The fact was Jesus had bigger plans for Pastor Eddie than overcoming his desire for chocolate. Yet, that night, we were all nice people who did nothing more than help Pastor Eddie wallow in his "addiction." We offered sympathy and compassion. James would not have done this. He would not have enabled such self-centered behavior that ignores the real suffering and sorrow in the world. James demanded that his congregants move from focusing on their problems to doing the work of God.

6

God's Slaves—James 1:1a

James, a servant of God and of the Lord Jesus Christ . . .

—JAMES 1:1A

The Sunday following the first study group meeting, I was pausing in my office to catch my breath between church services when I looked up to see Helen with her adorable twins in tow. The twins pulled out a bucket of toys, which I kept on my shelf for just such occasions, and began playing with them. Helen was glowing as usual and carrying a leather journal with an intricate Celtic knot embossed on the cover. The leather journal was where she was recording what the Holy Spirit revealed to her while she meditated. Helen opened her journal and showed me how God had been speaking to her. Rather than having a monumental lifetime revelation, the Holy Spirit had used her daily prayer time to reveal to her particular people who needed her. In turn, she had been faithful each day in reaching out to them. She was really enjoying the whole process.

For example, as Helen was praying one morning, she thought of a particular bride whose wedding she had coordinated as a church volunteer this past June. She realized that she had not seen the bride or groom in church recently. Helen felt the Holy Spirit was placing this woman on her mind for a reason. Normally, Helen would have just phoned, but since it was a Saturday, she drove by the couple's house with a loaf of freshly baked rosemary bread. The couple came to the door together looking somewhat wounded. It turns out that they had had a second trimester miscarriage and were struggling to overcome the grief of losing their first child. Helen spent some time offering comfort. She was thrilled to have this kind of connection with such "nice" people. I was very happy for Helen—it was a sign that she was listening to God speak into her life.

However, when Helen left the couple's house, she had driven to downtown Atlanta where her younger unmarried sister lived in a high-rise condo. As she entered her sister's parking garage, she was troubled at the sight of a young Latina teenage girl who looked like she was in serious need. The teen was terribly thin. From what Helen could see of her face, extending between the tattered coat collar and knitted hat, there was a nasty bruise on her cheekbone. The girl was lying on the ground asleep under the awning of the garage. It was cold and the teen had to be very uncomfortable. Upon seeing the teen, Helen felt God calling her into action—just as God had done during her prayer times. She felt compelled to care for the girl. Despite that, Helen refused. She walked right past the teen to the elevator. The memory of this teen was etched in Helen's mind and had been bothering Helen ever since. She wanted to know what I thought.

Before I could form my thoughts into words, Helen suggested to me what I might think, "My therapist says that I need to set boundaries for myself. Don't you think she is right? I am not comfortable with people like this. And it isn't safe." Long pause. "So this is a boundary I am setting." In essence, Helen wanted me to give her permission to limit her ministry to "nice" people like the couple who had had the miscarriage.

"Helen, did God reveal this boundary to you or is this a boundary that you are staking out?"

"I think God did. It is what I am comfortable with," she said as her enthusiasm diminished.

I told Helen that this new question about setting boundaries should not lessen how she feels about what the Holy Spirit had been doing during her prayer time. She should continue to ask God's guidance and listen for answers. I sent Helen to a website that had a list with a good description of the five most common mental and physical problems that vulnerable populations face. I asked her to select one of these problems each day, read about it, and then ask God which side of her boundary line people with this kind of problem fell on. Then I told her that we could get together again and see how the Holy Spirit had spoken to her. I helped Helen pick up the toys the twins had dropped on the rug at seeing their dad in the hallway. Helen was such a great mother with lots of patience. She hadn't minded the twins' dirty diapers or their drooling lips as baby teeth made their first appearance. Yet, she minded dirty teenagers and adults who didn't fit into her idea of "nice." Watching her walk away, she reminded me of an angel whose halo had slipped over one ear.

Though it wasn't initially obvious to me, the study group lesson, which was to be on the salutation of James's epistle, would be an opportunity for Helen to think through her boundary setting. In James's salutation, he announces himself to his readers not as a "follower" of Jesus, but as a "slave" of Jesus. We tend to want to sweep under the rug the strong image in his salutation. In fact, the more popular translation of "servant" instead of "slave" drives my point home—even the translators wanted to soften the meaning.[1] Nevertheless, the Greek word, *doulos*, did not mean servant or someone hired for pay. It meant someone who was owned by the master who had no identity of his or her own.[2] Nonetheless, to use the word "slave" sounds jarring.[3] To the modern person, it brings up images of the Civil War and human sex trafficking. Yet, being a slave of God is different. It is a voluntary taking on of the mission of God, knowing that God alone is worthy of our ultimate commitment. A God who loves us, values us, and sent Jesus for us would never mistreat us.

Despite the negative images of slavery, the word "follower" or even "servant" does not cut it for James or for the other writers of the New Testament; Paul, Simon Peter, and Jude also introduce themselves in their epistles as "slaves." Even the salutation in Revelation says it was written by "Jesus's slave, John" to "show Jesus's slaves what must take place."[4] In fact, none of the writers of the New Testament ever introduce themselves as "followers" of Jesus. The word "follower" doesn't indicate the complete and ultimate commitment that they had made, willingly giving up their own rights, desires, and preferences.

Furthermore, the idea of slavery to God is not a New Testament idea. In Leviticus, the author describes the entire Hebrew people as "slaves of God."[5] The psalmists often refer to the people of God as "God's slaves."[6] The Old Testament refers to certain individuals (Moses, David, Jeremiah, and Amos) who were tasked with carrying out important aspects of God's mission as "slaves."[7] The concept of slavery to God is an ancient one.

1. Glancy, *Slavery in Early Christianity*, 24–25.

2. Beavis, "Ancient Slavery," 37–54.

3. In fact, the word "slave" is so jarring that the word "servant" will be used in this book after chapter 7.

4. Rev 1:1.

5. Leviticus 25:42 is translated literally as God saying, "For they are my slaves, whom I have brought out from the land of Egypt: they are not to be sold as slaves."

6. Psalm 32:22 and 113:1 are just two of more than a dozen examples in the Psalms.

7. Num 12:7; 2 Sam 7:5; Jer 7:25; and Amos 3:7.

Our understanding of James's epistle, in fact our understanding of our relationship with God, hinges on our acceptance of this level of commitment. James's epistle brings into sharp contrast that faith in God is not believing that God will do something for us that we want done, but faith in God is what spurs God's slaves into action, doing what pleases their master. Faith, for a slave, is not believing that the master exists. Faith, for God's slaves, is taking on a sacrificial way of living on behalf of the master.

Voluntary slavery was what James understood to be the basis for living the Christian life, and yet our suburban churches never advertise the commitment to follow Jesus as slavery. We rarely start our personal stories with "God called me into slavery." Our church websites don't invite people to "come and worship with the slaves of God." How would evangelism change if right up front we told people that following Jesus is where they would, of their own free will, give up their desires and replace them with Jesus's desires? It is a hard sell. Yet, that is where James begins this epistle.

However, there is more to slavery than serving the master. Not only are we to be slaves to God, but we are to be slaves to one another. In no way does this mean that God condones one human being owning another human being. The disciples learned what being slaves to each other meant when the sons of Zebedee, disciples of Jesus, along with their mother, asked Jesus to give the sons the best seats in Jesus's kingdom. This request angered the other disciples, because they wanted the best seats, too. Jesus straightens them all out by saying, "Whoever wishes to be great among you must be your servant."[8] On another occasion, Jesus tells his followers a parable of a slave who does not take his responsibility to care for the other slaves seriously. Jesus warns that when the master returns, this slave will be dealt with severely.[9] Jesus doesn't stop there. On the last night of Jesus's life, in what would be one of his very last lessons to the disciples, he demonstrates what it means to be slaves to one another by taking on a slave's job and washing the feet of each disciple. Slavery to God compels us to put both God's desires and others' needs before our own desires and needs.

Before I knew it, the first Thursday in March rolled around and it was time for our study group to meet again. As I taught about slavery, I realized from the looks on their faces, with the exception of Rodney and Liz, the others had never considered the sheer breadth and depth of God's call upon their lives. Being a slave of God was a stretch, but somewhat reasonable given the awesomeness of God. However, the concept of being a slave to each other was way out there. They were seriously questioning if this was

8. Matt 20:26. Note the translator's choice of servant rather than slave.
9. Matt 24:45–51 and Luke 12:41–46.

what Jesus was really teaching the disciples. They were used to pastors offering them comfort by telling them of God's love, mercy, and power to help them. They liked getting hopeful messages that they could apply to their problems. They liked knowing God loved them despite their sins. They liked hearing about how God's power could bring them blessings. They might have even been okay with a pastor who Sunday after Sunday gave them a list of rules to follow, but promised them God's blessings if they complied. However, they were not used to a pastor promoting God's rather huge, unending demand of servanthood on their lives. I could tell that they weren't sure they believed me.

Olivia spoke with surprising honesty, "I have to say that this is new for me. I was taught that being aggressive in pursuing my own goals was what smart, successful people do."

Olivia had never studied the Bible before—never been a member of a church before. It was going to be exciting to see how the Epistle of James would unfold before her unencumbered by the preconceptions of someone who had grown up in the church.

As I looked around the room, I was pleased with how the study group was quietly reflecting on the salutation. Eventually Joe broke the silence. He specifically didn't buy that God wanted him to be a slave of those who worked for him, "If this is true, then we might as well sell all our belongings and move in together." Rodney muttered something about how that might not be a bad idea, but Joe overlooked the comment and went on to explain that he did feel employees should be treated well. In truth, Joe's company did have a reputation of providing good benefits to its employees.

Then, as if on cue, Pastor Eddie went where no one could have imagined that he could go. He jumped the entire gist of the conversation and blurted out, "I think God meant for some people to be slaves—they'd be better off."

Not even here in the South did people speak, at least to me, of slavery being an acceptable way of life. I assumed for a moment that Eddie must have something profound to say and was just going for shock value. I guess the others did, too, because, other than looking confused, no one immediately reacted.

Eddie elaborated by telling the story of receiving a summons to be on jury duty last month. On the appointed day, he had left the comfort of the suburbs and had gone down to the courthouse in downtown Atlanta. He told of a conglomeration of problems that arose as he tried to check in. The problems were really of his own making. He had forgotten the paperwork they had sent him and requested he bring with him. He had his pocketknife in his pocket when he tried to go through security. And so on. Of course,

Pastor Eddie didn't recognize himself as the source of these problems. Instead, he blamed them on the men and women working at the courthouse. At the end of his story, I still didn't understand how Eddie's story related to slavery.

However, Rodney had recognized where Eddie was going, "Eddie, were the people African Americans that you were dealing with?" Rodney was only slightly holding back his outrage.

Eddie, not discerning that he was about to make Rodney's righteous indignation flare, casually replied in a low whisper, "I don't think it is a race issue, but yes, they happened to be African Americans."

In ten seconds, just long enough for people to comprehend Eddie's nonsense, the room exploded with both verbal and nonverbal expressions of disgust. Liz shifted in her chair, turning her back toward Pastor Eddie and waved her arm saying, "Oh Eddie. How could you even think such a thing?"

Sophie, my Great Dane, had been sleeping curled up next to Eddie as usual. She was an expert at sensing when someone was in trouble. She sat up straight and then wandered over to Liz, looking eye to eye with her in order to sum up Liz's last exclamation. When Liz did not react to Sophie, Sophie went back to Eddie's chair and sat on Eddie's feet, staring out at us as if to put herself between Eddie and the rest of the group. She was prepared to soften the verbal blows she sensed that he was about to receive. Rodney held nothing back as he expressed exactly what he thought.

Rodney and his wife had been students in the nineties at Guilford College, a social justice–oriented Quaker liberal arts school in North Carolina. They had married shortly after graduation. Rodney had gone on to attend Emory to become a doctor specializing in infectious diseases, while his wife supported them on her social worker's salary. Sometime during Rodney's medical education, his father had been transferred from North Carolina to the Atlanta area. This was when his parents had begun to attend The Church in the Suburbs. Rodney and his wife were not really thrilled with organized religion, but they had attended The Church in the Suburbs whenever time had allowed—mostly to spend time with Rodney's parents. Then, one Sunday during their visit, a representative spoke about the denomination's international mission work. Rodney's wife, a bubbly, tall, beautiful blonde with endless energy, had volunteered to organize the church's first international trip. She had been hooked.

Upon Rodney's graduation from medical school, his now-inspired wife had gone to seminary, while Rodney had spent three miserable years cloistered in a lab doing research at the Centers for Disease Control (CDC). During those years, Rodney had realized that he needed direct contact with patients to be happy. His wife, on the other hand, was thriving in seminary.

While pondering what to do next, they had taken a month-long trip to Malawi, where they had worked in an orphanage for children who either were diagnosed with HIV/AIDS or whose parents had died from AIDS. The trip had been a godsend. Literally. They had found their passion. Rodney had resigned from his lucrative job at the CDC and together they had headed to Malawi. Since that time, they had had three children of their own while adopting five African children, all of whom had special needs.

Rodney, his wife, and the children were back in the states only because the denomination required that every missionary come home for a three-year furlough to raise funds for their mission work and recharge their batteries every ten years. Rodney hated being forced to come back. He felt restless knowing there was much work to do in Malawi. Coming here also made him face the disgust he felt for American Christians, the majority of whom, in his opinion, lacked the desire to care for those in need. Nor did they feel compelled to demand justice for the mistreated and forgotten.

As I watched Rodney talk to Eddie, I realized that I had not actually heard Rodney's words. I didn't need to hear them. It was enough just to see his expression. Rodney was a very good-looking man. He didn't have to work for his looks like Eddie did. Rodney was tall, athletic, and rugged. Eddie was groomed. He had his nails done and went to a tanning salon. Rodney was comfortable in jeans, a t-shirt, and a canvas jacket. Eddie wore starched shirts tailor made for him. When Rodney worked out, he played soccer with the young men in his village. Eddie went to a gym and worked out in air conditioning. I couldn't help but like Rodney. Eddie, on the other hand, exasperated me. In watching Rodney lay into Eddie, I did wonder how the gentleness of the Quakers had not rubbed off on Rodney during his years at Guilford. In stark contrast, there sat Eddie, calmly waiting with a smile glued on his face until Rodney was finished. Eddie, to his merit, never got angry no matter what someone said to him.

"Come on Rodney. I am not a racist. I have a lot of black friends." This was typical Eddie. He just didn't get it.

I looked over at Joe, afraid he would see this kind of exchange as a waste of his very valuable time, but he was busy watching Rodney. I didn't know what to make of it at the time, but now I think Joe was doing what he did best—making a mental note of Rodney's passionate side and evaluating how he might use it for his own advantage later on. Meanwhile, Pastor Eddie was still smiling like one who had no clue. He caught my eye and shrugged his shoulders.

7

A Kingdom of Slaves—James 1:1b

To the twelve tribes in the Dispersion: Greetings

—JAMES 1:1B

It would have been great that night if Helen had shared with the group the questions about boundaries that were raised for her when she walked away from that Latina teenager in downtown Atlanta. It would have been interesting to see the group address how a slave sets boundaries. Obviously, some boundaries are good—especially those that keep us focused on God's work. Others are just a way of staying within our comfort zones and avoiding anything difficult. However, she didn't bring it up. Perhaps she was too distracted because of the little scene Eddie had created with his racist remarks. Nonetheless, I suspected that she wouldn't be able to find "her ministry" until she was willing to step out of her comfort zone and follow the Holy Spirit across her boundaries into the difficult places that the Spirit likes to take us.

Unfortunately, Helen's boundary setting was far from unique to her. In fact, it was in vogue for Christians to set boundaries under the auspices of caring for themselves. At The Church in the Suburbs, we knew a lot about caring for ourselves and precious little about being slaves to God. In fact, we knew a lot about forming the homogeneous community we called the church and caring for its members—as long as the membership list was made up of people with like economic status, theological beliefs, and political leanings. We were good at setting up programming, complete with worship services, Sunday school, Bible studies, choir rehearsals, senior citizens' outings, children's activities, and youth groups. We knew how to entertain and enhance our lives at every stage of human development. Then again, the question I was pondering was how appropriate the activities of The Church in the Suburbs were, considering we were supposed to be a community of God's slaves. Were we doing the work of God together or were we simply a country club with a religious hook?

For many of us, thinking of the church as a unit that does God's work together was difficult. We had been raised to be rugged individualists. Often loyalty to our church was only in effect as long as we benefited from it. We didn't see that the commitment we had made to Christ included the stipulation that we build a community with other followers of Christ. However, James did. And the remainder of James's salutation "to the twelve tribes in the dispersion" described this community and it was like no other. With these thoughts in mind, I set about writing the lesson for our next group meeting.

The dispersion, or *diaspora*, was a Greek word meaning "scattering." It was first applied to what happened on several occasions to the Jewish community long before the coming of Christ.[1] God had told the Jews to live together in a community of twelve family tribes. They were to be a kingdom that was a beacon of God's righteousness and abundance. They were to be a kingdom of God's slaves who were a blessing to the world.

Unfortunately, they never quite became the beacon God meant for them to be. The Old Testament prophets proclaimed that God had told them to live righteously and justly, and they had not.[2] God had told them to care for the poor and needy, but they were consumed with their own riches.[3] God had told them to be a blessing to other races and even invite them into fellowship with God, and they had not.[4] Because of their repeated disobedience and faithlessness to God, the prophets declared that God would allow other nations to conquer them.[5] The kingdom of God's slaves never fully bloomed.

The conquerors of the twelve tribes had a brilliant plan to keep power and order among the vast number of cultures that they conquered. They would send part of the population into a different city-state and mix the

1. Barclay, *Letters of James*, 36–40.

2. Amos 5:24.

3. Isa 10:1–3.

4. Gen 12:2–3; 18:18; 22:18; and 26:4.

5. Amos 8:5–10 and Hosea 2:8–13 prophesied the Assyrian invasion of Israel in which the northern kingdom ceased to exist. Jeremiah 17:21–27 prophesied the invasion of Nebuchadnezzar. Ezekiel prophesied the Babylonian invasion of Jerusalem.

remaining population with those exiled from another conquered area.[6] This way those they had conquered would be forced to reform their society completely. They'd lose power and cultural identity. They'd have to learn new languages in order to speak to their new neighbors. Their heritage would be destroyed. This was the situation in the original diaspora. The once abundant life, now completely abolished. The temple destroyed. Yet, the prophets of the time offered the twelve tribes hope. The prophets told of a Messiah who would one day come and reunite God's kingdom, and it would be populated with—not just Jews—but as God had always intended, Gentiles, too.[7]

By the time Jesus arrived, the scattered tribes were much less distinguishable units. Many had stayed in the countries where they had been dispersed. Some had returned home to Jerusalem, where they had rebuilt a portion of the temple. The ones in Jerusalem were living under Roman rule—still not an independent nation.[8] Now add to that mix the Jews who had begun to follow Christ. These Jewish Christians started out worshiping in the temple and synagogues alongside the rest of the Jewish population. However, that was short lived. In some places, the Jews expelled the Jewish Christians; in other places, the Jewish Christians left of their own accord.[9] In some places, the Jews also began to hunt down both Jewish and Gentile Christians and persecute them.[10] This new diaspora was described in Acts 8 as a severe persecution against the church where the Jewish followers of Christ had been scattered—fleeing for their lives throughout the countryside of Judea and Samaria. This new scattering was different from the original diaspora in that the Gentile and Jewish Christians, unlike the Old Testament Jews, did not believe that they were being scattered because of their sins, but because of their loyal faith in Christ.

So when James addressed this epistle "to the twelve tribes in the dispersion," he was writing to a persecuted people unlike those of us in the suburbs. On the other hand, James was also writing to a people like us. We, too, live with the hope of a dispersed people waiting to be gathered into the coming kingdom of God.[11] We retain the same hope that they did in a Messiah who will one day gather us into his kingdom: a kingdom of slaves who serve God and others.[12]

---

6. Bamberger, *My People*, 27–29.

7. Isa 49:46.

8. Murphy, *Early Judaism*, 213–327.

9. Cohen, *From the Maccabees to the Mishnah*, 228.

10. Murphy, *Early Judaism*, 328–436.

11. Isa 66:22–23.

12. Matt 25:31–34.

The interesting thing about this kingdom of slaves is that it is already and not yet.[13] It is already within us, but not yet in its ultimate conclusion.[14] The church lives in an in-between place. We pray for, live in a desire for, and work for "thy kingdom come, thy will be done."[15] Yet, we also await an event—the grand finale of Christ's return when the kingdom will finally be fully manifested on earth. We both pursue the kingdom and wait for it.

Living out the kingdom of God was a strong theme among the early Christians, who were confused as to why Christ's return was taking so long. In Acts 27, the Apostle Paul beckoned the suffering tribes of the diaspora *to pursue* Christ's kingdom. This was in harmony with James, who was teaching the scattered slaves *how to pursue* it. This pursuit of the kingdom of God is a community effort—the work of the entire church. We cannot accomplish it as individuals.

Therefore, the question I would put before the group was this: Did The Church in the Suburbs seek the kingdom of God in order to serve God and *all* others—including those who might never enter our doors—or did our church just seek to serve its members? Were our church's programs worthy of a kingdom of slaves? These were questions without easy answers—questions that James's epistle addressed, but not head on. He taught his congregants to be slaves, but he didn't mention buying and maintaining a church building. Nor did he talk about the need for the first-century equivalent of a weekly church newsletter, a church bus, fancy communion ware, or stained-glass windows. Perhaps the fact that he didn't mention these types of things was important also—could it have been that James wanted the followers of Jesus to be focused on being a community of slaves above all else?

The conversation that followed was complex. Liz and Rodney lamented that we didn't do enough to serve others. Joe and Eddie pointed out the practical need for all the things that make a church run smoothly, like printers and office managers. Helen brought up an interesting point that the art within the church—the banners, the stained glass, the flowers, the crucifix, and the paintings—lifted our hearts to God in a way that nothing else really could. Though these artistic creations were expensive, the work of artists should certainly be valued and compensated. Olivia quietly listened, taking it all in. We agreed to look for answers within the epistle in the coming weeks.

That evening, I talked far longer than I had meant to talk and then hurried to close the meeting, but before I could, Rodney spoke up: "In honor of

13. Ladd, *Gospel of the Kingdom*, 24–51.

14. Luke 17:20–21.

15. The Lord's Prayer, Matt 6:9–15.

living as slaves to one another, I feel that I owe Eddie, in particular, but the rest of you, an explanation."

Rodney had chosen his words well. They were not an apology to Eddie, but an explanation as to why life on furlough was so difficult. He explained the conditions that he and others live under in Malawi. He went on to name all the luxuries they could not have. Yet, they willingly and happily lived like this in order to help the people in Malawi. When he would come home and experience the materialism of American churchgoers, coupled with the lack of concern for those in need, he had a very hard time not speaking out. Although Malawi was a peaceful country, the other African countries where his associates lived experienced persistent persecution. They experienced diaspora on a monthly basis, moving their medical supplies from one place to another trying to stay hidden from bullies who wanted to steal the valuable medicines and resell them to the highest bidder.

Rodney was astonished that Americans did not even realize the hardships some have taken on to live out the gospel. He complained that we had no sense of being part of a worldwide kingdom of God where we were to care for others outside of our comfort zones. He confessed that he had no tolerance for those who whine about first-world problems while others die of starvation. He was struggling with knowing that he must speak up, but at the same time, he struggled with knowing how to speak up without being abrasive. He said he needed help showing God's love as he spoke the truth to The Church in the Suburbs and other churches where he needed to raise money for his work in Malawi.

Astonishingly, Pastor Eddie, with only the inconsistency he could pull off, stood and held out his hand to Rodney. When Rodney reached for it, Eddy pulled Rodney out of his chair and hugged him. That ended our meeting.

8

The Problem of Having Problems— James 1:2-4

My brothers and sisters, whenever you face trials of any kind, consider it nothing but joy, because you know that the testing of your faith produces endurance; and let endurance have its full effect, so that you may be mature and complete, lacking in nothing.

—JAMES 1:2-4

James begins the body of his epistle by addressing the problem of having problems. James doesn't try and tell his congregation that there wouldn't be problems. Nor does he try and tell them that every trial is God making way for something better. He tells them the truth: there will be trials. However, James does not see trials as we have been programmed to see them—as obstacles to enjoying life fully or maybe even obstacles to doing the work of God. James sees them as occasions for joy!

We think of problems as things that we should walk away from; James sees them as things we should endure. We think of them as things that hurt us—even things that we must carefully heal from—but James sees them as things that make us mature and complete. No wonder we have had such a hard time getting past our problems and on to a life that produces good works. While James joyfully endured his problems, meanwhile doing the work of God, we run away, looking for a holy place to hide and lick our wounds, begging God to comfort us. We think that maybe one day, if we finally get enough of that comfort and overcome our problems, we will have

45

enough energy to serve God. Yet James would soon tell us that getting God to fix our problems is not what servanthood is all about. To this end, in the coming verses, James does not give advice on *how to fix* our problems, but instead *how to deal* with them.

Between the months of March and April, the Atlanta suburbs had begun to green up and the days had grown longer. We had a few cooler days every now and then, but spring was decidedly here. Dogwoods and azaleas would be in bloom soon and lots of things were happening around The Church in the Suburbs. Probably because of my immersion in the Epistle of James, I had recently begun to observe that many of the programs at The Church in the Suburbs went toward trying to fix our problems rather than living the lives of servants.

For example, a few congregants had formed a group they called "Modern Mystics." The group had started in the fall and was causing somewhat of a stir. The stated purpose of the group was to promote a closer walk with God, but rumor had it that the Modern Mystics had been getting closer to God sitting barefoot in yoga-style positions with the lights turned off, in the dark church parlor, while staring at candles, burning incense, and chanting. It seemed that they danced every now and then, too. This was way too much for many people, but Liz and Helen had both been attending the meetings and loved them. So when they invited me to try out one of the meetings, I decided to tag along. If something was encouraging people in their relationship with God, then I was all for it.

The meeting started with the instructor, a congregant who had recently received a certificate in spiritual disciplines from a nearby seminary, talking about how to get centered so that one could enter into a state of experiencing God's love. She promised this state would make us feel peaceful and energized. I took my seat in the floor in between Liz and Helen. We were sitting in yoga positions with our hands resting on our knees and palms toward the ceiling. The rumors were true. The meeting had a distracting wannabe New Age feel to it.

Liz leaned over and whispered in my ear, nodding toward the instructor, "She is the Mystic Momma!"

"Liz!" I feigned disapproval at the nickname. "Does she know you call her that?"

Shifting back into her own space, she opened only one eye as she answered me, "Yes! She likes it." Liz sat in a perfect yoga pose looking serene.

I kept my eyes open for another moment, looking around, and then closed mine, too, and began to pray. With our eyes closed, the instructor melodically reminded us to concentrate on God's love for us. She helped us picture God's love in various ways. The whole goal of the activity was to relax and let God's love make us feel good. Peeking, I noticed that both Liz and Helen were really getting into it. Liz looked especially adorable. The lights from the candles danced in her silver hair as she sat on the floor praying, barefooted in the semi-dark room.

There was certainly nothing wrong with taking time to concentrate on God's great love for us. In addition, I had long felt there was a huge need for the twenty-first-century Protestant followers of Christ to reclaim the ancient practices of meditation, silence, prayer, fasting, confession, pilgrimages, liturgical dancing, and worship—many of which had been lost over the centuries since the Reformation.[1] Scripture told us to "be still and know that I am God."[2] King David danced "with all his might" as an act of worship.[3] I was all for creativity in practicing spiritual disciplines. Yet something I couldn't quite put my finger on was missing here.

After we continued praying in this manner for a while, the teacher closed the prayer segment of the gathering by asking for our attention. Next, she gave a mini-lecture on the importance of keeping Sabbath. The instructor said that we should pick one day a week to practice Sabbath and for a twenty-four-hour period, we were to do only what made us personally happy. She described Sabbath as a day of indulgence to look forward to each week where we would forget all of life's commitments and just live. She told the young mothers in the group to find someone to keep their children for as much of the day as was possible, to find a restaurant with good food and wine to indulge themselves in, to get a massage, and to gather a group of girlfriends to relax without husbands around. For the Mystic Momma, the whole point of Sabbath keeping, like the whole point of the earlier prayer exercise, was to leave one's problems behind and to feel good. With that observation, I suddenly knew what was missing. I remembered what the prophet Isaiah wrote:

> If you refrain from trampling the sabbath, from pursuing your own interests on my holy day; if you call the sabbath a delight and the holy day of the LORD honorable; if you honor it, not going your own ways, serving your own interests, or pursuing your own affairs; then you shall take delight in the LORD, and I will make you ride upon the heights of the earth. (Isa 58:13–14)

These spiritual disciplines were focused on making ourselves feel good, not on moving us toward servanthood.

---

1. Rice, *Reformed Spirituality*, 9–11.
2. Ps 46:10.
3. 2 Sam 6:12–23.

As I left the Modern Mystics, I headed toward my office. The church was filled with people coming and going. I loved the welcoming community feel the church had when lots of people were around and things were happening. It felt like church should feel—upbeat, friendly, lots of laughter. As I passed one of the conference rooms, I spotted Rodney just as he spotted me. His short straight brown hair was always headed in different directions as if he had just woken up and his beard always looked slightly untrimmed. Seeing him made me smile. I got a big welcoming grin back from him. He was part of the group volunteering to build a Habitat house and this morning they were doing some resource planning. There was no doubt by the look on Rodney's face that he was glad to be doing something purposeful during his furlough. Upon seeing me, he waved me into the room. I went in and sat down at an empty seat around the big conference table filled with retirees.

All of the men were a good thirty years older than Rodney was, but they were clearly looking to him for leadership. These retirees were not the type I would consider truly retired. They might not be working for pay any more, but they hadn't stopped working. They were always doing something good for someone who needed it. They all said hi to me at once. After I said hi back, Rodney began to speak for the whole team. He complained that one of the main team members, whose name was George, had sent word this morning that he could no longer take part, even though he had agreed to be the lead on this next project. George was a retired residential builder whose second (and much younger) wife had left him just after he retired. Unfortunately for George, his wife leaving and the economy falling apart had gone hand in hand. Most builders had suffered a setback. It seemed like George had just decided to retire instead of fighting with the economy. Yet, I was surprised to hear that George had quit the Habitat team. It wasn't like George. He had very little going on in his life right now to keep himself busy, so this Habitat work seemed like it would be good for him and right up his alley. I asked why George wasn't going to be able to take part. One of the men sitting across from Rodney explained that George was seeing a Christian counselor because he still hadn't gotten over the divorce. The counselor had told him that he needed to take a break from life and focus on getting back to spiritual health. Before the first man could finish the story, another man popped up and mocked George in a less than flattering rendition, "I can't do any work for a 'season' until I am spiritually focused."

The all-male flannel-plaid-shirt-wearing planning team was greatly amused hearing this "sissy" talk from big burly George. Many jokes followed as they poked fun at George. In truth, they really admired him and were just amused, but also they were greatly disappointed because they had been counting on his expertise and leadership to make the Habitat build go smoothly. I didn't want to take part in mocking poor George, though I couldn't help but smile at their amusement.

George's counselor was apparently under the impression that until George had adjusted to the divorce he was off the hook from being God's servant. This was not unique to George. Somehow, most of us were under the impression that we needed to fix our problems before we were able to be servants. We thought taking a break from life whenever things weren't going our way was the thing to do. Yet James tells us that our problems "produce endurance"—the ability to keep on serving God even in hard times. James would not have agreed that a servant should wait until he or she is problem free before serving the master.

No sooner than I had left the Habitat meeting, my thoughts turned to the two groups that I would be working with that evening at the church: the Prayer Warriors and the Fortnight Bible Study. The Prayer Warriors, a group of faithful Christians, had been praying for whatever was on the church prayer list for as long as anyone could remember. They gathered together weekly in the church library to tell God what they thought God should do for other people—often for complete strangers whose names had been put on the prayer list by well-intending members. If a person had a broken leg, the Prayer Warriors would tell God to heal it. They simply told God to do whatever the person requesting the prayer asked for.

The meetings more often than not spiraled into benevolent gossip sessions, with each prayer warrior disclosing what they had heard about the person or situations on the prayer list. A lot of sympathetic wagging of heads back and forth occurred. Their prayers were about fixing problems—not the holistic prayers of servants seeking to take part personally in God's mission. For instance, they never asked God to show them how they might personally intervene to help the person who was in need. They simply brought a wish list of needs and wants to God each week. It was more or less offering the person being prayed for a blessing. There was a place for this, but somewhere our prayers needed to extend beyond fixing problems and venture into servanthood, asking for wisdom and power to serve God.

Similarly troubling was the Fortnight Bible Study. I loved teaching the Bible, and these participants were avid students of Scripture. Despite their faithfulness, factual knowledge of God was not the same as experiencing God and certainly not the same as doing the work of God. One more Bible study that focused on gaining more information instead of going out and living a servant's life was not going to solve our problems. Collecting facts about God but never focusing on putting what was learned into action was just another recipe for chronic self-centered problems.

If I summed up all of these observations, I'd have to say The Church in the Suburbs was stuck trying to get God to fix our problems. We had forgotten who we were in Christ: servants. If the spiritual disciplines practiced at the church, if the counseling at the counseling center, if the prayers of the Prayer Warriors, and if lessons of the Fortnight Bible Study never moved the participants into servanthood, then it might explain why our problems seemed to consume us. After thinking prayerfully about this for a while, I concluded that I, too, was contributing to keeping my congregants sick by coddling them instead of teaching them to deal with their problems. I was actually hindering their ability to become fulfilled as the servants of God.

At the same time as I seemed to be discovering what was plaguing us, I prepared for the next study group by rereading a variety of commentaries. In doing so, I now found myself at odds with the great majority of scholars who had written about James's epistle. Most, if not all, believed that the epistle was random wisdom literature, much like the Old Testament book of Proverbs.[4] These scholars believed that the epistle just happened to start with instructions on how Christians should deal with their problems. However, I no longer thought anything about James's epistle was random. I had come to believe that the early church, even in the midst of persecution, had the same kind of self-indulgent focus that my congregants and I had. I believed that they had become so consumed with their own problems (albeit more legitimate problems than we often had) that their faith had become focused on seeking to escape their trials—their persecution—rather than actively pursuing lives of servanthood. Perhaps they had become paralyzed in fear—scared to death even. We, on the other hand, had become paralyzed by our lives of privilege. The result was the same. Both then and now, the followers of Jesus were in danger of never becoming his hands and feet—of having no works to show for our faith.

James says, "Faith by itself, if it has no works, is dead."[5] Dead faith sits around believing God will fix our problems, give us more of what we want, and be on our side in any conflict. Faith that is alive serves God and others regardless of any problems we might face. To that end, James starts his epistle with instructions on how to deal with problems. That is not random, because after he has dealt with his church's problems, then he instructs them on how to live the servant's life.

I am not sure that James would have thought of the next verses as a five-fold strategy for dealing with our problems, but I did. And I would present James's strategy at the next study group meeting.

4. Palmer, *Book That James Wrote*, 13–16; Clifford, *Wisdom Literature*, 167–68.
5. Jas 2:17.

9

James's Strategy—James 1:2–5

My brothers and sisters, whenever you face trials of any kind, consider it nothing but joy, because you know that the testing of your faith produces endurance; and let endurance have its full effect, so that you may be mature and complete, lacking in nothing. If any of you is lacking in wisdom, ask God, who gives to all generously and ungrudgingly, and it will be given you.

—JAMES 1:2–5

One spring evening, my husband and I ventured out to the movies. *Silver Linings Playbook* was showing. It struck me that the main character, Pat, played by Bradley Cooper, had the same problem that many of us have: we don't have a strategy to deal with our problems so that we can get on with the business of living. In the movie, Pat has an angry and violent reaction to finding his wife with another man and nearly kills the man. Not only does Pat lose his wife, lose his job, and end up in a mental hospital, but he also has a hard time coming to grips with the reality of his situation. Even after he is released from the hospital, he has the unwavering belief that he will reconcile with his wife.

Pat tells his psychiatrist, "Nikki's waiting for me to get in shape and get my life in order, and then she's gonna be with me." In other words, he thinks that if he works at it hard enough, his problems are all going to go away. He is ignoring the fact that Nikki has taken out a restraining order against him and doesn't want to see him.

The psychiatrist has a wise response, "Pat, there's a possibility, and I want you to be prepared for it, that she may not return . . . I don't want you to fall apart. So get a strategy, okay? You need one."

James was giving his congregants the same advice: their problems weren't going to go away so they needed a strategy to deal with them so that they could going on living—serving God—despite their trials. James used the word "trials" to describe anything that had the potential to keep the followers of Christ from serving God. Trials could manifest themselves as challenges, temptations, tragedies, or even personal interests placed before God. I use the word "problems," but whatever we call them, James had a strategy—not for fixing them, but for dealing with them:

- Accept problems as a servant's way of life

- Understand the problems

- See problems as joy

- Endure problems

- Ask for wisdom

I planned to cover the first four bullets of James's strategy in this month's study, but the final bullet, "Asking for wisdom," would be a whole lesson of its own the following month.[1]

ACCEPT PROBLEMS AS A SERVANT'S WAY OF LIFE

. . . whenever you face trials of any kind . . .

—JAS 1:2B

It is important to note that "trials" is plural. James wanted his congregants to know that they could expect that they would have more than one. Furthermore, in order to accept problems as their way of life, they needed to come to the realization that God would not usually make their problems miraculously disappear. This was true whether they were innocent or guilty in causing the problem. It was also true whether they had faith that God could fix their problems or not. In fact, they could have been entirely free of fault while fully believing God could do a miracle and still God might not have intervened. We need to accept this, too, because our faith is not measured by how much we believe but by our service to God even in the face of adversities. Part of accepting that there will be problems means that

---

1. Likewise, chapter 9 covers all of James's strategy except for "Ask for Wisdom," which is covered in chapter 11.

we realize that God does not give up on us even when our problems are of our own making. James says "trials of *any* kind." Even when they are our own fault, God wants to use them to make us mature and complete.

Around six hundred years before James wrote his epistle—right before the original diaspora[2]—God had sent the prophet Ezekiel to the Jews to tell them that God would no longer tolerate their oppression of the poor and needy, their idolatry, or any of the other sins that they were blatantly committing before God.[3] The Jews believed that because they did not heed Ezekiel's warnings, the *diaspora* came to pass. Daniel was a young man of the first diaspora. Because of the sins of his community, God allowed him to be taken by the Babylonians from the land that God had given them into a land where he would be held captive.[4]

For Daniel, the diaspora was a somewhat different experience than for most Jews. Daniel, because he was handsome and smart, was forced directly into the king's service.[5] The king would kidnap the cream of the crop with the best physical and mental potential and bring them into his own palace. There he would re-educate them to the Babylonian ways while feeding and housing them in luxury. When they were ready, the king would make these young men leaders in his kingdom often sending them back to govern their homeland. This way, the cultures of diverse conquered people would assimilate quickly. In addition, the conquered nation could take pride that they had one of their prized young men in charge. In contrast, it wasn't all fun and games for these young men. They were routinely castrated so that their loyalty to the king would not be compromised for the love of a hometown girl. They were stripped of their previous identity, taught a new language, and even given a new name. They were separated from their families, friends, and religion. In this new homeland, these were just a few of the problems they faced that had been brought on because of their community's unfaithfulness to God.[6] Nevertheless, God did not turn away from Daniel. God used Daniel's problems—being served unhealthy food, being forbidden to pray, and being forced to face lions in the lion's den and fire in the furnace—to make him mature and complete. Likewise, God will not turn away from us when we face trials that are brought on by missteps.

Joe was the first to speak up after I told Daniel's story at the study meeting. Not long after Joe had graduated from the University of Georgia with

---

2. See chapter 7 for a discussion of the Diaspora.

3. Ezek 17:12–24.

4. Dan 1:1–6.

5. Longman and Garland, *Daniel*, 49–54.

6. Smith-Christopher, *Biblical Theology of Exile*, 65–74.

an MBA, his college frat mate, Dave, had taken a job managing the daily operations of a multi-million dollar hotel chain. There were plenty of perks in Dave's business. One of them was getting free hotel rooms when he traveled. The only rule that Dave really had to follow was not to share a room with anyone except his immediate family. This rule was meant to protect the company against what Joe called "funny business." In a moment of extremely poor judgment, his friend Dave had invited a member of the opposite sex, who was not his wife, to stay with him in his room. It was the end of Dave's rather short career in hotel management and plunged him into deep depression.

I interjected into Joe's story, "It seems that Dave experienced a sort of diaspora of his own."

"Yes. An exile for sure! His playboy ways weren't what his company wanted to promote to its customers or employees. He was out on his ear."

Dave had a lot of problems on his hands. How to pay the mortgage, how to resolve things with his spouse, how to provide for his kids, how to get another job. Sadly, Joe went on to tell us that Dave lost everything, including his house, wife, and kids. It was years before Dave got back on his feet. Joe pondered whether it might have helped Dave if he had known that God wasn't done with him even though he had messed up.

There are plenty of examples in the Bible of people who messed up. In fact, King David was an adulterer—perhaps a rapist—and a murderer.[7] Paul was a murderer, too.[8] What these men had in common was that after they asked God to forgive them, they forgave themselves. Then without looking back, they became God's faithful servants.

There will be problems—maybe a whole lot of problems. Some we cause. Some we don't. Accepting this is the first step toward dealing with our problems and moving toward a life of service.

UNDERSTAND THE PROBLEMS

. . . consider it . . .

—Jas 1:2c

The Greek word for "consider" means to think through or to measure. James didn't want the followers of Christ to distract themselves from their problems or pretend there weren't problems. He wanted them to look at the truth of their circumstances and understand them. This means looking at the facts and being aware of one's options.

7. 2 Sam 11:1–24.
8. Acts 22:20.

The spiritual exercises that the Mystic Momma had been teaching her group were comfort techniques at best, distraction techniques at worst. Both had some merit, but if these techniques never led us to a place where we could look our trials straight in the eye, then the techniques were only enabling us to avoid dealing with our problems and life. Alternatively, James was telling his readers to think their problems through and measure them out.

Along these lines, I knew I needed to follow James's lead and instead of coddling my congregants, offer some kind of pastoral guidance to the Modern Mystics. About a week before the study group meeting, my opportunity arrived. I happened to be in my office at the church when Helen, Liz, and the Mystic Momma passed by on their way home after their gathering. They were chatting away as they headed down the hall passing by my office, when they suddenly got quiet. The next thing I knew, Liz, who was walking in the middle of the two women, had latched arms with Helen and the Mystic Momma. Like little girls, they were giggling while backing up into the door of my office. The door wasn't wide enough for all of them to enter at once so they eventually turned around, came on in, and one by one sat down. They wanted to know why I didn't come to the meeting of the Modern Mystics that morning.

Liz noticed that I was searching for the right words and demanded, "Out with it girly! Was the chanting too much for you?"

"No. That isn't really it. I can't make it every week, but I'll come by again sometime. " There it was. I was starting down a path of coddling—enabling, instead of speaking the truth gently. Taking a deep breath, I stepped back and boldly explained that I saw an opportunity for the spiritual exercises of the Modern Mystics to go beyond basking in the love and comfort of God toward discerning how they can serve God and others.

"Hmmm," said Liz while the Mystic Momma stared at me with a concerned look on her face. She was young, attractive, and had no idea that her spiritual exercises might be considered odd by anyone. After a few more moments, Liz said, "Could you say a little more about that?"

"I made no sense at all—did I?"

Liz, looking at the others, laughed and said, "No dear. But we are still listening."

The birth story of one of my children popped into my mind and on the spur of the moment, I decided to tell it. Without a doubt, I knew that these three nonconformist women could handle my own non-conformity. Therefore, I began, "Life is sort of like labor . . ."

When I was preparing for the birth of my first child, I took a childbirth class that taught distraction and comfort techniques to cope with labor. One technique used a variety of breathing rhythms. The distraction techniques worked for a time, but the great majority of mothers using distraction techniques reported that they would eventually turn to pain medication for comfort. This was the case in my first son's birth.

When I had my second child, I hired a midwife. I asked her about using breathing techniques during labor. She said that there was a place for them, but she wanted me to get comfortable with facing labor head on. It was going to be a lot of work and I needed to accept that right up front. Instead of using anything to distract me, she would help me embrace labor, trusting that God had made my body to work properly and that the contractions would guide me.

I finished my story. The women stared at me.

"Well I guess that was clear as mud!" Finally, without beating around the bush further, I asked the women if we couldn't expand the spiritual disciplines they practiced beyond comfort techniques toward more directly helping people do the work of God.

"You think we are distracting ourselves from dealing with life?" Liz always had a way of putting things out there in black and white. She was a great listener.

"Well, there is nothing wrong with being still and feeling the love of God. Yet if that is where our relationship with God stops, we aren't maturing. I think that opening up a space to contemplate both our problems and how we can serve God despite them would take the Modern Mystics to a whole new level."

"Why not?" the Mystic Momma shrugged her tattooed shoulder. She seemed pleased with the suggestion.

Liz saw the relief on my face and laughed, "You intellectual types are always overthinking things." Liz stood. Pointing her finger at me she added, "Helen and I are on our way to buy a couple of yoga mats for our prayer time. I am getting you one, too!" It was hard to disagree with Liz! What she had to say was always coated in wisdom.

SEE PROBLEMS AS JOY

. . . nothing but joy . . .

—JAS 1:2D

When I was in labor, despite the best efforts of my midwife, I have to admit that I became tired and fearful at some point. Graciously, my midwife did not give up reminding me that I needed to see that the labor pains were a gift from God. It changed everything. When I stopped telling God to take away the pain and started seeing the pain as something purposeful, I was able to relax and get on with the work I needed to do to usher my son into the world.

Humans tend to experience problems with stress, fear, and even panic. It is no wonder that we have developed a myriad of ways to distract ourselves from our problems. I have to admit, the comfort techniques of the Modern Mystics were far better than turning to alcohol, sex, or drugs! Despite that, James, in stark contrast, gave his congregants an outlandish coping technique. He, like my midwife, told them to have a radical attitude toward the pain. James said to experience problems as "nothing but joy."

It helps to understand that joy and happiness are two very different things. Happiness in the face of difficult problems is likely impossible. Joy is not. In English, we can distinguish "joy" from the word "happiness" by considering the Old English roots of the word "happiness." "Hap" means "chance or luck." Happiness, like "happenstance," depends on one's circumstances—whereas, joy does not. Joy doesn't happen to us. It is a choice. Joy is the choice to be positive, praising God in every situation while knowing God is in control. We can be happy when we get a raise, see a beautiful flower, lose ten pounds, or get to spend time with a friend. Joy, on the other hand, can be chosen even when happiness is impossible—for instance, when we face loneliness, illness, death, unemployment, and even persecution. The people James was writing to were facing persecution, a condition where I don't imagine happiness can exist, but James told them to be joyful! Not because they were faking themselves into believing that God was miraculously going to take the persecution away, but because they could trust that their trials had a holy purpose.

ENDURE PROBLEMS

. . . you know that the testing of your faith produces endurance; and let endurance have its full effect, so that you may be mature and complete, lacking in nothing.

—Jas 1:3–4

James told his congregants to endure because there was purpose in their problems. He wanted them to look beyond their trials and see God at work. He promised that if they endured, they would be "mature and complete." The word "mature" is also translated as "perfect" in other places in Scripture. It is the same word that Jesus used in the Sermon on the Mount: "Be perfect, therefore, as your heavenly Father is perfect."[9] God doesn't cause our trials, but God uses our trials to mold within us a godly character. James intended for the followers of Christ to understand that in their endurance of problems, they would be empowered to become who God created them to be.

There is a New Testament story about a man named Stephen that also drives home James's point.[10] Stephen's story is one of faithful endurance. He was a young servant of Christ in the first-century church who performed great signs and wonders among his fellow Jews. Although many Jews became servants of Christ, following Christ was a very unpopular thing among the leaders of the Jews whose power and authority was threatened. Therefore, the leaders confronted Stephen and brought him before the council for a trial. Stephen did not endure his trial by shutting down. Stephen spoke the truth of the gospel. The Jewish leaders became enraged at Stephen and decided to kill him by stoning him. Immediately, Stephen was facing an even greater problem—death. Again, Stephen did not use comfort techniques nor did he simply endure the stoning, waiting to die. We are told that he rejoiced as he "gazed into heaven and saw the glory of God and Jesus standing at the right hand of God."[11] Stephen saw what the physical world saw and accepted that he was about to die. Then he looked through his circumstances into the spiritual world and saw Jesus. He began to pray aloud that God would forgive the men who were stoning him. Stephen's death left an indelible mark on the early church of someone who took seriously the teachings of Jesus to love his enemies. His death also had a profound impact on the conversion of the Apostle Paul, who witnessed it.[12]

Consider Moses. He killed an Egyptian in passionate anger while standing up for his fellow Jews, who had been enslaved by the Egyptians.[13] Afterward, Moses was forced to run for his life into exile in the wilderness. He experienced a lot of problems in exile, but he endured every one (homelessness, learning to be a shepherd, and integrating as a husband and father into a foreign culture). He could have been overcome with guilt knowing that he had committed murder. He could have decided that murder was unredeemable and given up, but he didn't.

Because he endured, God called him to lead the Jewish people out of Egypt. However, Moses didn't want to face the problems of being God's representative to the Pharaoh and tried to play his disability card: "I am slow

9. Matt 5:48.

10. Acts 6:8—8:2.

11. Acts 7:55.

12. Acts 22:20.

13. Exod 2:11–15.

of speech and slow of tongue."[14] The Jews have long believed that Moses stuttered, and yet, God picked him to be the one to talk to Pharaoh.[15] Moses saw his circumstances very clearly, but he looked through his physical circumstances and saw the spiritual reality, in which God had a purpose in putting him through these problems. Endurance is not sitting tight and waiting for a miracle. Endurance is serving God despite our disabilities.

As I wrapped up the lesson that month, Liz shared a story from her teenage years. Liz had grown up in a tumultuous neighborhood in the Deep South where her father was a pastor. The Ku Klux Klan (KKK), a hate group, was active against immigrants there. One night, on Liz's way home from work, she cut through the parking lot of a locally owned immigrant grocery store where she spotted the older brother of one of her friends. He was a known member of the KKK. At that moment, he was dousing the backside of the store exterior in some kind of liquid. There were other men with him. Liz was still in high school and just barely sixteen. She told no one what she had seen.

The next day, the morning paper carried the story that the store had burned to the ground overnight. She knew by name who had set the fire, but still she told no one. Liz was afraid for herself and her parents, but she regretted all her life that she had never come forward. Enduring problems by hiding in fear was not what James had in mind. Endurance meant serving God. In this case, it meant standing up for justice.

The study group meetings were lasting longer than I had anticipated, but no one seemed to mind. As Olivia was leaving, she pulled me into the entrance hall of my house and asked if she could come by and see me in two weeks. She was leaving on a business trip the next day and then to see her husband who was still spending most of his time in Chicago. However, she wanted to talk when she got back.

I said, "Of course," wishing she would talk to me now. Her brown eyes looked—not exactly sad—but more vulnerable than I had ever seen them look. Something was wrong.

14. Exod 4:10–12.

15. Scharfstein, *Torah and Commentary*, 167.

10

Applying James's Strategy

Two weeks later, Olivia and I got together. Olivia had gone into work that morning but was taking a midmorning break to drive over to my house. She was impeccably dressed as usual, with the I-am-climbing-the-corporate-ladder pencil skirt, sweater, and scarf. Though she was direct, she was not her usual bull-in-a-china-shop self.

"I think I am being pushed out," she said matter-of-factly.

"Out of your job?" I asked, already knowing the answer. She was the third female executive from our church who Joe had pushed out of his company. It was hardly a believable scenario, but it was what it was. He had fired or replaced some secretaries and non-executive personnel, too—almost always women. The turnover was very high at the corporate office among people who Joe did not consider his long-term associates.

"Yes. By Joe," she answered.

"Olivia, what has happened?"

She told me that getting promoted to the executive suite as Senior Vice President of Marketing had been very exciting. It was exactly what she had hoped for and been groomed for. She knew the business well. Upon her arrival, Joe had paraded her around to customer sites and board meetings. He told people that she was the answer to taking the company to the next level. She felt she had gotten off to a good start, but then it was time to get down to business.

Her organization's job was to define new features and products for engineering to develop, but also to provide sales with the resources to take the product to market and to win contracts. However, there were company practices that were old fashioned, worn out, and no longer working. She needed to revamp these immediately. Actually, she was shocked with how bad things were and truly surprised that the company had been able to get the kind of big government contracts it was winning. She wanted to make changes before it affected the business. Even so, she needed Joe and the board to back her because it would require some expense and reorganizing of the whole marketing organization. Some of the engineering organization, which she did not manage, would be affected, too. At the same time, it would put marketing closer to customers and in the field with sales. In the long run, it would make products better, sales more lucrative, and contracts easier to win.

She had talked her strategy over with Joe, but could never get him to commit. This went on for some months. Frustrated, she decided to talk to a few of her peers about her ideas, one of whom was the Senior Vice President of Engineering. It turned out that he wasn't open to anything that would affect his engineering group. He reacted poorly and seemed threatened. She knew he had been at the company for several decades, but little did she know that he considered himself Joe's best friend. But then again, what did it matter? Her ideas were not a secret.

It was then that she saw a different side of Joe for the first time. He came into her office and unashamedly shouted at her. He was mad that she had shared her ideas. Joe berated her and accused her of trying to go behind his back. He even went so far as to tell her that she would not last at his company. Since her office had mostly glass walls, the entire executive suite had both witnessed and heard Joe's tirade.

Not only did she find Joe's behavior over the top, but she also felt there was absolutely nothing wrong with sharing her ideas with her peers. Good plans usually required collaboration. Talking with another executive wasn't tantamount to going behind Joe's back. Joe's reaction seemed odd to her. Then even more disturbing was that he called her late that night at home and apologized. The apology was over the top, too, showering her with an embarrassing amount of praise. She had begun to doubt that working with Joe was even a possibility.

After relaying the story, she said, "I want to try handling this problem using James's strategy instead of strategizing over whatever is best for my career. Will you help me?"

"What an honor to be asked." I shook my head yes.

"I brought the handout from our last meeting with me." She unfolded it and we looked at what I had called James's strategy. We began to step through the bullet points.

ACCEPT PROBLEMS AS A SERVANT'S WAY OF LIFE

This was easy for Olivia, not having grown up in the church where many of us have been taught that if we have enough faith, then God will address every problem with a miracle. She wasn't looking for a miracle, just God's direction. Olivia realized that she was experiencing something else for the first time. She was giving control of her problems to God. With that came unanticipated relief. In the past, she had felt alone as she had worked her way up the corporate ladder. Now she believed that God was with her.

UNDERSTAND THE PROBLEMS

Olivia had already explained the situation to me very well. Obviously, she had put some thought into it and understood the facts. She wasn't in denial that there were problems. Moreover, she wasn't troubled over whether she was in the wrong or right. When things go awry, so many Christians immediately believe that they have done something wrong to deserve it. Olivia didn't bring this misplaced guilt with her. She had no doubt that Joe was acting without cause.

I asked her to state the problem concisely in one sentence.

"I have taken a position where I may not be able to do my job because of my boss."

I asked her to consider all of her options. She laid them out one by one in detail. In summary, they consisted of staying and quietly trying to make the best of it, going to the board and making them decide how they wanted the company run, leaving immediately, or staying just long enough until she found a job.

"Out of curiosity, Olivia, what would be the best thing for your career?"

"Formally sending my plan for the marketing organization to Joe and copying the board. Then offering my resignation if they are unable to support my ideas. This would have the same effect of making my ideas public both within the leadership of the company and to anyone who mattered outside the company. As far as resigning, there really is no need for me to continue at this company if I am going to be forced to watch it degrade when their problems are either solvable or preventable. If Joe is not going to take sound expert advice, waiting around would do nothing for my career and nothing for the company. As my ideas found their way to the outside technology community, the experts would see me as smart and no-nonsense. Joe would be seen as a fool."

"Are you certain that is *not* what God wants you to do?"

"It is one of my options, but if this is what God wants me to do, I want to know for sure."

SEE PROBLEMS AS JOY

Olivia wasn't exactly happy, as this threw a big wrench into her career plans, and she expressed her disappointment over what she had thought was a great opportunity. It could potentially set her back in her career and be a financial hit. Nevertheless, she wasn't fearful either. We talked about the difference between being happy and joyful again. Olivia said that she wouldn't exactly call what she was feeling joy either. For her it felt more like peace—like contentment that God had her back.

Olivia, like the rest of us, may never see how God is at work within her problems. On the other hand, God's presence may become obvious. Either way, James promises that our problems are never without purpose. There is a scene in the Gospel of John where Jesus compares the Holy Spirit to wind—we can't see it, but we can see it at work.[1] Over the years, it had become a hobby of mine to watch for the Holy Spirit at work. I told Olivia to keep her eyes open for rustling leaves and swaying branches.

Then she asked the kind of question that makes me want to blurt out an answer, but ethically, I can't.

"Have you ever seen or heard of Joe raking anyone over the coals before? And then afterwards offering an over-the-top apology?"

Yes. I had. I wanted to tell her all that I knew so badly. "Olivia, I can't talk about another congregant to you. Just like I can't talk to Joe about anything that you have said today. You could ask others who have worked for him."

If the past repeats itself, it was only a matter of time until Olivia was out the corporate door. The story was always pretty much the same. The woman had been—in Joe's mind—disloyal to him or the company in some way. It appeared to insiders as paranoia. The less confident women would work hard to make him like them despite his abusive behavior, which seemed to get worse the harder they tried. Some would see the writing on the wall and start looking for a new job while tolerating his mistreatment. The more confident ones would just quit. The story Joe always put out was that the woman was somehow either incompetent or mentally disturbed. I wondered how, after this situation had occurred with so many women, his board of directors could back him. Surely, by now there were obviously both

---

1. John 3:8.

legal and ethical issues at play. All the same, the board seemed very protective of Joe. Perhaps it was simply that he had made them a lot of money.

Despite his terrible treatment of women in the workplace, as far as I knew, Joe had always been good to his wife when she had been alive. Yet, for some reason, he could not tolerate having a woman in the executive office. It seemed to me that Joe had a deep psychological problem that was way beyond my training to diagnose.

ENDURE PROBLEMS

I could see that Olivia had already made up her mind to do what God would tell her to do. I had no doubt that when God's will was clear to her that God would also give her the power to endure. We discussed how having patience in waiting for God's direction and timing would be important.

ASK FOR WISDOM

As if on cue, Olivia asked, "How will I know that God is speaking to me?"

I had planned to teach about asking for wisdom at the next study group meeting, but went ahead and gave her the simple answer. "Ask and then listen." I suggested that she spend time meditating daily in a quiet place where no one would distract her. I asked her to lay the problem out before God—tell God all about it. She wasn't to ask God to handle it a certain way, but to simply tell God what was going on. Then she was to listen, letting God speak into her mind and heart concerning the problem. Olivia was to repeat this time of prayer and meditation daily until she felt God had spoken to her. She shouldn't expect an immediate answer. However, an answer would come. It might come during her prayer time, but it could come at any time in any form. Setting aside time to allow God to talk to her about her problem would open her heart to hearing God whenever God was ready to speak.

I watched Olivia walk slowly (at least it was slow for Olivia) up my driveway to the street where she had parked her car. It wasn't a sad walk. It was as if she was taking time to breathe in and enjoy the fresh air. It was as if she had never noticed the breeze on her skin before. She was enjoying it. Something was happening to Olivia. This is why I had become a pastor. I wanted a front row seat where I could catch a glimpse of the breezes created by the Spirit.

11

Asking for Wisdom—James 1:5

If any of you is lacking in wisdom, ask God, who gives to all generously and ungrudgingly, and it will be given you.

—JAMES 1:5

James's strategy for handling problems was incomplete until we turned to God for wisdom. However, getting God's wisdom should be easy since James told us that if we ask for it, we would receive it. Asking God for wisdom was not a new practice. Ten centuries prior to James's epistle, Scripture recorded the story of King Solomon, a king with a nation to run.[1] Things weren't going badly for King Solomon at all. In fact, things were going quite well. Still, he didn't want to run his nation any old way. He wanted God's guidance. So he gathered up his leaders and took them to a holy place on top of a mountain where they had a big blowout party worshiping God. Then, when nighttime came, Solomon went to sleep on the mountain. I picture cool dry desert mountain air and cozy good sleep. Somewhere in the night, Solomon began to dream.

God must have enjoyed the party Solomon and his leaders had thrown, because in the dream, God spoke to him and said, "What do you need from me?"

Solomon answered, "Give me wisdom so that I can lead this people of yours."

---

1. 2 Chr 1.

God was extremely impressed with King Solomon's request. Solomon demonstrated that he cared more about others than himself. Solomon didn't ask for protection for himself or harm to his enemies or even riches. Therefore, God gave him wisdom in spades. King Solomon became known as the wisest man to have ever lived. Centuries later, James wrote that followers of Christ get wisdom in exactly the same way as King Solomon: they ask.

James also wrote that the followers of Christ could ask for wisdom knowing that God offers it generously and ungrudgingly. God doesn't hold back. God doesn't say, "If you do this for me, then I will give you wisdom." God doesn't check an ethereal list somewhere to see whether we deserve wisdom or not. God wants us to have it and gives it generously to those who ask.[2]

Working with Olivia to think through James's strategy for her particular set of circumstances had made preparation for the next study purposeful with a direct application. I couldn't wait to teach it. It was a rainy evening when everyone showed up at my house.

I began by posing a question to the group, "How often do you lack wisdom in dealing with the situations that you find yourselves in?"

Most of the group answered in unison, with several saying, "Often!," or, "Almost always." Except for Pastor Eddie and Joe, of course. Pastor Eddie commented proudly that wisdom was one of his spiritual gifts. I accidentally raised my eyebrows for a second, then without comment caught myself. I looked away embarrassed at my unguarded reaction and went on with the lesson. Joe said nothing.

Going through life without feeling that one had the benefit of God's wisdom was obviously a common problem among followers of Christ. Congregants would often tell me that they had asked for wisdom for particular problems, but never seemed to get an answer. One reason was that they asked, but never really listened for the answer. Most of us have the habit of asking God for direction, but not taking time to let God speak. Maybe we feel that we need to make a decision right away rather than waiting for clear direction. Maybe we just don't understand that part of prayer is being quiet in the presence of God and letting God speak into our thoughts. Either way, we need to ask, but we also need to listen.

Another reason we ask for wisdom and don't get it is that often we don't know what wisdom is and therefore don't recognize it.

"So what is wisdom?" I asked the group.

In one of those awkward moments for a pastor, Helen, who had been pretty quiet in the Bible studies so far, spoke up first with an answer that was

2. Perkins, *First and Second Peter*, 98–99.

doctrinally questionable. She quoted the Dalai Lama: "This is my simple religion. There is no need for temples; no need for complicated philosophy. Our own brain, our own heart is our temple; the philosophy is kindness."[3]

It was one of those teaching moments, but I didn't want to embarrass her. I approached it positively. "That quote parallels much of Christian doctrine. Plus I love the call in it for simplicity." I went on to explain that we agree with the Dalai Lama that it is our heart that is important and not the building where we gather to worship God. We also agree that kindness—though we might call it love—has everything to do with being a follower of Jesus. However, where Christianity differs from Buddhism is that we do not believe that our own brains and hearts are enough to give us wisdom. Christians really do depend on the supernatural Spirit of God. I cringed inside, hoping I was affirming enough to Helen, but she smiled, reassuring me that all was well. It is a hard line to walk between being respectful of other religions and, at the same time, preserving beliefs that are distinctively Christian.

I told the group that I thought what I was saying would make more sense if I started by talking about what wisdom is *not*. Throughout Scripture, wisdom is neither human logic nor a body of knowledge, which, once mastered, helps us make a decision. Believe it or not, we can accurately know all the facts and figures—use our finest logic derived from years of experience—and still not have wisdom.

Consider the prophet Hosea.[4] God told him to marry a tramp.[5] This is clearly not advice I would give my sons. It makes no sense. It isn't logical. Hosea knew that the woman God was telling him to marry was and would be unfaithful. Hosea knew all about her. However, God told him to marry her and Hosea did. Hosea was wise, not because he studied the facts and did what was reasonable. He was wise because he followed what God told him to do. To the rest of us, it looks ridiculous, even foolish, to choose a wife who is going to break your heart. However, God asked Hosea to do this for the sake of teaching Israel the pain they were causing God through their unfaithfulness. Through Hosea, we learn that wisdom will not always lead us to a place that makes sense to the world. Wisdom doesn't promise a successful marriage or career. If bettering yourself financially or finding happiness was what you were expecting from wisdom, you might not recognize wisdom when God gives it to you.

3. Piburn, *Dalai Lama*, 38.

4. Hos 1:1—3:5.

5. Hos 1:2.

Joe listened politely, but when I was done, he spoke up. He had a way of speaking that quashed any further thoughts or ideas that anyone else might venture to share. He was attempting to quell my lesson this time. That put me on edge. Furthermore, I had been dumbfounded all evening at how Joe did not show any discomfort at being around Olivia despite their recent row. He didn't act more friendly to her, but he didn't act less friendly either. I guess in his mind, he had apologized and all was well with the world. I wondered if he was even fully aware of how he had behaved toward her and the other women he had run off. Olivia, on the other hand, was well aware of the situation, but, in turn, did not act in the least bit emotional about it.

Joe went on to inform us, as if making a declaration, "God would never ask us to do something that logically seems incorrect." He didn't offer another interpretation of Hosea. Instead, in a booming authoritative voice he declared that he had grown his company on logic and reason. He thought these were God-given gifts and we should use them. He claimed proudly that he had never asked God for wisdom in running his business, but had just stuck to making sound decisions and staying ahead of his competitors. He sat with his arms and legs crossed. Joe had spoken and no one need give a different opinion. His tone was meant to dress me down and intimidate me.

And I *was* momentarily intimidated. Even with Joe's stern opinion laid out in front of us, I think most of us could relate to what Joe was saying. None of us wanted God to tell us to marry an unfaithful spouse. None of us wanted to look foolish either. Joe was bringing up some interesting thoughts. If they just hadn't been so strongly stated, we might have had a great discussion, but he just shut it down. Except for Helen. Helen, unpredictably, not the least bit worried about Joe, expressed yet another side of what some of us were thinking. She had been pondering the Dalai Lama's quote. She said that it was actually a relief to her that there was a supernatural component to wisdom and that it wasn't just based on our limited understandings. She found comfort in the fact that it wasn't all up to her and that she could go to God with questions and expect answers.

Her comment was a welcome voice over and against Joe's. She set me back at ease. I went on with the lesson citing another thing that wisdom is not: wisdom is not following a list of rules. Almost anyone can be motivated to follow a list of rules for any number of reasons. Rule following doesn't require wisdom nor does it require a loving heart that is focused on serving God. It may require discipline if you actually desire to break the rules, but it doesn't require wisdom. Furthermore, just about any rule can be justifiably broken under the right circumstances. In fact, sometimes keeping a rule is unwise.

I shared a story that I thought might resonate with Joe. There was a big technology company, not unlike his own, in the Silicon Valley that had given all of its employees badges with a digital strip. They were to use the badges to enter and leave the building. The employees would slide their badges through the reader and it would record their coming and going. There were two rules. First, employees were not allowed to let anyone in or anyone out who didn't have a working badge. Second, everyone without exception was to run his or her badge through the reader before entering or leaving the building. The company wanted to track employees' movements in and out of the building, thus improving security in a highly classified lab. It also kept their employees safe. The theory was that if the building ever needed to be evacuated due to a fire or disaster, security would know who was in the building, where people were located, and how to get people out quickly. One day there was a fire in one of the labs. People tried to flee from the building. Masses huddle at each door trying to run their badges through the badge reader as they left. Due to the sheer number of people throughout the facility trying to access the badge readers, the readers crept to a snail's pace. Smoke filled the hallways. People were collapsing. The situation became dire. Finally, a truly wise person yelled with great authority, "Move immediately out the door! Please do not run your badge through the badge reader." This wise person was a new college intern. He had no authority, but, as my grandmother would have said, "he had lots of horse sense." The young man was credited with saving the lives of several hundred employees. My point was that following even good rules does not necessarily demonstrate wisdom.

Joe spoke up again, perhaps even more authoritatively this time. He said my example applied to human rules, but not to the rules in the Bible. He firmly stated that the rules in the Bible weren't meant to be broken under any circumstance.

Rodney pointed out to Joe that although many people claim to follow the rules in the Bible, no one really does. He began to list the ones that The Church in the Suburbs breaks: divorced elders and deacons, a female pastor who teaches both men and women, Wednesday night dinners that serve shellfish, congregants that wear fabrics of mixed fibers, and women who don't wear hats to church—but do wear makeup.

Rodney's list was running on when Pastor Eddie inserted, "Joe, you have to admit that this world would be a much gloomier place if women didn't wear makeup." There were a few snickers from the group, and Liz kicked Eddie's shin with her toe, but Joe's demeanor showed no leeway—no chance of respecting our theological differences.

Joe and Rodney ignored Eddie and went right on arguing over the rules. I didn't want to spend the rest of the meeting stepping through every rule and evaluating why we followed it or not, so I moved on by giving an example of wisdom from Scripture this time. There is a New Testament story of Jesus healing on the Sabbath.[6] The Pharisees pointed out to Jesus that this was against God's law. Jesus answered their complaints against him by asking, "Are you angry with me because I healed a man's whole body on the Sabbath? Do not judge by appearances, but judge with right judgment."[7]

Wisdom is not the same as following a list of rules. Wisdom understands that true righteousness comes from demonstrating God's love to others. If we are expecting that wisdom will always follow a set of rules ignoring situations where the rules lack love—where they trample on or hurt others—then we may not recognize wisdom when we see it.

Joe was still not buying it. Unexpectedly, he was turning out to be a legalist who saw the Christian life as black and white. I wondered if this had anything to do with his issues with women. Perhaps he was dedicated to a rule that women shouldn't work. His wife, Annie, had never worked. My mind drifted in different directions as I thought about what was going on in Joe's mind.

Armed with more examples and knowing that Joe would not like them, I proceeded with caution. The first was contained in the Old Testament book of Job. Job was a man who truly relied on God's wisdom and not his own. Unfortunately, within a day's time, Job lost everything—his wealth, his health, and his family. Job's friends tried to convince him that he had committed some unknown sin and should repent. Nevertheless, Job held firm in the wisdom that these problems were not a result of his personal sin and that God was still on his side. His friends, however, had bought into the prosperity gospel that taught that if you did what was right and had enough faith you were guaranteed health and wealth.[8] Job's friends falsely believed that God would not allow a person who had followed God's wisdom to have problems or suffer in any way. If it were true that Job had not sinned, then this would be evidence that they had no control over God and no guarantee of the kind of life they wanted.

---

6. John 5:5–16.

7. John 7:23b–24.

8. The prosperity gospel teaches that if a Christian keeps a list of rules, verbalizes to others their belief that God will bless them, and gives financially to the church, then God will reward them with financial wealth and good health. Most churches who teach the prosperity gospel are independent, non-denominational churches. Kroesbergen, *In Search of Health and Wealth*, 22–25.

Job did not accept the prosperity gospel that his friends were teaching. Job had a different understanding of wisdom than his friends: "But truly it is the spirit in a mortal, the breath of the Almighty, that makes for understanding."[9] In other words, Job believed that his wisdom was a result of God breathing into him the Spirit of God.[10]

Listening to the Spirit of God instead of his misguided friends probably saved Job years of counseling trying to sort through what he had done to cause such calamity. James knew what Job knew. Wisdom takes us down God's path, not to make us successful or popular or even to protect us from problems. Wisdom takes us to a place where we can serve the master. If we are expecting that wisdom will be advice that will keep us from all problems or even solve our latest problem, we may not recognize wisdom when it is given to us.

When I was done with the example, the whole group—without really meaning to—including myself, looked over at Joe, waiting for him to tell me how wrong I was. But he was done with me. He had determined not to say another word. When he realized we were all looking at him waiting, he rotated his hands upward, shook his head, and said, "I give up," and laughed. It was a good moment and we all laughed with him. Looking back on that conversation, I think we all felt Joe was adding a level of unwelcomed pressure to the group, but at that second, when he laughed, we felt relief.

Well, if wisdom is not human logic or following a list of rules or a pathway to success, then what is wisdom? There is a similar story from King Solomon's life. King Solomon's wisdom became legendary after two prostitutes came to him with a problem. They had each given birth, but one of the two babies had died. Now the women were disputing whose child had lived. They both claimed the living child as their own and wanted Solomon to decide the identity of the real mother. In a colorful display, the king said, "Bring me a sword!" He proposed to chop the child in half so each could have part of the child. The real mother of the child immediately became overwhelmed with the desire to protect her child from harm, offering the child to the other woman. It was then that Solomon knew the true mother by her sacrificial love for her child. Scripture says, "All Israel heard of the judgment that the king had rendered; and they stood in awe of the king, because they perceived that the wisdom of God was in him, to execute justice."[11] Solomon was not just smart, not just able to analyze data and form

---

9. Job 32:8.

10. Nystrom, *James*, 50–51.

11. 1 Kgs 3:15–28.

a plan, but Solomon had the wisdom of God in him. This wisdom enabled him to deal with problems in a faithful way.

Later King Solomon wrote a book called "Wisdom" that is not part of the Protestant Bible. In it, he also writes about wisdom as a gift from God: "Therefore I prayed, and understanding was given me; I called on God, and the Spirit of Wisdom came to me."[12] Wisdom, as it turns out, is the living Spirit of God.[13] It enabled King Solomon to solve and deal with problems. This kind of wisdom does not come from experience or knowledge. It is not fact or logic. It is alive and knows the very heart and desires of God.

My final example was odd, somewhat spooky, but kind of fun, too. I asked the group if they remembered Daniel, the young man of the first diaspora from one of our early meetings.[14] He was faced with many trials while in forced service to the King of Babylon. On this occasion, the king was throwing a party when he decided to serve his guests with the sanctified goblets, the ones his army had stolen from the temple in Jerusalem.[15] Not a good idea! Fingers of a disembodied human hand suddenly appeared and began to write on the plaster wall of the palace. Of course, this was frightening—something right out of *The X-Files*—unexplainable and eerie. The words written on the wall were not in a language that anyone knew. It was then that the king was encouraged by his advisors to send for Daniel to interpret them: "There is a man in your kingdom who is endowed with a spirit of the holy gods. In the days of your father he was found to have enlightenment, understanding, and wisdom like the wisdom of the gods."[16] Even Daniel's kidnappers knew that his wisdom was the living Spirit of God indwelling him. Daniel went on to demonstrate his wisdom by interpreting what had been written on the wall.

No doubt, James knew the stories of Job, Solomon, and Daniel. He knew that wisdom was a living spirit that indwelled followers of God. This living spirit, the Holy Spirit, was the eternal and perfect source of wisdom. It indwelled believers and revealed to them everything they needed to know to serve God faithfully. When James told his readers to ask for wisdom, he was teaching them to do more than verbalize the words. He was telling them to open their lives to the Holy Spirit's presence so that the wisdom of God could be active and alive in every aspect of their lives.[17]

---

12. Wis 7:7.

13. Winston, *Wisdom of Solomon*, 178–83.

14. See chapter 9.

15. Dan 5.

16. Dan 5:11.

17. Nystrom, *James*, 50–51.

12

Doubting—James 1:6–7

But ask in faith, never doubting, for the one who doubts is like a wave of the sea, driven and tossed by the wind; for the doubter, being double-minded and unstable in every way, must not expect to receive anything from the Lord.

—JAMES 1:6–7

I had given the study group two reasons why we ask for wisdom and don't get it. One was that we don't take time to listen for the answer. The second was that we don't recognize God's wisdom when it is given to us. However, James gives yet another reason. James says our asking must be done "in faith, never doubting." It is important to know that in the Epistle of James, faith is not the belief that God will do whatever we ask. Faith is action that follows the Holy Spirit's wisdom.[1] When we "ask in faith, never doubting," we do not ask for what we want to happen and try to believe hard enough that God will make it happen. Instead, we ask for wisdom to do what God wants us to do, believing God will give us both the wisdom and power to do God's work.[2]

On hearing this, Olivia told us of a former coworker, Doug. He was a thirty-something single businessman who held the executive position in

---

1. *Merriam-Webster Dictionary*, s.v. "faith," makes an interesting note that in the 1600s when the King's James Bible was translated, *faith* was a verb rather than the noun it has become in modern times.

2. Nystrom, *James*, 51–53.

the customer service department of an up-and-coming dot com. She had met him years ago while she was interviewing for a sister position over the marketing organization of the same company. She described Doug as a clean-cut, nicely dressed man who pushed his works-oriented religion until he turned everyone off around him.

"He must have thought that I was a Christian, because during the interview process he confided in me that God had told him . . ."

I interrupted, "So God had given him wisdom?"

"Exactly. Doug believed that God had told him—given him wisdom—that this job would be his last. God had also told him that this company, which we both would own a small part of, was going to make him—and me, if I took the job—wealthy. He seemed to have no doubt that God was going to bless the company right into a public offering where he would sell his stock and retire into the lap of luxury."

From Olivia's description, Doug seemed to have a lot of what is mistaken as faith. However, the kind of faith James was talking about was not an unwavering belief that God would bless us. Faith, for James, was the action of a servant doing the work of God. Doug suffered from the prosperity gospel.[3] This false gospel had led him to think God's goal was to make him happy, successful, and wealthy in exchange for his faith and obedience.

"After the interview, I took the job, not based on Doug's claims, but because it was a good job. I got to know Doug pretty well over the next couple of years. I doubt that Doug had any concept of a God who would call him into servanthood. He was asking for wisdom to succeed in his job because he wanted to retire and still be able to afford his million-dollar home and cute little sports car. Faith came into play only because he thought he had to believe hard enough to get what he wanted."

Doug, like most of us, had no idea that servanthood might mean living with less, working harder, and maybe even never retiring. Doug had overlooked that when Jesus invited people to follow him, Jesus never mentioned his followers getting wealthy. He did mention them selling all that they had.[4] Jesus described poverty, suffering, trials, rejection, etc. as a follower's way of life.[5] He even told some of his followers that they would be martyred on his behalf.[6] Doug's faith, on the other hand, was about his personal success. However, James's definition of "asking in faith" means the followers of Christ are to ask for wisdom, believing that God will give them wisdom so

3. See chapter 11 for a discussion on the prosperity gospel.
4. Matt 19:21–24.
5. John 15:20.
6. Matt 20:22–23.

that they can serve him. We are to ask for the sake of serving God, not for our own benefit.

Olivia finished her story by saying, "Sadly, and rather unjustly, within a year or two, Doug was asked to leave the company before it ever made him rich." Doug had missed the point of "not doubting." Not doubting had nothing to do with believing hard enough that God would make him rich.

As we read further in the epistle, it was especially fascinating to me that James compared the doubter to "waves of the sea." I shared with the group a surreal vacation experience from years earlier. My husband, sons, and I had spent more than six weeks together sailing the Caribbean in a three-masted schooner. We had sailed in calm seas and in rough ones. On one occasion in particular, the seas had been stirred up by a constant wind, which caused the waves to build and build to more than sixteen feet. These sixteen-foot waves furiously splashed over the top deck of our ship. One day, we had been sailing in these waves on open sea since early morning trying to reach Buck Island Reef National Park. Ships were not allowed to anchor at Buck Island for fear that they would interfere with the underwater ecosystem of the park. The authorities on the island had told us to anchor some distance away from the island and then they would send out a boat to bring us to shore, but as the waves seemed to get more violent, it became obvious to us that transferring from our schooner to a Buck Island boat would be impossible. The waves would have bounced the Buck Island boat back and forth in one direction while continuing to rock our larger ship in another direction. Changing ships in this situation would have been exceedingly dangerous if not completely impossible. We had no control over the stability of either vessel. If we were tossed from one of the boats into the water, we could have been crushed between them.

These were the images in James's mind when he described the instability of those who ask for wisdom without having faith that God will give them wisdom. There isn't anything stable under their feet. The kind of person who seeks wisdom, but doesn't believe God will give it to them, bounces around all over the place. In one moment, they are flung in a westerly direction thinking that surely God is sending them west. In the next moment, they are flung toward the northeast thinking that surely God is now sending them northeast. The wind blows them around into this wave and that wave. They have no understanding of where they are going or why. They assume that when the waves are pleasant they have followed God's wisdom, but when the waves are angry God is not pleased with them. There is no point in God giving this person wisdom, because they are not anchored. They are constantly second guessing themselves and God.

James calls people bounced by the waves "double minded." This is a word that James appears to have coined, since it has never been found in any other first-century literature.[7] Translated literally, it means, "split soul." If we doubt that God has given us wisdom, then our souls are split and James says not to expect that God has spoken. Even if God should give the doubter wisdom, then they will never really be certain that they have it. Moreover, if the followers of Christ aren't certain they are following the wisdom of God, then they can't experience the peace and joy of being guided by God. James not only says doubting is anathema to receiving wisdom, but he goes onto say that the one who doubts is "unstable in every way." It is a strong warning. Those who doubt are not just unstable in dealing with a particular problem, but completely unstable. To act when we are unsure that God has given us wisdom makes us completely unstable.

The lesson was coming to a close when Olivia jumped in with an important question. She had been praying fifteen minutes a day, as we had discussed on the day she had ventured over to my house. She had been asking for God's wisdom about the situation with Joe for two weeks now. She didn't give anything away to the group, but subtly asked, "I feel God's presence in my prayer life, but I do not have an answer yet to a question I have been posing to God. Am I doing something wrong? How long should I expect this to take?"

"Patience, Grasshopper," said Pastor Eddie in an Eastern accent, sounding like Mr. Miyagi from *The Karate Kid*. Next, he touched his hands together into a prayer position, bowed his head toward Olivia, and added in the same accent, "It may take long time. God's timing not your timing."

Pastor Eddie was politically incorrect as usual, but theologically correct this time. God is not going to answer until God is ready. We can't hurry God along. God doesn't work on our deadline. We just have to wait, meanwhile serving God. The *meanwhile* is very important. While we wait, we don't put our service to God on hold. We serve God while we wait.

This seemed to wake Rodney up from deep contemplation. He said, "I am a living example that we can create problems for ourselves if we are not willing to wait for God's wisdom. In the early days on the mission field, my wife and I tried to make decisions by asking God for guidance, but when God didn't answer fast enough, we picked whatever path we wanted the most."

Not long after Rodney and his wife had gone to Africa, they asked God for a piece of diagnostic equipment that Rodney had found useful in the States. It wasn't absolutely necessary, but Rodney wanted it to simplify

---

7. Motyer, *Message of James*, 40.

diagnoses. He had enough funds to buy it, but it would mean they couldn't get other things that were also important to the clinic. They started talking to God about the decision. In reality, Rodney said that they prayed for about thirty seconds and expected the answer to show up. Forty-five seconds later, when God hadn't spoken, they debated it, made a list of pros and cons, and stressed out. Then they decided to make a choice based on what they wanted the most and ordered it. Of course, before they acted on their choice, they shot up a prayer saying, "Stop us if this isn't your will."

Looking back on it now and laughing, Rodney said, "I call this the 'Stop Me' method of serving Jesus." It really was pretty funny when you thought about it. Something most of us could relate to. How could we *follow* Jesus if we were *running out ahead* of Jesus, daring Jesus to chase after and stop us?

"Believe me," Rodney went on, "when our decision enabled me to make a quicker diagnosis, we'd say, 'God gave us wisdom when we bought this machine!' Those ocean waves that you spoke of would be gentle. Life was good. But when the equipment began to have problems due to the lack of air conditioning at the clinic, we'd say, 'We made a big mistake.' And those waves would kick up and make us queasy. We'd change direction and bounce around some. We'd regret all the money we had spent and ask God for forgiveness. Then, when we found a way to protect the machine from the heat and moisture, we'd be back to thinking we had done the right thing. Then we'd see another way we could have spent our funds and we'd be regretting our purchase all over again. We were the perfect picture of the double-minded couple! Our souls, instead of knowing that God had given us wisdom, always doubted because we didn't wait until God spoke."

Rodney was right. It is very hard not to doubt whether you have received wisdom if your game plan is to wait and see if things go well for you. So many times, when we are seeing and following God's wisdom perfectly, things are awful if you look at them from a human perspective. When we follow God, there are going to be negative things that happen, as well as hardships. In fact, James had just gotten through telling his congregants to expect problems. Just because we have problems doesn't mean we have failed to follow God's wisdom. Just because it looks like a disaster to the world, doesn't mean God hasn't been leading us. Jesus often calls us to follow him into disasters. How—if you are waiting for God to stop you—will you know the difference between a wrong step that caused a disaster and a right step taken intentionally into a disaster for the sake of Christ? You will always wonder if you have chosen the right path if you are running ahead of God instead of following.

The group disbanded and we all headed home. The next morning, I drove over to the church an hour or so before I was committed to being there and walked down Church Street to where it crossed Main. There was a classy little coffee shop on Main where I could hang out with my computer and write for a while. This morning I found Rodney working. While he was home on furlough, he was to raise funds for his clinic, as well as rest. He waved me over and I snuggled into the red leather chair next to him.

"Wazzup?" I smiled.

"Going to ask you the same thing."

"I asked first," not really having anything exciting to share.

"Joe took me hunting last Thursday?" He spoke it as if it were a question—as if I got to determine if it was exciting enough news to share with me.

"Did you shoot anything?"

"Between the two of us we brought home three turkeys. I shot two of them!"

"No way!"

"Actually, I hunt small game quite often in Africa."

"I had no idea."

Then Rodney got serious, "What do you know about Olivia?"

"You know I can't talk about other congregants except what is public knowledge. She just transferred down from Chicago into the corporate office of Joe's company. You know all of this. She runs the marketing organization there. Why?"

Rodney went on to tell me that Joe had casually mentioned Olivia on the drive to the hunting lodge. In typical Joe fashion, he was putting out some ugly innuendoes about Olivia. No hard facts. Nothing that could be checked out. Just insinuations that she wasn't capable. She'd upset some of the people in the corporate office. Didn't fit in. Wasn't making the changes fast enough that they had brought her in to make. Doubts about her competency were topped off by Joe's questioning her mental stability. He thought she was too emotional for the job. He quoted rumors that she had gotten fired from her last company.

Rodney finished and I sat with my eyebrows raised. I could see that Joe was up to the same old tricks. How could he be so cold-hearted, manipulative, and have absolutely no shame? He came across as charming when he wanted to be. He had the ability to make one feel important, but I was beginning to see that it was all an act. Joe's charm was superficial. Underneath it, he had a high sense of self-worth, but he was nothing more than a cunning manipulator. For the life of me, I could not understand why the board of directors put up with him.

"What?" Rodney inquired.

"What do you mean?

"You were thinking awfully hard about something."

"Yep," I replied shaking my head slowly up and down, eyebrows still raised, staring at the wall behind Rodney. There was nothing I could say except, "Rodney, before you tell anyone else this—before you even believe it yourself, I would suggest you and your wife get to know Olivia. If she is crazy, you can help her. If she isn't crazy, it sounds like she is going to be unemployed soon and needing friends."

"So you are saying that she isn't crazy."

"I am saying nothing." I got up, smiled mischievously, and waved goodbye to Rodney. I walked back down Main Street to Church Street, turned right, and went to my office wondering how this would manifest itself at the June study group.

13

Two Common Problems—James 1:9-12

Let the believer who is lowly boast in being raised up, and the rich in being brought low, because the rich will disappear like a flower in the field. For the sun rises with its scorching heat and withers the field; its flower falls, and its beauty perishes. It is the same way with the rich; in the midst of a busy life, they will wither away. Blessed is anyone who endures temptation. Such a one has stood the test and will receive the crown of life that the Lord has promised to those who love him.

—JAMES 1:9–12

Pastor Eddie had a way of making just about everyone uncomfortable at one time or another. A few days following the study on wisdom, it was my turn—again. Eddie and I both entered the parking lot at the same time that morning and he waited for me to get out of my car. He had been to the gym and was standing there in spandex shorts and a tight t-shirt holding his gym bag. Eddie was particularly muscular, but there wasn't a whole lot floating around upstairs. Even intelligent women swooned over him until he opened his mouth. Then they couldn't run away fast enough. I wanted to run, too, but it was too late, he had seen me. No matter how I tried not to express it, he exasperated me with his political incorrectness and arrogance.

"Hello Eddie." I tried to sound friendly.

Eddie moved inside my personal space and said, "Can you come to my office. We need to talk."

"About what?" I was still trying not to sound annoyed.

"About the Bible Study."

"Eddie, why don't you tell me what is bothering you right now?"

"Okay, but you aren't going to like this."

I always took everything Eddie said and divided it by ten to make it less dramatic and more representative of the truth. I knew whatever he had to say was not the end of the world. Despite that, I also knew he wanted me to think it was the end of the world, which infuriated me.

"What's up Eddie?" This time I showed my annoyance.

"You need to tone down some stuff at the Bible Study."

"What stuff?"

"Well, for a starter, the stuff about wisdom not being logical. And then the stuff about how wisdom doesn't come from keeping a list of rules."

"Why?"

Eddie hemmed and hawed as if what he had to say next was really going to be devastating to me and didn't want to hurt me. In truth, he enjoyed creating drama. "Joe is upset. He thinks you aren't orthodox."

"Did he tell you this, Eddie?"

"Yes. He told me this." Eddie ended his sentence by capping it off with my name just like I had done to him. It was his way of mocking me. Tactics of seventh graders.

"What did Joe say?"

Eddie went on a long rambling explanation. From what I gathered, at a meeting with the senior pastor in which Eddie was present, Joe got off the subject at hand and mentioned our study. Joe said he thinks I am too liberal. Instead of conforming to rules of the Bible, he says I am touting a gospel where everyone does whatever they want under the guise of the Holy Spirit leading them.

"Well, does Joe know you are telling me this?"

"No."

"Thank you for telling me, but I have to teach what James taught. Eddie, I think Joe is—heck, I think we all are—going to struggle with what James taught a lot more as we progress through the book. The whole epistle calls out our way of living and calls us into a new way of living. If Joe wants to blame me for taking him out of his comfort zone, he is wrong to do so. The Scriptures are challenging him. I am just the facilitator. If he disagrees with my interpretation, then he is more than welcome to share his own interpretation—that is why the group was formed. Shoot—we might all decide we agree with him! But my goal can't be to teach the study so it makes Joe happy."

With that, I walked into the building, leaving Eddie stretching his calves in the parking lot. Eddie yelled after me with a smile on his face and a tone in his voice. His words said, "I think you are underestimating the problems you are stirring up. You need to back off," but the tone said, "Nee-ner-nee-ner," daring me not to take him seriously.

This illustrated precisely why Eddie had been at the church for so long despite his often offensive and un-pastoral behavior. He knew who to snuggle up to and make happy. He made that a priority above all else. I shook my head, reminding myself not to be judgmental toward Eddie. I wondered if Joe was upset or not. Honestly, there probably was some amount of truth to Eddie's story, but there was no way of telling how much. Perhaps Joe planned to go after Olivia and me in one fell swoop. Thinking of how Olivia took her situation so unemotionally and with so much determination to serve God, I figured the least I could do was practice what I preached and deal with this problem just as James had taught. I took a few minutes when I got to my office to think through James's strategy, applying it to this situation. Afterward, I was determined to plow ahead, letting God lead my teaching, refusing to be afraid of Joe or irritated with Eddie.

Preparing for the next lesson was easy. I could understand how at first glance the verses appeared as random advice, having something to do with economic justice, but, once again, I did not believe that anything about this epistle was random. A common misinterpretation of these verses is that they make a promise to the lowly believer (God would give them more) and a warning to the wealthy non-believer (God would make them poor). However, a careful reading shows that this is not where James goes, nor does James do what he will do later in his epistle, where he encourages the followers of Jesus to fight injustices against the poor.[1]

Instead, James follows up what he has just written by giving two examples to ponder. One example is the trial of having too little. The other is the trial of having too much. James is not the first to teach about these two types of trials. Jesus taught these lessons before James. To those who did not have enough, Jesus said, "Do not keep striving for what you are to eat and what you are to drink, and do not keep worrying. For it is the nations of the world that strive after all these things, and your Father knows that you need them."[2] To those who had too much, Jesus said, "Sell your possessions, and give alms."[3]

I had begun the meeting by laying out James's first example, the trial of having too little. Those who did not have enough (enough money, enough power, enough friends, enough of a job, enough of anything) were going

1. See Jas 5:1–6, and chap 24 of this book.
2. Luke 12:29–31.
3. Luke 12:33.

through a very common trial. Rather than fretting over when, where, and how their needs would be met, James has already taught them that all problems should be counted as joy. Here, he even writes that the poor should boast. Left to our own logic, most of us have made the mistake that the impoverished should pray for more of whatever they are lacking, but James does not tell either the rich or the poor to ask God to change their circumstances. The poor are not raised up by God giving them whatever they lack, nor are the rich brought low by God taking whatever they had too much of. All are made whole by being faithful servants who endure.

Furthermore, the poor are not to see themselves as being looked at unfavorably by God because they are in need of help. Even the rich perish like a flower in the field—it is the human condition of both the rich and the poor to be helpless in the scheme of life and death.[4] Neither poverty nor wealth can be seen as punishments or gifts from God. Even if we are lacking what we need because of a bad decision or some fault of our own, we are to know that God can still use our trials to make us mature and complete.[5]

I didn't get very far with my example before Rodney took over. He explained that Malawi, with a poverty rate of forty percent and an ultra-poverty rate of fifteen percent, had a great need for sanitized water.[6] Diarrhea due to contaminated drinking water was the leading cause of infant mortality, with more than a quarter of all Malawians lacking access to clean drinking water.[7] Through a partner church in the United States, a scholarship was made available to send a native from the village where Rodney's clinic was located to Mzuzu University in Malawi where they would study Water Resource Management. The most promising young person, a woman who had excelled in high school, was chosen. She, her husband, and their two children packed their bags and headed off to the university. Rodney described them as a beautiful family always sitting in the second pew at church on Sunday mornings. The scholarship covered the woman's tuition, but not their living expenses. Jobs were hard to come by and the one her husband was able to get near the university did not meet all of their financial needs. They were persistently struggling financially and constantly asking God for a miracle. Every week after church, their large extended family would come to the reception area at Rodney's clinic and wait for this little family of four

---

4. Barclay, *Letters of James*, 58.

5. See chapter 9.

6. Clancy, *Republic of Malawi*, 9.

7. Sudeshna and Morella, *Africa's Water*, 1. Further, as of February 12, 2014, WaterAid listed on its website, www.wateraid.org, that 2.4 million people in Malawi do not have access to safe water. Over half of the population does not have adequate sanitation, and 3,500 children die each year from diarrhea caused by poor sanitation.

to call home. Then whatever news they had would be relayed around the room until everyone knew all there was to know. Afterward, their family would stay and pray for them.

The miracles came one after another, always just enough to pay the latest bill. Never a windfall, but they never went hungry or without clothes or shelter. When they would have a decision to make, the whole village asked God to send them wisdom and waited for God to direct their steps. Month after month God provided. Rodney said that the family approached each trial with joy. They would find out about some unplanned fee at school and Rodney would listen on the call as the mother's voice lit up. She would tell the crowd her latest problem and then laugh! Not sarcastically. There was joy in her laughter. She saw the Holy Spirit as the mischievous person of the Trinity who couldn't wait to delight her with another surprise. In fact, the whole village laughed with her. They were all excited to see how the Holy Spirit would show up each and every time.

Because this little family knew that they had followed God's will by going to Mzuzu, when trouble hit, they never doubted that God would provide. They didn't bounce around on the ocean, because their faith was stable. Even when their grocery money for a week's worth of groceries was stolen, the little family still praised God. As they endured the trial of having too little, Rodney watched God make them mature and complete. Their faith was so strong that they would even take the miracles God gave them and spread them around to those who had bigger financial needs than their own. They often told stories of how they had helped those in need. They were mature servants of God.

Rodney seemed to come to the end of the story, so I began to talk about what it meant to experience the trial of having too much. Before I could get very far down that road, Rodney took over again.

The day came when the mother of this little family graduated from the university. Not only did she return to her village to begin work, but the work she was doing to bring clean drinking water to the region would be completely funded and she would be given a good salary. What a celebration! Rodney glowed as he told about that first Sunday when they came home for good. The husband had told Rodney, "You know, doctor, now that we have enough to take care of ourselves, we are afraid we will stop seeing the miracles of God."

In truth, the job was anything but high paying by suburban standards, but it would cover all of their basic needs and a few luxuries. For them, they had now entered into the trial of having too much. This trial applies to those with too much of anything (clothes, food, money, etc.). Although the goal of the wealthy followers of Jesus is not to become needy, it is also not to retain their wealth or obtain more. For those that have too much, their trial is to put all that they have to good use in service to their master. For this, they need to seek wisdom too.

The trial of having too much, unlike James's followers who faced severe poverty, is the hardest trial many of us will ever go through in the suburbs.[8] Yet, most of us in the suburbs would be unaware that we are even facing a trial. We assume we are either to spend our blessings on ourselves or save them for our future. We hold dear pithy sayings such as "the one with the most toys wins," "pay yourself first," "save for a rainy day." But James calls us to lay down the wisdom of the world and seek the wisdom of God instead.[9] The trial of having too much will be before us every time we collect a paycheck, every time our investments increase, and every time we are given money or resources of any kind. Each time, we need to ask God for wisdom to show us how to bless others with our resources. This is our sacred responsibility.[10] Would we decide to hoard our money away for a rainy day, ignoring people who need it now? Could we trust God to supply our future needs or would we need to feed our 401(k)s? The questions are difficult. The solution is simple:

> A certain ruler asked Jesus, "Good Teacher, what must I do to inherit eternal life?" Jesus said to him, "Why do you call me good? No one is good but God alone. You know the commandments: 'You shall not commit adultery; You shall not murder; You shall not steal; You shall not bear false witness; Honor your father and mother.'" He replied, "I have kept all these since my youth." When Jesus heard this, he said to him, "There is still one thing lacking. Sell all that you own and distribute the money to the poor, and you will have treasure in heaven; then come, follow me." But when he heard this, he became sad; for he was very rich. Jesus looked at him and said, "How hard it is for those who have wealth to enter the kingdom of God! Indeed, it is easier for a camel to go through the eye of a needle than for someone who is rich to enter the kingdom of God." (Luke 18:18–25)

The solution might have been simple, but the challenge was whether we would be obedient to Christ's teachings. Rodney had covered the two

---

8. Moo, *James*, 69 indicates that a famine had struck Palestine at this time (Acts 11:28–29) and that it was probable that Christians would have suffered particularly severely because they were ostracized by the majority population.

9. Nystrom, *James*, 69.

10. Motyer, *Message*, 45.

examples James gave so well that I didn't feel a need to elaborate and I moved on to the final verse in this section.

> Blessed is anyone who endures temptation. Such a one has stood the test and will receive the crown of life that the Lord has promised to those who love him. (Jas 1:12)

The words that both James and the translators use in this verse are fascinating. First, the word *blessed* is the same word that Jesus uses in the Sermon on the Mount to describe those who follow him. I think this demonstrates the closeness of James to Jesus and that perhaps he even heard Jesus preach that sermon.[11] Second, the word *temptation* is the same word that the translators translate as *trials* in James 1:2.[12] I do not understand why the translators were inconsistent in using two different words in the same section of verses. It gives the impression that James is changing the subject in this verse from our "trials" to our "temptations." This is not the case. James does not distinguish between trials and temptations. It is more likely that James intentionally chose one word and used it in both places to emphasize that every trial—every problem—is a temptation in which we have an opportunity to endure, counting it as joy and letting God use it to make us mature and complete.

Finally, James ends this section with a promise. Those who endure are blessed with an award, the crown of life.[13] However, there are night and day differences between the way God gives awards and the way our culture gives awards. God has promised the crown of life to those who endure trials. On the other hand, the world only gives out awards to those who succeed. The world isn't very impressed as to whether you endured a trial or not. The world is impressed by measurable success. Be that as it may, worldly success is not what is important to God.

To many people the life of Christ looked unsuccessful. Instead of playing his cards right and staying on good terms with authorities until he had gained enough popularity to beat them at their own game, Jesus died the death of a cursed criminal. Crucifixion is not a mark of worldly success, but Scripture says that Jesus endured—obeying and following the wisdom of God to the very end. Our trials, even though we follow God's wisdom and endure, may not meet the world's idea of success. Therefore, we must leave the outcome up to God and not worry about meeting the

11. Matt 5.

12. Moo, *James*, 73.

13. Barclay, *Letters of James*, 48–49, describes four images the crown invokes: flowers worn at a wedding, precious metal worn by royalty, a wreath worn by the winner of a competition, and a figurative crown indicating good qualities.

world's expectations. God does not require that we be successful, only that we endure.

Remembering the difference in what God sees as important and what the world sees as important is a good thing for us to hold dear for our own spiritual and mental well-being. Humans rarely admire people who have a track record that looks unsuccessful. But God does.

14

The Potential of Problems—James 1:13–18

No one, when tempted, should say, "I am being tempted by God"; for God cannot be tempted by evil and he himself tempts no one. But one is tempted by one's own desire, being lured and enticed by it; then, when that desire has conceived, it gives birth to sin, and that sin, when it is fully grown, gives birth to death. Do not be deceived, my beloved. Every generous act of giving, with every perfect gift, is from above, coming down from the Father of lights, with whom there is no variation or shadow due to change. In fulfillment of his own purpose he gave us birth by the word of truth, so that we would become a kind of firstfruits of his creatures.

—JAMES 1:13–18

Pastor Eddie had been using Sophie "to pick up babes" at the local dog park. I am not proud of going along with this. And I am not the one who called the unsuspecting women "babes." That was Eddie's word. To him every woman was a babe. He had dated the "banker babe" he met at the bank and the "software babe" who wrote code at Joe's company. There was even the "bid'ness babe" who taught in the MBA program at Georgia Tech. Once he called me the "babe of the cloth," but I quickly put an end to that.

Walking Sophie started when my husband and I went away for the weekend and couldn't find a pet sitter. Eddie volunteered. I really didn't want Sophie spending time with him, but my husband said that was ridiculous so

I eventually came around and let her go to Eddie's house for the weekend. Ever since then Eddie had been coming by several times a week to take her to the doggie park. Sophie adored Eddie and the attention that he gave her.

However, I noticed that Eddie was coming around less on the weekends and going out of town a lot—taking Friday off and coming back late Saturday night in time for Sunday worship. I figured that he had a girlfriend out of state. I wondered why he was still trying to meet women at the park. I knew better than to ask Eddie these sorts of questions. The inane conversations that ensued always made me regret asking, but curiosity got the better of me this time.

Turned out he was running errands for Joe. A few months back Eddie had run into Eddie's old college roommate having dinner with Joe at a local restaurant. Eddie hadn't seen his roommate in a decade. It was a great reunion, which ended in the wee morning hours. Joe, of course, had left the two of them to party alone and had gone home early in the evening. Eddie's old roommate was a Pentagon employee doing some business with Joe's company. Neither Eddie nor his roommate had been aware that the other knew Joe.

About a month later, Joe had called Eddie and asked him if he might like to take a trip to Washington, DC, where Eddie's roommate lived, and pick up some papers that Joe didn't want to trust to the post office. I queried Eddie as to when the post office had become unreliable. He explained to me unconvincingly that the post office could be fairly unreliable. Whatever. At any rate, Joe said he would pay for all the expenses so Eddie went. He had done this for Joe several times now. Joe was paying for his trips and Eddie was getting to hang out with his old friend and meet "politico babes" living inside the DC beltway.

"Stop calling women 'babes' Eddie!"

"Why? They like it."

"No they don't. Anyway, why can't you pick one woman and just settle down?" I teased.

"One woman is one problem too many. And I stopped manufacturing problems for myself a long time ago," Eddie's eyes sparkled as he served back his reply knowing it would rile me up.

"Well it is a good thing this month's lesson is on using problems to their full potential. Maybe this will help you figure out how to handle your one-woman problem."

"Handle babes?" He asked, befuddled, as if I had just questioned his manhood. "I know how to handle babes."

"Problems, Eddie. Not babes. How to handle problems." There I was again, regretting having started the conversation. Yet, I couldn't help but laugh. Eddie could be so annoying and yet, I hated to admit, at times I found him loveable, too. Even Sophie saw the good in him.

In these verses, the first thing James teaches about problems is that God does not manufacture problems for us. I doubt that knowledge would actually help Eddie with his one-woman problem, but nonetheless, we'd study this aspect of problems anyway.

We began with the story of Job that we had studied earlier, but looked at it from a different angle this time.[1] This story seemed to contradict exactly what James taught. Job was blameless and upright. He had everything going for him: a good family, a thriving business, and perfect health. Then one day there was a gathering before God of all the heavenly beings. Somehow, Satan had slipped into the party. God noticed Satan hanging around in the background and asked Satan what he was up to. Satan used the opportunity to trash talk Job, saying that the only reason Job was God's servant was because things had gone so well for Job. Satan declared that Job's faith would crumble under hardship. He accused God of having put a protective fence around Job. Satan wanted God to remove the protective fence. It was then they'd see if Job was still God's servant.

Disturbingly so, God gave Satan permission to attack Job. Technically, James had been right. God didn't manufacture hardships for Job, Satan did. However, God had allowed it. On one hand, it was comforting to know that Satan could do nothing to Job that God was not aware of and had not allowed. On the other hand, it was a harsh thing to know that God would allow Satan to attack someone as righteous and innocent as Job.[2] That wasn't an easy pill to swallow.

Within a few hours, all that Job had, including his family and his health, were gone. Job's temptation came in the form of a choice over how he would react to these horrible tragedies. Would he embrace the supernatural wisdom that God loved him and continue to worship God or would he embrace the human wisdom of his friends and curse God?[3] This is the essence of every trial. Will we embrace God's wisdom and pursue it as servants or will we be tempted by desire, lured, and enticed by it? Job's desire was to end his suffering. His friends encouraged him to admit he had sinned and to curse God and die. The problem was Job hadn't sinned. Job knew God loved him and was not punishing him. Job didn't curse God, but endured. In fact, he worshiped God. When I finished this example during the study group, I looked around to find nothing but silence.

1. See chapter 11.
2. Andersen, *Job*, 64–72.
3. Walton, *Job*, 441–42.

"The story of Job is hard to grasp on a good day," voiced Liz on behalf of everyone. "The answer as to why bad things happen to good people is not pleasant when you believe God has the power to control everything."

We all stared at one another, hoping someone could come up with a better explanation for problems than the author of Job gave. No one could, so we let it stand. I moved on to the next section of verses where James points out to his congregants that there are two possible outcomes when we go through a trial. We can choose to follow God's wisdom, experiencing a birth that leads to life, or to ignore God's wisdom, following our own desires and experiencing a birth that leads to death. James isn't talking about births that lead to heaven or hell. He isn't answering the question "What do I have to do to get to heaven?" He is talking about our lives in the here and now. A birth that does not serve God is a dead end. A birth that serves God leads to a purposeful work-filled life—the life of a servant—and a soul that is alive.[4]

The birth that leads to life is generated by the "word of truth"—God's wisdom—the Holy Spirit.[5] Wisdom is a perfect gift from the Father of lights. It has no imperfections—no darkness—no shadow. It is pure. It fulfills the promise Jesus made that God would send his followers the Holy Spirit, who is the embodiment of perfect wisdom. It is through this Spirit that we are born. In arising from this birth and following the wisdom of the Holy Spirit, we become God's firstfruits. Like the firstfruits of any harvest, we are eagerly awaited. Those who approach trials with joy are a special treat to God—like the firstfruits of the season.[6] Problems have the potential to spiral us downward toward spiritual dead-ends or to mature us into the tasty firstfruits of the season.

Next, I posed the question, "Have you ever watched someone on a path that led to a dead end?"

Liz had. She shook her jeweled finger at her clavicle bone and named herself openly to the group saying, "I was once on a downward spiral toward that dead end you just spoke of. I guess I am ashamed of this, but then maybe I am too old to be ashamed. And I don't want others to behave the way I did."

Liz told the group that after her husband had left her for another woman, she was devastated and suffered a huge lack of confidence. "It was the 70s and a pretty wild time anyway. I guess I needed to prove that I was worth something to a man. But I always hooked up with the wrong men—men who were not good to me."

---

4. Moo, *James*, 76–77.

5. Perkins, *First and Second Peter*, 102–3.

6. Ibid.

Liz would eventually leave one rotten man for another rotten man, repeating the same scenario over and over. "I came to blame all men for problems that anyone else could see were brought on by taking up with the wrong kind of man in the first place." She reflected that the same trials seem to come before us repeatedly until we learn the right lessons.

Liz had learned the wrong lesson—that all men were bad. Instead of learning to wait for a godly man, she followed her latest desires and settled for someone whose character was lacking. She didn't ask for wisdom in finding a partner. In not doing so, she had chosen not to "endure." She was following her own desires. The whole matter resulted in a lot of unpleasant drama. She wasn't taking on the mindset of a servant in any way. Nor was she concerned about how this was affecting her son. She made the choice that James describes as giving birth to sin and heading down a rocky road toward spiritual death.

She summed it up by saying, "I went from a woman who loved life and men to one who was jaded and cold. And one who was mad at God, another male, for not giving me what I wanted." At the time, she had no comprehension of what it meant to serve God. So she became mad at God for being like all the other men and not serving her like she deserved.

The study group showed Liz a great deal of compassion when she finished. Helen reached over and hugged Liz teasing, "You don't really think God has a gender do you?" We all laughed.

Desires are not a bad thing in and of themselves. In fact, they are God-given. The desire to love, to be loved, to live, to laugh, and to know others intimately are good things. I wished that it were true that our desires always led us to the same place as God's wisdom, but they don't.[7]

We see this conflict between human desires and godly wisdom never more clearly than on the night before Jesus's death.[8] Jesus has the Holy Spirit—the wisdom of God—upon him. God's wisdom is directing Jesus to a death on the cross. On one hand, Jesus wants to reconcile humanity to God through the cross, but on the other hand, suffering death on the cross doesn't sound fun to Jesus for the obvious reasons. Jesus goes to God and asks God to plan another way. Still God says no. Jesus's desire not to suffer emotionally, spiritually, and physically are normal and healthy human desires. Nevertheless, they were not God's will for Jesus. Jesus knows this so he prays, "Your will, not my will." Your desire, not my desire. Your wisdom, not my wisdom. Jesus's immediate desire was to avoid the cross. Despite that, he was willing to endure what God wanted at all personal costs. This is

7. Moo, *James*, 76–77.
8. Matt 26:36–42.

an attitude of a servant. Jesus was the picture of perfect spiritual maturity, but on the night before Jesus was crucified, he struggled. He showed us that there would be times when our immediate desires will be different from God's desires. Like Christ did, we need to go to God, discuss it with God, and yield to God's will.[9]

Following Liz, Pastor Eddie shared a little of his past, too. Eric was part of the middle school youth group where Pastor Eddie had grown up. Eddie described Eric as a good-looking boy with a normal desire for friends. Of course, the desire for friends was not a bad desire. There was nothing wrong with a preteen (or anyone of any age) wanting a group of friends. Unfortunately, Eric had only just recently moved to Eddie's town, leaving behind all of his lifelong buddies in Florida. The move put Eric into a time of trial. He was terribly lonely. Eddie hung around with him for a while, but Eddie was on the football team so he was too busy to see much of Eric most of the year. Apparently, it was only a gentle urge that nudged Eric when a group of older classmen offered him drugs. He'd never tried drugs before.

James calls this "being lured and enticed" by desire. Pastor Eddie said that he had personally learned what "being lured and enticed" was all about when he had spent a summer living with his grandparents on a lake in North Carolina. Every day that summer, he had gone down to the lake to fish. He had learned how to dig for worms and to bait his hook. Outside of Pastor Eddie giving us way too much detail about what it was like to put the worm on the hook, he actually made a great point. Seeing a worm on the hook *lured and enticed* the fish to bite down on the hook. Once the fish had been hooked, the poor fish was done for—ending up on Eddie's table that night for dinner. The fish had a healthy desire for food, but looked for it in the wrong place. Like us, when our healthy desires are not satisfied in right ways, evil has a way of luring and enticing us until we are hooked.[10] The wife whose husband isn't attentive is lured outside of the covenant with her husband by her desire to feel special. The business owner's desire to keep their business afloat lures him to lie in order to get more business.

Eddie said that looking back at his friend Eric, it wasn't the drugs that lured and enticed him. It was a legitimate desire for friends. However, the legitimate desire for friendship became defiled when Eric pursued it through friends who did drugs. James writes, "When that desire has conceived, it gives birth to sin, and that sin, when it is fully grown, gives birth to death." Eric, if he had been thinking in the way of Jesus, would have seen that his desire for friendship could not be fulfilled by this crowd of druggies. His

---

9. Guthrie, *Hearing Jesus Speak*, 11–22.

10. Nystrom, *James*, 81–87.

perfectly good desire for real friendship must be honored—a desire so important that he needed to endure patiently and wait for God to provide the right kind of friends. If God did not provide, Eric needed to put God's way before his desire.

Instead, Eric's desire gave birth to sin, and then to death. Eric went from dabbling in drugs occasionally to turning to them for respite whenever things didn't go well. This continued until he was captured by their destructive power and became a full-fledged drug addict. Eddie said Eric overdosed and died their senior year in high school. Eddie's retelling of this story showed another side of Eddie that conflicted with everything else. His voice choked up. His eyes blurred. Who would have guessed that the big, goofy, irritating tough guy had real compassion buried just under the surface?

Eddie made a very important point. Often in the suburbs, we raise our children to believe that God will grant all of their healthy desires. We don't teach our children that God might not force the world to give them what is fairly theirs. They might not get enough of the love, food, or belongings they desire. We don't teach them that God may call them to live in want and that following Christ is dangerous and hard. There will be trials. They will have legitimate desires for things that will not be granted.

There is danger in venturing into the world as a servant of God without this knowledge. If you have not been raised with the understanding that following Christ means giving up your desires and replacing them with Jesus's desires, then when your desires are unmet, you might feel you have the right to fulfill them any way you can. Yet, as servants, we should seek God's desires for our lives, not our own desires. The marvelous thing about God is that as God transforms us—as we mature and learn to pray over our trials—our desires become aligned with God's desires and we leave behind our own desires, which would never have satisfied us anyway.

15

Turning Point—James 1:19–25

You must understand this, my beloved: let everyone be quick to listen, slow to speak, slow to anger; for your anger does not produce God's righteousness. Therefore rid yourselves of all sordidness and rank growth of wickedness, and welcome with meekness the implanted word that has the power to save your souls. But be doers of the word, and not merely hearers who deceive themselves. For if any are hearers of the word and not doers, they are like those who look at themselves in a mirror; for they look at themselves and, on going away, immediately forget what they were like. But those who look into the perfect law, the law of liberty, and persevere, being not hearers who forget but doers who act—they will be blessed in their doing.

—JAMES 1:19–25

An inescapable turning point in James's epistle was upon us just like the miserable July heat. In July, the air does not move in Atlanta. It hangs over the city and the suburbs with suffocating humidity. Luckily, in the suburbs we had air-conditioning. We could turn the thermostat down low and forget about what was going on outside our climate-controlled homes and churches. Even so, every now and then, our air conditioners would break and jolt us into the reality of life in the real world. Mine broke the morning of the July meeting and the repairman couldn't fit us in until the next day. I called Joe and asked if we could meet at his offices. He agreed. We loaded ourselves into our climate-controlled cars and headed to Joe's private conference room.

Before this turning point, everything in the first eighteen verses had been directed toward teaching how to deal with problems so that Christ's followers could get on with the business of serving God. Everything in the rest of the epistle would teach what it meant to serve God and others.[1] Yet, so many Christians get stuck in the first eighteen verses. They reach this turning point and make the choice to wallow in their own concerns, never becoming the servants God intended for them to be. They do not realize it, but their faith is dead.

While teaching in various churches, I had heard a particular minister preach several times over a span of a few years. During one of her sermons, it suddenly dawned on me that I had heard all of her sermons already. They all had the same general theme: her personal confessions and laments. This pastor was stuck. She must have thought that confessing her problems and grieving over her imperfections summed up the practice of the Christian faith. Yet, her problems weren't even significant ones. They were on the scale of the common cold versus a real problem like stage four cancer. The unconscious message she delivered from the pulpit each Sunday morning was that Christianity was about moving from one personal trial to the next and generally failing at them. All the while, her confidence was that God loved her anyway. She offered appealing comfort and compassion for those battling similar trials, but no direction other than to try harder next time. She offered no advice to help them deal with their trials and get on with a life of servanthood. Nothing about her sermons ever took the listener beyond themselves toward living out the kingdom of God. This was a terribly incomplete view of the gospel. The gospel does not stop with us accepting the unconditional love God has for us. It moves us forward to serve God and others. This pastor was stuck in the first eighteen verses of James, unable to cross the turning point into a life of service—a life of living faith.

Let me contrast this pastor with a minister I knew who had a church just a few miles away from the first pastor. He had had some really big problems—in particular, his surgeon wife had left him for her coworker, another doctor. He was left to raise his teenage kids alone, all the while pastoring a church. Still, I never once heard him lament over his problems. Every sermon was a challenge to make life count for the kingdom of God. He even practiced what he preached, building a church that was active in the community around it. He, like James, called others to pick up their crosses and serve God despite life's problems. James knew that we, like these two pastors, have a choice to stay focused on our problems or to serve God despite them.

1. Nystrom, *James*, 88, describes this turning point as a link between faith and practice, where James now begins to call for the observance of a practicing faith rather than a confessed faith.

To get his readers' attention, James starts by shouting, "You must understand this, my beloved!" If that were not enough, James then tells them to listen up, "Let everyone be quick to listen, slow to speak, slow to anger; for your anger does not produce God's righteousness." James wants their attention, but he doesn't think he has it yet, so he goes even further now, "Rid yourselves of all sordidness and rank growth of wickedness." When interpreted literally, this seems to be some first-century sarcasm. James was using a medical word, *rhyparia*, translated "sordidness," to tell them to get rid of their earwax![2] At this point, James feels he has their attention. He then gives them the key to being able to turn from their problems toward servanthood:

> Welcome with meekness the implanted word that has the power
> to save your souls. (Jas 1:21b)

The implanted word is *not* Scripture or memorized Scripture. It is so much more than that. In the same way that John spoke of Jesus being God's word, Jesus in turn spoke of God sending the person of the Holy Spirit to remind us of God's word, and Paul spoke of the Holy Spirit living within us.[3] The Holy Spirit has been implanted within every servant of God. The key to serving God is to welcome the wisdom and power of the Holy Spirit into our very being.[4]

James even told us how to welcome the word: "with meekness." Meekness is strength under control. When we are meek, we recognize that the wisdom and power of the Holy Spirit resides in us not because we deserve it or have earned it. Nor can we control it. Instead, we welcome it allowing it to use us to serve God.[5]

I paused to get my breath. The lesson was going smoothly in the glass conference room. The headquarters of Joe's company was not trying to hide its success by any means. They had spent a fortune on its sleek modern design. Most importantly, the air inside was cool and dry.

Next, I moved into the latter part of this set of verses, where James writes about two kinds of people: those who are doers of the word and those who are merely hearers. Those who are merely hearers are the easiest to describe. They know exactly what God is telling them to do, but they fail to do it. Their faith is verbalized and well intentioned, but there is nothing to show for it. They hear, but don't act. Doers, however, are a little more complicated.

2. Barclay, *Letters of James*, 64–65.
3. John 1:1, John 15:26, and Rom 8:9–11.
4. Nystrom, *James*, 159–60; Moo, *James*, 85; Smith, *Indwelling Spirit*.
5. Barclay, *Letters of James*, 58.

Doers of the word are quick to listen to the word, slow to speak their own needs and opinions, and slow to anger. Most of all, they act on the implanted word's guidance. It is important to note that doers of the word are not necessarily people who *do* a lot, but what they *do* is in reaction to the implanted word. In other words, they don't practice random acts of kindness; instead, they do intentional good works as led and empowered by the Spirit.

The story of Mary and Martha is a perfect example.[6] When Martha opened her home to Jesus, she got busy preparing a meal for him. Her sister, Mary, didn't even offer to help Martha, but instead sat down at Jesus's feet and listened to him. Mary was listening to the word of God—Jesus himself. Mary was quick to listen. Martha, on the other hand, was a doer, but *not* a doer of the word. She was not quick to listen. In fact, she had been too busy to listen to the word. Then to make matters worse, she had the audacity to complain to Jesus about her sister's lack of attention to the chores that needed to be done. Martha was quick to speak out about her needs to Jesus. She needed help. She needed Jesus to set her sister straight. When she got absolutely no support, she was angry—first with her sister and then probably at Jesus. Jesus, instead of reprimanding Mary, as Martha had hoped, pointed out that Mary had "chosen the better part." Mary was listening to the word. Martha was not listening—she was just "doing." Being a doer is different from being a doer of the word. One must first listen to the word in order to follow up with right action.

Rodney started to say something. Then stopped. I waited to see if he would continue, but he didn't. He looked smug. Rodney had a heart of gold, but he also had the propensity to jump to conclusions that weren't always accurate. There was a lot of injustice in the world that needed to be called out and discussed, but as Rodney himself had pointed out, he oscillated between stewing over it in silence and aggressively pouncing on possible offenders without forethought. He seemed to be in "stew" mode at the moment, but, unfortunately, not for long. Rodney looked down at his feet and then pounced.

"Would a doer of the word drive a Jaguar?" His voice was soft, knowing he shouldn't say it.

Jesus might not have driven a Jaguar, but Olivia did. In fact, she had just bought a new Jaguar. It was a $112 thousand car. There was no doubt that Rodney was attacking Olivia. The women in the group were all taken aback, including Olivia. Her mouth opened. Liz and Helen immediately supported her by saying in unison, "Rodney!" Their tones were a mixture of surprise and confusion. Rodney was so likeable, but every now and then, his

6. Luke 10:38–42.

uncontrolled self-righteousness would rear its ugly head. The three women looked at him waiting for an explanation.

Eddie looked at me and then spoke up as the one in authority. "I think Rodney has a point. I think Olivia should answer."

"I think so, too," chimed in Joe as he crossed his arms and stared at Olivia with his nose in the air. Here we sat in one of the most expensive buildings that I had ever been inside, in which the architecture fees alone would have paid for ten of Olivia's Jaguars. Didn't anyone else see the hypocrisy in Joe picking on Olivia? Of course, I didn't dare say any of that out loud.

Olivia looked at Rodney, whose head was still pointed at his shoes, but whose eyes were raised, looking up at Olivia. She looked at Eddie and then Joe, her mouth still open. She was obviously thrown. So was I. Rodney had acted badly enough, but Eddie and Joe were acting like two jealous little boys. I knew neither of them was on a justice crusade like Rodney. They just wanted her to enjoy her new car a little less.

My heart immediately went out to Olivia. The study group was supposed to be a safe place. However, Bible study rarely is. People get all bent out of shape over matters of faith. Being new to church, she hadn't expected this. Yet, Olivia could stay calmer than any man or woman I have ever met, so when she spoke, her tone was level and authoritative, too. She confirmed that they were out of line by sitting back in her chair and crossing her arms, matching Joe's pose. Then she asked innocently, but not naively or falsely, just as matter-of-fact as possible, "Have I broken one of the Ten Commandments?"

Silence.

"Of course not, dear," said Liz, while Helen shook her head in agreement with Liz.

Her accusers began to back down when they saw that Olivia wasn't rattled. Olivia went on, "This year—and it is the first year in my life I have ever tithed at all—I tithed more than ten percent." She raised her eyebrows and looked directly at Joe, "And I worked hard to earn my money." She didn't come across as bragging. Nor was she shaken or angry. She simply spoke as one who had nothing to hide.

I noticed Rodney glance at Joe to see what he would say. Joe was stone cold and stared back at her. The inappropriateness of it all was hanging like thick smoke in the room.

"I assumed that I could spend what was left over any way I wanted as long as I didn't break any of the Ten Commandments," added Olivia. Then she looked at me to tell her if her assumption was right or not. The look was not one of "you better back me up," but of sincerely wanting an answer.

My answer would need to be carefully worded. What Olivia had just voiced was a common misconception among the servants of God. We'd like to believe that if we tithe our ten percent, then everything that is left over is ours to spend in any way we want as long as we don't break any of God's commandments. Olivia's keeping of all the commandments might make her a doer, but that didn't necessarily make her a "doer of the word." She needed to listen to the wisdom of the Holy Spirit.

Unfortunately, Rodney was not done. Struggling to keep his voice calm, he whispered, "You could have bought a twenty-thousand dollar car and used the other ninety grand to pay a year's salary of two childcare workers at an inner city nonprofit daycare just eighteen miles from here that helps families get back on their feet." There was judgment in his eyes. Ugly stuff.

I decided not to let this go any further, "Rodney, I think one of the reasons James is going to tell us later in his epistle not to judge each other is because you and I can't know what the Holy Spirit has told Olivia to do. Perhaps the Holy Spirit did guide her to buy the Jaguar."

Olivia said quietly, "It is okay. Maybe Rodney is right. I am just learning how to be a servant." The sincerity of her words broke Rodney's self-righteousness in two and he got a grip on himself.

After a moment, he sat up, looked her in the eye, and said, "No, I am out of line. I am really sorry." Their eyes locked in a sudden deep respect for each other. Olivia looked away—now blinking away tears. She didn't get emotional over being beat up, but it seemed to touch her when Rodney softened. Joe on the other hand seemed smug—happy to witness her tears. Eddie just made that dumb smile unconscious of his contribution to whatever little drama was going on.

Trying to move forward on a positive note, I said, "You know Rodney, I believe we will be surprised at how many blessings God will want us to have—not so much as an award, but just simply because God enjoys giving us gifts."

In fact, James also goes on to say that doers of the word look into (are guided by) the perfect law—the law of liberty. James's use of the words "law" and "liberty" together should be a clue that he is not focused on a law that is a set of rules—not the Ten Commandments or any other Old Testament Law. The Law of Liberty is the law that the implanted word has written on our hearts as prophesied in Jeremiah.[7] It is not a following of rules, but a following of the Spirit. Doers of the word are not those who serve a set of rules. Doers of the word have been set free from serving a set of rules

7. Perkins, *First and Second Peter*, 105–6.

and have been liberated to serve God directly. This is a shocking statement. Theoretically, anyone can keep a list of rules—that doesn't mean they are servants of Christ. God wants us in a relationship with God where those rules become obsolete, because our guidance comes directly from listening to the implanted word of God—the Spirit.[8]

Joe spoke. I cringed, but he wasn't particularly upset. He was on his home court. In his mind, he had proof all around him that God was pleased with him. He didn't believe that he could have this much success if God didn't think he was a great guy. Taking the home court advantage, he gave his opinion as he highlighted my supposed foolishness, "Look, society and the church have to have rules that everyone agrees to follow. We can't have every church member deciding for himself what God teaches. Christianity has a set of rules and we need to make sure they are followed—not just by Christians. They need to be reflected in our government, which was founded on Christian values, too."

Helen spoke up. She didn't interject herself into the conversations very often. When she did, it was usually very motherly, trying to help others get along. Now she was going to run interference between Joe and me. She said, "Joe, this idea of liberty is a new idea for me, too, but it resonates with me."

She gave a very insightful example of the early days of her marriage before the twins had come along. She told us that she and her husband really didn't have a very good relationship. Perhaps it was because her husband was quite a bit older and that intimidated her in some ways. She said that she put together a list of "rules" that she thought would make him happy—things like keeping the house super clean, taking him a hot homemade meal at the store when he worked long hours, etc. All the rules were making her exhausted.

Unconsciously, she had rules for him, too. He needed to be home by a certain time after the store closed. He needed to buy her gifts that made her happy. He needed to remember her birthday and anniversary. When he didn't keep his side of the unspoken rules, she said she would become very judgmental to the point of thinking he didn't love her.

One day, they met another couple where both partners were simply dedicated to serving one another. They didn't keep count of who did what and how often. They simply wanted what was best for the other and put the other before themselves. They'd go the extra mile for the other partner and not because they had to, but because they wanted to. This was when she realized that she could simply love her husband. All the preconceived rules and role-playing had been dragging her down. God wants this type of

8. Smith, *Power of the Blood Covenant*, 12, 192–203.

relationship with us too—a direct relationship based on love and not a set of rules.

James had already told those who endure trials that they would be blessed.[9] Now he goes on to tell those who persevere in being doers of the word that they, too, will be blessed. This was a turning point; would we become doers of the word or remain hearers only?

9. Jas 1:12.

PART 2

Servanthood: A Life of Pure and Undefiled Worship

The Parable of the Good Samaritan—Dissecting the Levite

One morning, I ran into a distinguished member of my church. He said, "There was a man who was going down from the city to the suburbs, and fell into the hands of robbers, who stripped him, beat him, and went away, leaving him half dead. When I came to the place and saw him, I passed by on the other side."

I asked, "Why did you pass by on the other side without helping him?"

The church member replied, "I have big problems of my own. If I stop taking care of myself to take care of him, what will happen to me?"

—ADAPTED FROM LUKE 10:30–37

16

Pure and Undefiled Worship Defined—
James 1:26–27

*If any think they are religious, and do not bridle their tongues but deceive
their hearts, their religion is worthless. Religion that is pure and undefiled
before God, the Father, is this: to care for orphans and widows in their
distress, and to keep oneself unstained by the world.*

—JAMES 1:26–27

My cell phone rang as I was finishing my early morning hiking adventure
on the Stairmaster in my basement. Indoors was my least favorite place to
exercise, especially in the fall when the weather had turned nice outside, but
sometimes it was necessary to keep an otherwise hectic schedule on track.
It was Joe on the phone.

"I understand that Pastor Eddie told you that I called you unorthodox?"

"Yes, I guess he did," I replied, somewhat cheerfully despite shaking my
head in disgust knowing how much Eddie was enjoying stirring things up.

"I don't agree with some of the things you are teaching."

"Can you explain a little more about that?"

Joe explained that he believed that there is no need to pray about what
God wants us to do because God has already spoken in Scripture. He said
he believed that everything we needed to know was there in the "good book"
and we just had to do it. He said he didn't really believe prayer was necessary
since we had the Bible.

"Joe, let's say you are in the market for a new house. How would you know which house God might want you to buy?"

"For Pete's sake, if it isn't specifically in the Bible, then I can buy whatever I want. God doesn't care."

Until we had started this study group, I had never seen this do-not-mess-with-me attitude in Joe before, although I had heard about it. His tone was one of authority and not the least bit interested in what I thought. I could tell it was going to be a waste of my time to present my view, but unexpectedly Joe softened a bit. It was as if he desperately wanted to have a conversation about these matters, but didn't want to have to ask. Asking my opinion would have lowered his self-worth.

"Look," he demanded. As if he didn't already have my attention. "I just want to know what I have to do to go to heaven when I die. What does James say about that?" The thought crossed my mind that he wanted to go to heaven when he died to be with Annie, his wife. I wondered if that was why he was so upset.

"Joe, James wasn't writing his churches to answer the question of how to go to heaven. He was writing about how followers of Christ should live in the here and now."

"I just want to know the minimum. What is the minimum?"

"The minimum isn't exactly a question that the Epistle of James answers."

I went on to explain that even Jesus didn't give us a minimum standard. Instead, Jesus invited us into an all-encompassing relationship with God where we would give up our own lives so that he could live out his life within us. Despite the focus of American Christianity today on getting people saved, even Jesus was focused more on what it meant to live in right relationship with God and others in this life than any part of the afterlife.

Joe was mad again. "I have been going to church all my life." He punctuated each of the last three words "ALL . . . MY . . . LIFE" in a way that felt like he was poking a finger through the telephone and into my neck. "I expect my pastor to teach the Bible's rules so that people will follow them—not teach them to pray about what God wants them to do."

Then he hung up on me.

"Seriously?" I said out loud, looking at my dead phone. Hard to believe that I had just made the international technology giant *that* angry. "Wow!"

Whether Pastor Eddie was stirring up this problem with Joe or not, I had a problem. Unfortunately, for me, it appeared that James was vicariously going to offend Joe again in the next lesson. So once again, as I prepared the lesson, I also steadied myself, waiting for the messenger—me—to be shot.

The word "religion" showed up in the verses we would be studying next. I have always disliked the word when it refers to my faith. In my mind, religion is what humanity does to try and commandeer God's blessings. It usually comes with a set of rules and rituals that, if done properly, are said to please God, and in turn, God sends blessings. The first-century Jewish religion, for instance, was full of rules, rituals, and sacrifices, which, if practiced, made the Jews pure and undefiled before God. Yet, even their own prophets told them that these things were useless if they did not do justice, love kindness, and walk humbly before God.[1] In essence, Joe wanted me to tell him which rules, rituals, and sacrifices he needed to follow in order for God to bless him. In reality, God wanted Joe's heart.

As I had told him on the phone, I don't believe that the Epistle of James intends to tell us how to commandeer a place in heaven. James was more interested in how we serve God than in how we get God to serve us. Our culture sees Jesus as having started a new religion when in truth, he was inviting us into a relationship with God—a relationship of servanthood that starts in the here and now.[2] For me, religion and servanthood are opposites. In fact, there are those who are part of the Christian religion and then there are those who are servants of Christ. The two might overlap, but they aren't the same.

Because of my dislike of the word religion, I started my exegetical study of these verses by looking at the Greek word translated as religion. Lo and behold, the Greek word also meant worship.[3] It was even translated "worship" where it was used elsewhere in the New Testament.[4] Now I can get into that! If I translate what James says using *worship* instead of *religion*, then the Scripture comes alive for me:

> If any think they are worshipers, and do not bridle their tongues but deceive their hearts, their worship is worthless. Worship that is pure and undefiled before God, the Father, is this: to care for orphans and widows in their distress, and to keep oneself unstained by the world. (Jas 1:26–27)

The life of a servant of Christ is a life of pure and undefiled worship. This life starts when we stop talking—stop telling God what to do and who to be—and listen to what God wants and who God is. In our worship, we bridle our tongues so we can hear God speak. We can't serve God and others

1. Isa 1:10–17; Mic 6:6–8.
2. McGee, *First Corinthians—Revelation*, 643.
3. Barclay, *Letters of James*, 61.
4. Acts 26:5; Col 2:18.

if we come to a conclusion about what God is saying to us without first hearing the implanted word of God speak. If we think we know the wisdom of God, but have not listened to God, we deceive our own hearts and our worship is worthless.

The story of the Pharisee praying in the temple immediately comes to mind. He had so much to say to God, "God, I thank you that I am not like other people: thieves, rogues, adulterers, or even like this tax collector. I fast twice a week; I give a tenth of all my income."[5] He was so busy telling God what was what that he never thought to listen to God. We can't worship God until we bridle our tongues and listen. The story goes on to say that it was the tax collector who was worshiping God, not the Pharisee. The Pharisee had missed the whole point. His heart was not right.

In Luke 9:59–62, Jesus, the living word of God, meets up with a man whose father was either approaching death or had just died.[6] The man has culturally binding obligations rooted in the Ten Commandments to honor his father by burying him.[7] By all Jewish standards, Jesus should have encouraged the man to fulfil his familial responsibilities. At least Jesus could have exercised compassion and either healed the man's father or resolved all the issues around burying him. Instead, Jesus says, "Follow me." The man answers, "But Lord, first let me go and bury my father." Jesus says to him, "Let the dead bury their own dead; but as for you, go and proclaim the kingdom of God." The man is slow to listen and quick to tell Jesus what his priorities are. In addition, he will likely become quick to anger at Jesus's next words. They are harsh. Jesus says, "No one who puts a hand to the plow and looks back is fit for the kingdom of God." He tells the man that he is unfit! If we are going to be servants of God, we can't do it without listening. Otherwise, we will remain focused on our problems. We must hear God's wisdom and plow ahead.

Though a life of pure worship starts by listening to God, it is established when, after listening to God, we act on what God tells us. This is the faith act of a servant. Worship is not a passive act—it is what we do with our lives. Worship is the working out of our faith. Worshiping and serving God go hand in hand. One can't exist without the other. The life of a worshiping Christian is a life of servanthood.

James follows this up by giving us an example of a life of worship: "to care for orphans and widows in their distress and to keep oneself unstained by the world." This example is not all-inclusive. It doesn't mean that if we

5. Luke 18:11–12.

6. Bock, *Luke*, 979–80.

7. Wright, *Luke*, 118.

give some money to an orphanage and help a widow change a flat tire, then we are good to go. It isn't a one-size-fits-all directive. It is an example.[8] We each have to listen to God to know which pure and undefiled acts of worship God is calling us each to do. Yet, one thing we know for certain. From James's example, we know that worship is accomplished by serving others.

In addition to serving others, those who worship God live a life that is unstained by the world.[9] The world stains us when we come to accept its ways and culture as God's ways and culture; when we accept discrimination, consumerism, looking out for number one, hatred, retaliation, war, sexism, and even "the American way" as God's way; when we measure our success by the world's definition, letting it define us and shape us; when we value others and ourselves less than God does. The world stains us when we think living in the suburbs is the dream life—a place where we do not have to see the suffering of this world, do not have to address neighborhoods of high crime, and do not have to be around people who do not look like us. The world stains us when we do not respond to a gospel that invites us to enter into the pain and problems of the world with the message of God's love.[10]

Teaching the servants of Christ about a life of pure and undefiled worship is James's main goal in the rest of this epistle.[11] James will give us example after example.[12] In fact, he will give us ten distinct examples. Each example shows us what it means in different situations to engage in worship. This is not a new set of commandments—not a new set of rules to follow. It is not all-inclusive. They are examples. We will find our particular paths of servanthood by being intentionally available to the Holy Spirit's guidance.[13] The following list shows how I divided James's examples for the group to study over the next few months.

A Life of Pure and Undefiled Worship:

- Is impartial (2:1–14)

- Has faith that produces good works (2:15–26)

- Speaks words that bless others (3:1–12)

- Sows seeds of peace (3:13—4:10)

- Does not judge others (4:11–12)

8. Moo, *James*, 90.

9. Plantinga, *Not the Way*, 39–51.

10. Jordan, *Practical Religion*, translates James 1:27b: "keep one's self free from the taint of materialism."

11. Nystrom, *James*, 112–13.

12. Moo, *James*, 90.

13. Smith, *Indwelling Spirit*.

- Knows God is control (4:13–17)

- Gives resources to others (5:1–6)

- Endures until Christ returns (5:7–11)

- Speaks truth (5:12)

- Prays (5:13–20)

I saw Joe at church services that week and tried to be warm and friendly. We never mentioned our last conversation or that he hung up on me. Nevertheless, I was quite worried that this lesson on worship would come across as preachy and directed at him, so I decided to call him the morning of the next Bible study and warn him.

"You worry too much," he said, as if he was talking to a hysterical female.

I really didn't appreciate the condescension in his voice, but I had called to make peace so I let it go. He said that he would see me that evening. The evening came. Instead of meeting in my living room, we gathered on my back porch around a barn-red table under centuries-old hickory trees. The heat had dissipated because of an early afternoon thunderstorm, and with the help of the ceiling fan, it was very pleasant. I presented the study—it was shorter than usual and uncharacteristically uneventful. Everyone stayed and talked until the fireflies came out to dance around the cluster of tract mansions in the valley below my house.

17

A Life of Worship Is Impartial—James 2:1–13

My brothers and sisters, do you with your acts of favoritism really believe in our glorious Lord Jesus Christ? For if a person with gold rings and in fine clothes comes into your assembly, and if a poor person in dirty clothes also comes in, and if you take notice of the one wearing the fine clothes and say, "Have a seat here, please," while to the one who is poor you say, "Stand there," or, "Sit at my feet," have you not made distinctions among yourselves, and become judges with evil thoughts? Listen, my beloved brothers and sisters. Has not God chosen the poor in the world to be rich in faith and to be heirs of the kingdom that he has promised to those who love him? But you have dishonored the poor. Is it not the rich who oppress you? Is it not they who drag you into court? Is it not they who blaspheme the excellent name that was invoked over you? You do well if you really fulfill the royal law according to the scripture, "You shall love your neighbor as yourself." But if you show partiality, you commit sin and are convicted by the law as transgressors. For whoever keeps the whole law but fails in one point has become accountable for all of it. For the one who said, "You shall not commit adultery," also said, "You shall not murder." Now if you do not commit adultery but if you murder, you have become a transgressor of the law. So speak and so act as those who are to be judged by the law of liberty. For judgment will be without mercy to anyone who has shown no mercy; mercy triumphs over judgment.

—JAMES 2:1–13

Septembers are still warm in Atlanta—sometimes downright hot. The leaves don't change that early. In fact, some of the hottest temperatures on record in the South are in September. I remember our first September back in Atlanta after living up North. The temperatures reached over one hundred degrees for five days in a row and all of the newly planted boxwood bushes in our front yard turned brown and died. It was not quite that hot the day of the next study group meeting, but it was still unbearable, and the heat sometimes felt inescapable even though we knew summer could turn into autumn at any moment.

I found myself surprised that everyone was continuing to attend the study group meetings. It was a miracle that no one had run screaming into the night with hurt feelings. The study had turned into more than even I had bargained for, but I was not deterred.

I started off the September session by reading to the group the first verse in the set of verses that we would be studying, "My brothers and sisters, do you with your acts of favoritism really believe in our glorious Lord Jesus Christ?" Then I told them a story of a man who I had never met named Mike McQueary.[1] A national news story that he played a part in had broken in the spring. However, his involvement in the story had started a decade earlier when he was twenty-eight years old and had landed a graduate assistant job for the Nittany Lions football team at Penn State. It was not long after getting this position that he entered the locker room at the Penn State campus to catch Jerry Sandusky, a prominent, powerful assistant football coach, sexually assaulting a child. At that moment, Mike McQueary made a decision to practice favoritism. He chose to favor the powerful coach over the powerless ten-year-old boy. More accurately, he chose to favor himself, protecting his own career over helping the child. That day, McQueary, in his physical prime—athletic and six feet five inches tall—didn't even attempt to stop Sandusky, who was thirty years older and had far less physical strength. McQueary let the assault continue. He didn't call the cops. He went home. Even the next day, rather than taking action by reporting the incident to the police, McQueary followed the chain of command (another act of favoritism) and went to see the head coach. From there things only got worse. Leader after leader practiced favoritism, protecting their careers, their school, their friends, and ignoring the well-being of the child. It was not for another decade that the incident and other assaults by Sandusky would be exposed.

Favoritism is a type of discrimination where we choose to support the powerful over the powerless, the important over the marginalized, our

---

1. Durantine, "Penn State Aide."

family members over strangers, and even our neighbors over our enemies.[2] Favoritism goes against everything Christ taught and is against the character of God.[3] It is no mistake that James makes abolishing favoritism the first example of pure worship.

James believes that favoritism is so abhorrent that he wonders out loud in these verses if those who practice it even believe in Christ. In addition, the example of favoritism that James uses, giving a poor person a bad seat, seems tame compared to my McQueary-Sandusky example. Yet, to James, even that small amount of favoritism is incompatible with the kingdom of God.

In all but a few sectarian Jewish communities, where being poor was considered a blessing, being a poor person in first-century Palestine was a disgrace.[4] In general, for the first-century Jew, poverty had spiritual and religious implications.[5] The poor person was thought to have done something that caused them to lose favor with God. James emphasized this point by using a word to describe the poor person's clothes that also meant defiled.[6] The implication was that the poor person was not just poor, not just dirty, but morally filthy. Still, James teaches us that even this person should not be pushed to the margins of the Christian community. They should be invited in, given a seat at *our* table, and valued. If these Christians in James's example had been living lives of pure and undefiled worship, they would have seen themselves as servants to this person. However, they didn't see it that way at all.

Liz spoke up with her usual boldness, "This is exactly how we treat the poor in our church today!" Liz had been an advocate for the poor long before I met her. Even though people sometimes mistook Liz's boldness as eccentric and failed to see her accomplishments, Liz was never daunted. She was well aware of how people perceived her, but she did not let that stop her from speaking out and working for those in need.

Liz went on to give us some background. You wouldn't think there would be a lot of homeless in the suburbs. Usually there aren't. However, a few years ago a community of homeless moved into a park that was built on uninhabited wetlands near The Church in the Suburbs. The City of Atlanta

2. Hartin, *Spirituality of Perfection*, 158–62.

3. Lev 19:15–18; Deut 10:17–18; Rom 2:11; Eph 6:9; Col 3:25.

4. Maynard-Reid, *Poverty and Wealth in James*.

5. Hartin, *Spirituality of Perfection*, 116–17.

6. The Greek word, *rhypros*, is used to describe the clothes of the poor man. The only other place it is used in the New Testament is in Rev 22:11 where its meaning, though still translated "filth" becomes clearer. The man's clothes are defiled, which makes him not only dirty, but also morally filthy.

had gotten tough on vagrants, so a group of homeless ventured out of the city and into the parkland. After one of their own died, they sought a pastor to do the funeral service and ended up knocking at the door of The Church in the Suburbs. This, of course, was no problem. The senior pastor gladly performed the funeral and the church even pitched in for a coffin, a burial plot, and the related expenses. This act of kindness made a headline in the local papers and gave The Church in the Suburbs the kind of publicity it liked. Be that as it may, what the church quickly discovered was that this homeless community now felt welcomed at the church. The homeless began to show up on Sundays for worship. They smelled and looked bad. The wealthy congregants were appalled.

Then one church elder came up with a "great" idea. She wanted to offer the homeless their own church service. It would be held in the afternoon, still on church property, but away from the sanctuary where the homeless could be controlled and contained. A separate service meant that the homeless wouldn't come and sit on *our* pews smelling up *our* church with their unwashed clothes and bodies. Liz was on the church board at the time and spoke out against this idea. From all she knew of Jesus, it just wasn't right. She knew without doubt that Jesus would have welcomed the homeless as equals in the congregation.

Liz felt that worshiping together had other benefits, too; the congregation could get to know the homeless, understand their problems, and offer them real compassion and help. She fought this "homeless church service" idea good and hard, but when the vote was taken, Liz was the only one voting against it. And so the church service for the homeless began.

It was soon obvious that the people who had voted for the separate service had no intention of taking part, other than supporting it with their money. They hired a person to preach on Sundays and washed their hands of it. Despite her disappointment, Liz got busy. She worked tirelessly to make it a good service. She found a praise band that would sing and she collected clothes and food to pass out afterward. She never missed a Sunday worshiping with the homeless. This had gone on for many years.

However, recently with the economic downturn, the elders decided that they could no longer afford the salary of the pastor who preached at the homeless service. Nor did they actually want the homeless hanging out on church property on Sunday afternoons. Therefore, they voted to shut down the service. Liz found out after the fact. She had been madder than a hornet's nest. To make matters worse, the church, instead of welcoming the homeless back into the regular worship services, had hired an off-duty police officer to guard the doors and keep them from coming in at all. In Liz's view, The Church in the Suburbs was guilty of practicing favoritism.

Liz voiced her anger in the study group that evening. In the weeks to come, she would voice it again when the church board met. She would continue to speak out at every opportunity. Her anger was just, but she was also getting up there in years and her body was fragile. I worried about her. I could see the situation was having an effect on her health. It didn't take much for Rodney to get behind what Liz was saying and doing. He backed her at every turn, speaking at the church board meetings alongside her, but the church leaders dug their heels in. Liz and Rodney's voices were to become lost in an economic crisis where the church felt it was more important to protect its own wealth than to support those in need.

By watching Liz and Rodney become activists at the church board meetings, I grew to see that being impartial is perhaps the most important way we worship God. It defines what it means to love others. We can't really love others if we do not put their well-being as a priority above our own. We cannot serve others if we do not open ourselves up to them and enter into relationship with them so that we can know their needs. We cannot know their needs if we push them to the margins of society. At The Church in the Suburbs, Christians were saying to the poor, "You are not good enough to have a seat on *our* pews."

This was a somewhat unique situation in the suburbs. In most suburban churches, congregants rarely run into the poor. Instead of being in relationship with them, they try to answer the call to care for them by finding a charity where they might send a few dollars—or maybe send the youth group to pass out sandwiches once a year. We let these charities broker a relationship with the poor for us. Interestingly, neither James nor Jesus ever encouraged us to create a charitable organization to offer institutional care to the poor; instead, they told us to enter into a personal relationship with them, bringing them into our communities to be one of us. Institutional care may not be wrong, but no one should deceive himself or herself that in giving money to an institution, favoritism has been abolished. A life of pure and undefiled worship does not practice favoritism of any kind.

In fact, James tells us that favoritism destroys the Christian community. James says that we practice it because we are judges with evil thoughts. We aren't to be judges of the poor, judges of those wearing defiled clothes, or judges of anyone, for that matter. Christ is the only judge. This is great news. It frees us to treat everyone with love without the burden of judging them. We simply get to be deliverers of God's tangible love by inviting others into God's community.

As James moves on in his warning, he says that practicing favoritism is as bad as if we had committed murder or adultery. Nevertheless, there is a lot of favoritism that exists in churches. It is not just between rich and poor.

We have segregated ourselves economically, by race, and even by theological beliefs. We have withheld equality in the church from women, believing that they were cursed during the fall.[7] We treat homosexuals as though Christ withholds their complete reconciliation within the community of God. We have failed to recognize that Christ's blood covered all curses, healed all wounds, and left no second-class citizens. James was right, how can we "with our acts of favoritism really believe in our glorious Lord Jesus Christ"—unless we believe that his powers of forgiveness, of overcoming curses, of reconciling us to God and others didn't completely work?

Paul stated it this way: "There is no longer Jew or Greek, there is no longer slave or free, there is no longer male and female; for all of you are one in Christ Jesus."[8] James and Paul were against acts of favoritism based on any criteria. Christian communities should be places where discrimination of any kind is broken down and restoration takes place. Christians should speak a prophetic voice into the world condemning all acts of discrimination.

Joe interrupted, "I don't believe Paul meant that women should have the same responsibilities that men have in the church or in the workplace. In other places in the Bible, Paul says women have a place of submission. They aren't given the same competencies as a man."

I couldn't bring myself to look over at Olivia to see her reaction to her boss's take on women. However, I looked at the rest of the group who were all looking at her. No one was speaking. Slowly I gained courage to turn my head toward her. She looked down at her Bible and shook her head slightly, then looked Joe straight in the eyes. She was a woman who knew she was capable and had no problem standing her ground. He was staring back at her. I wasn't an expert in employment law, but I was pretty sure he had just crossed a line that could cause him legal problems. I tried to remember what my next point in the lesson was, but couldn't. In the silence, Rodney was the first to speak. Anger. Again. But it wasn't directed at Olivia this time. He was focused on Joe.

"Joe! It is the heart of the gospel that we are all created to serve each other—to be submissive to each other. God doesn't want women to be the doormat of the world. Women are just as gifted as men in leadership—maybe more so at times." Rodney looked at Olivia as he spoke.

"To be honest," said Joe arrogantly. "I am not really sure they should be pastors either."

---

7. Gen 3:13–16.

8. Gal 3:28.

Rodney, calmer now, spoke for a few more minutes, trying to convince Joe he was wrong by throwing out some Scripture references here and there.

Then, in trying to diffuse the situation and move on, I said, "There are many denominations that agree with Joe. Of course, our denomination believes that women are given gifts for leadership and ministry. We believe Paul gave evidence of women in key positions in ministry even in the New Testament."[9]

Joe countered, "The Church in the Suburbs has never embraced that idea. In fact, I believe that one of the things that made our church so stable over the years is the strong male leadership."

Years ago, The Church in the Suburbs had rejected the first slate of elders containing women. When the slate was read, a self-appointed nominating committee put forward their own all-male slate of elders. The all-male slate won. Joe told this story and ended by saying that even now most of the congregation rejects the notion that women are supposed to take part in the leadership of the church.

Liz spoke up, "Joe. That is not the opinion of the majority in this congregation. I have been an elder for more than fifteen years and while I have not *always* felt respected in my position, there are many who have treated me with great respect and honor." Joe wouldn't get in an argument with Liz. Why? I am not sure. But while Liz held Joe off, I went on with the lesson.

James doesn't end the chapter until he offers us a cure for favoritism. The cure is the Law of Liberty, which offers "mercy not judgment." In Jesus's death and resurrection, he fulfilled the Old Testament Law and exchanged it for the Law of Liberty.[10] Under the Old Testament Law, humanity carried a great burden trying to please God. We judged others and ourselves against these rules. Everyone failed—we always had to bring sacrifice after sacrifice to make things right with God. The whole situation was hopeless. It was laborious and defeating. However, when Jesus died and rose again, a new covenant and law was exchanged for the old fulfilled law and covenant. This new law was the Law of Liberty. Followers of Jesus are now under a new covenant, in a relationship with God where we have been set *free from* the rulebook and set *free to* love God and one another. In fulfilling the old covenant and giving us a new one, Christ showed us mercy not judgment. Therefore, like Christ, we, too, are to offer others mercy and not judgment.

I looked around the room and no one disagreed—at least out loud. Therefore, I offered the group what I hoped would be a shocking twist on the McQueary-Sandusky story. I reminded them that when the atrocious

9. Elliott, *Women in Ministry.*

10. Refer to the discussion on the Law of Liberty in chapter 15.

acts of Jerry Sandusky came to light, he was tried, convicted, and sent to prison. I asked them to pretend that a day came when Sandusky had served his sentence and had been set free. What would happen if the next Sunday, he showed up at our church? I wanted them to think about how they would treat him. Would it be with judgment and favoritism? On the other hand, would we see ourselves as his servant? Would we begin by finding him a good seat? Would we treat him with mercy and not judgment? How would we balance the practical aspects of protecting our children? A life of pure worship does not practice favoritism, but that doesn't mean it isn't going to be complicated.

18

A Life of Worship Has Faith That Produces Good Works—James 2:14–26

What good is it, my brothers and sisters, if you say you have faith but do not have works? Can faith save you? If a brother or sister is naked and lacks daily food, and one of you says to them, "Go in peace; keep warm and eat your fill," and yet you do not supply their bodily needs, what is the good of that? So faith by itself, if it has no works, is dead. But someone will say, "You have faith and I have works." Show me your faith apart from your works, and I by my works will show you my faith. You believe that God is one; you do well. Even the demons believe—and shudder. Do you want to be shown, you senseless person, that faith apart from works is barren? Was not our ancestor Abraham justified by works when he offered his son Isaac on the altar? You see that faith was active along with his works, and faith was brought to completion by the works. Thus the scripture was fulfilled that says, "Abraham believed God, and it was reckoned to him as righteousness," and he was called the friend of God. You see that a person is justified by works and not by faith alone. Likewise, was not Rahab the prostitute also justified by works when she welcomed the messengers and sent them out by another road? For just as the body without the spirit is dead, so faith without works is also dead.

—JAMES 2:14–26

I needed a vacation. Fortunately, I would get one between the September and October meetings. My husband and I liked to hike and we had planned a three-week international hiking trip. I'd be back in time for the next lesson, but I wouldn't have time to prepare to teach it. I was pondering what to do about my absence when I ran into Helen at church. It dawned on me to ask her if she would lead the next study group. I admit that she was an unusual choice. She wasn't really a born leader or teacher. Despite her outgoing half-flower child, half-sophisticate appearance, she rarely initiated conversations. She generally hung back to see what others had to say first. However, what made me think she might be a good choice was what had happened back in February when she had come to my office after ignoring a homeless Latina teenager. She had hoped I would give her permission to put boundaries on her servant life that would keep her inside her comfort zone. Instead, I had asked her to pray. I thought the section of verses we were going to study this month might help her discernment.

I had not told the rest of the group that Helen would be teaching. When time for the meeting came, we all gathered as usual at my house. Helen came prepared with some handwritten notes in her journal and her Bible. After reading the section of verses we were studying, she started us off with a question, "Can faith save you?"

The group looked down at our Bibles and contemplated the question. She let us sit in silence. James seemed to have said that works, not faith, led to salvation. Yet, that was the opposite of what we had been taught in Sunday school. We had all read the Apostle Paul's writings, "For by grace you have been saved through faith, and this is not your own doing; it is the gift of God—not the result of works, so that no one may boast."[1] Paul and James appeared to have different ideas.[2]

Therefore, we sat in silence.

To give us some encouragement, Helen said, "Maybe it would be helpful to review the definition of faith that we learned back when we were studying James 1:6–7."[3] Helen kept notes of each meeting in her journal. She read what she had recorded, "Faith is not the belief that God will do what we

---

1. Eph 2:8–9.

2. Moo, *James*, 103–4, states that the appearance of a conflict between Paul and James was created because they gave two key words—*faith* and *justify*—different meanings. When Paul referred to faith, he was assuming works were part of faith. When James referred to faith, he was separating it from works for the sake of conversation. He knew that separating the two was not actually possible. Likewise, when Paul spoke of justification or salvation, he spoke of the initial conversion into God's family. Whereas, when James spoke of justification or salvation, he spoke of the continuous work of God in our lives.

3. This discussion on faith is found in chapter 12.

ask God to do. Faith is action that follows the Holy Spirit's wisdom." Then she inserted the definition of faith into her original question, asking, "Can actions that follow the Holy Spirit's wisdom save you?"

More silence. I decided not to jump in until they had had a chance to think about it.

Pastor Eddie finally broke the silence by telling us a story from his youth. One of Eddie's stronger attributes was that he could tell stories in a way that made you want to roll around in the floor laughing. Sometimes you laughed at the story and sometimes at him because he seemed oblivious to how inappropriate some of his stories were. The story he told that night started when he was finishing up high school. He had been on the wrestling team, and according to his immodest account had been an Olympic-quality wrestler. Much to the disgust of his coach, he had gone through a grunge phase, letting his hair grow long, refusing to brush it, and only rarely using deodorant. He told us that he had gone around saying "dude!" a lot, smoking pot, and dabbling in a variety of other drugs. He said he had liked to go shirtless with his long hair matted around him sticking out in all directions, because "the chicks" liked his chest and his hair.

Yes. Eddie had just called women "chicks" and talked about his chest. Unbelievable. Then again, we all laughed, cringing in anticipation of just how inappropriate this whole story was going to get. He was a pastor, after all. We expected a little more from him, but knew we'd get considerably less.

As he went on, Eddie lowered his voice, making it masculine and quiet. He tightened both hands into fists, pounding them on the armrests of his chair matching each word he spoke. His words, just barely above a whisper, said, "I wanted adventure." He could have followed this up with a cave man growl, but didn't. Instead he added in a high-pitched cry, "And women!"

Despite pleadings from his mother, he had started hitchhiking across the country to random spots that he thought might be fun to live and where he might find loose women. The first place he had gone was Key West, where he had slept on the beach at night on top of one of his only possessions, a sleeping bag. He had kept himself fed by shinnying up palm trees and hacking down the coconuts that he would then crack open, spike with rum, and sell to the tourists. He'd make enough money each day to buy himself lunch—if not lunch and dinner.

He described the breeze at night over the sand dunes and the shirtless warm days. Yes, he was still talking about his muscles at every opportunity. It was crazy, but his descriptions of life in the tropics made us all wish we could pack up our sleeping bags and head to the beach.

Eventually he had harvested all of the coconut palms on public property and had run out of a way to make money. He had then made the mistake of climbing a privacy wall and chopping down coconuts in someone's front yard. The police had been called. They had caught him hanging from a tree with the owner's Doberman pinscher snarling at him. Once again, Eddie took time to explain to us his apparel, or lack thereof. All he had had on was his "spicy" low-rise Brazilian bikini-cut swimsuit that showed all his contours.

At that, Liz clapped and said, "Preach it, Eddie." Joe and I locked eyes and shook our heads in unison. I greatly approved of the chance for laughter, but like Joe, I wasn't quite hip enough to embrace fully Eddie's lack of restraint. Yet, he had all of us and we wanted to hear more.

The police had roughed Eddie up when he had admitted that he was living on the beach. Hence, he had spent the night in jail in nothing but his Brazilian knickers. Being locked in the tank scarcely dressed with a bunch of drunks was not exactly the kind of adventure for which Eddie had been looking. To make matters worse, the next day Eddie had returned to the spot where he had left his few belongings, including his sleeping bag. They were gone.

After that, he had decided to hitchhike to Asheville, North Carolina, where he had heard there were a lot of beautiful women and a high tolerance for street people. It had taken him two days to hitchhike from Key West to about four hours south of the Atlanta airport. It had been two days since he had eaten. His last meal had been breakfast in jail. Fortunately, the police department had released him with some clothing—ill fitting, but better than traveling in his bathing suit. While waiting for someone to take a chance and pick him up, he had decided to do what he called the "Magic Hitchhiker's Dance." Eddie said the word "magic" as if it had many extra vowels: "maaaagiiiic." Unfortunately, Eddie felt called to demonstrate the dance for us before going on with his story. He jumped up from my antique rocker and swung his hips around and around. While all of this was happening, Liz reached in her purse, pulled out a dollar bill, and tucked it into Pastor Eddie's belt. Eddie's hips kept swinging and every one of us were laughing hysterically. Truthfully, this was just the kind of Bible study session we needed! Eddie was a genius savant or crazy loon. Either way, I didn't care. For the first time, I saw Eddie in a way that made me sad at how badly I judged him most days.

The meeting was to get even funnier! Sophie, my Great Dane, had been sleeping in the entry hall on her bed. All of the commotion had gotten her attention. She could see us from her perch, but didn't dare venture into the room. Our laughter caused her to begin howling, "Awoo woo woo woo woo." She repeated the sound over and over, including a few rounds after we had all paused to watch her. As we started laughing again, she took a long look at us, put her head back down and went back to sleep.

Eddie's dance was finished, too. He sat down, going on with his story. He said that when no one had stopped to pick him up after several hours, he started looking for a pay phone to call his mom and ask her for help. Just about that time, an old beat-up station wagon driven by a Baptist preacher from South Georgia had stopped to pick him up.

Eddie made fun of the man's accent, "Boy, get EEyun!" Eddie had been glad for the ride and obeyed. The preacher was on his way to the Atlanta airport to pick up a traveling evangelist who would be holding tent meetings the following week at the preacher's church.

Pastor Eddie said that during the first five minutes in the preacher's car, the preacher had lectured him on what a "Tuhrrible sinnuh" he was. Eddie had learned that his sins were being unemployed, hitchhiking, having long hair, and living on the street. There were a whole lot of things that Eddie had done wrong according to the preacher's first impression of him. Eddie had been hungry, tired, and needed the ride, so he had just listened.

After the preacher was sure Eddie understood how sinful he was, he had demanded that Eddie "ADD-mit!" that he was a sinner. Eddie had agreed he was a sinner, not so much because of what the preacher had said about him, but because of things that the preacher didn't even know about him—things that the preacher wasn't ever going to know about him.

Next, the preacher had asked Eddie if he wanted to stop sinning and have "a Dee-cent life." Eddie said he had answered sarcastically, "That would be iDeeal," while looking out the car window so he didn't have to make eye contact with the man. The preacher had not been dissuaded by Eddie's sarcasm and asked if Eddie believed in Jesus. Eddie had said yes, though he had no idea who Jesus was other than a God who was born on Christmas.

The preacher had told Eddie he was going to "get'im saved." "Boy, if you bee-LAVE in JAY-sus an' AD-mit yo'a sinnuh, even you can be sAYved . . ." According to the preacher, all Eddie had to do was repent of his ways and believe the right stuff. Then the preacher had led Eddie in a prayer that Eddie had repeated, where he confessed the sins the preacher had judged Eddie guilty of and asked Jesus to save him. When the preacher was done, he told Eddie that it didn't matter if he sinned or not for the rest of his life, because now he was saved and going to heaven. This kind of "faith" required no desire or intention to follow Jesus at all.

Still standing in the middle of the study group, Eddie paused his story. Perhaps he was a genius. His story was a profound example of the kind of bad theology that James was exposing in his epistle. After a moment, Eddie got very serious and said, "I doubt that I got saved in that car, but I sure was turned off to Christianity for a long time. Plus, when the man dropped me off, I stole his M&Ms which were sitting next to me in the front seat unopened."

Helen greatly approved of Eddie's story. "I could be wrong," suggested Helen, "but I don't think James would have appreciated the preacher's attempt at getting Eddie saved. It seems to me that even as a young adult, Eddie knew in his gut that the preacher's definition of faith didn't jibe."

I agreed. James tells us that faith is not real unless it produces good works. Clarence Jordan, in the Cotton Patch version of James, writes, "A man is made whole by what he does, not merely by what he believes."[4] This is where Eddie's preacher was really missing the boat. He was not inviting Eddie to become a servant of God who would produce good works directed by the Holy Spirit. He was inviting him to pray a magic prayer to get a ticket to heaven. Apparently, the magic prayer had been less effective than Eddie's magic hitchhiker's dance.

Although we were unable to verbalize it yet, my congregants and I were making a very similar mistake. Though we were less focused on life after death than Eddie's preacher friend was, we were very focused on getting God to bless us in the here and now. Our faith was often limited to believing Jesus had come to help us navigate our trials successfully. We had no concept that our faith required a servant relationship to others with obligations to care for them.[5]

Helen guided us through the four examples that James uses to teach what faith is and is not. In the first example, James ties faith to social justice: "If a brother or sister is naked and lacks daily food, and one of you says to them, 'Go in peace; keep warm and eat your fill,' and yet you do not supply their bodily needs, what is the good of that?" When our worship of God is pure and undefiled, we have faith that cares for those in need. This idea is not unique to James. John instructs his church in the same way:

> How does God's love abide in anyone who has the world's goods and sees a brother or sister in need and yet refuses help? Little children, let us love, not in word or speech, but in truth and action. (1 John 3:17–18)

We don't just verbalize love, but we act on that love, clothing the naked and feeding the hungry simply because they need these things, not because

4. Jordan, *Practical Religion*, 8.

5. Perkins, *First and Second Peter*, 113–14, indicates that the obligation that faith has to serve others raises an interesting question. If works are necessary for living faith, then aren't relationships (which are necessary in order to serve others) also necessary for living faith? Can faith only be real when lived in community with others?

they deserve them. A life of worship doesn't just pray for a miracle; it knows that it is the miracle. It is the hands and feet of Jesus making sure the needs of those in trouble are met.

I was not surprised when Helen shared with the group the story of the day she passed the Latina teenager huddled in the parking garage. Instead of helping, she had defiantly told God that this was not her ministry. Tears flowed from Helen's eyes as she told about going back down to the parking garage after preparing for this lesson—months after seeing the girl—hoping beyond hope that she would see the girl again and could help her. But the girl was not there. She cried on the way home, praying both for the girl and for herself. She admitted to wanting to pretend that society's outcasts didn't exist and pass on by. Now she knew she couldn't and be a servant of God.

Liz cried with Helen. Olivia was simply absorbing their stories and thinking. I had really grown to admire every one of these women in many ways. Olivia wasn't ready to talk again just yet, but I knew without a doubt that God was working in her deep thoughts. This was the first time that I suspected that she was feeling called to something beyond being the VP of Marketing at Joe's company.

The second example James gives is about what faith *is not*, rather than what faith *is*. James teaches that faith *is not* about having a correct theology. He says that even demons know the truth about God, but having the right information about God doesn't mean demons are servants of God. In fact, they represent the opposite of servants. A life of pure and undefiled worship does not depend on knowing all the answers.

James's third example of faith is not so much about charitable good deeds, but simply obedience to God—obeying the wisdom of God.[6] James tells us an Old Testament story about Abraham, the father of the Jewish nation.[7] Helen led us through this story.

Abraham was a man to whom God had made very clear promises. In James's vocabulary, God had given him "wisdom." The thing about this wisdom was that as time went on, it became harder and harder to imagine the wisdom was true. For instance, God said that Abraham's wife Sarah, who was long past menopause, would have a baby. It was impossible by all human effort. So instead of relying on the power of God to bring the wisdom of God to pass, Abraham and Sarah decided to take matters into their own hands and began to collaborate on how to help God—as if God needed their help. They were soon to learn that it was a faithless gesture on their part and ended up creating a whole set of problems for themselves—an unwanted

---

6. Moo, *James*, 106.

7. Gen 22:1–19.

child, a mother with no husband, and family discord for centuries to come. However, when God was ready, through *God's* power, not *theirs*, Sarah had a baby and named him Isaac. They learned that faith was trusting in God's wisdom and power completely no matter how impossible or foolish it might seem.

It was an important lesson to learn, because one night, many years later, Abraham had a dream where the wisdom of God came to him and told him to offer his son Isaac as a sacrifice. By now, Abraham had learned to put his complete trust in God's wisdom and power, so he made plans to sacrifice Isaac the next morning even though it really made no sense at all. Why on earth would a loving God ask this? Nevertheless, at the same time, Abraham also knew that God had declared Isaac to be the one from whom a great nation will come. God could not take young Isaac's life and have him be the father of a great nation at the same time. Because of Abraham's faith, he knew that Isaac's life was safe in God's hands. So the next morning he woke up and took Isaac to the place where God had told him to do the sacrifice. Abraham was willing to put his complete and total trust in God. In the end, God substituted a ram for the sacrifice and Isaac's life was saved. A life of worship that was pure and undefiled does good works born of wisdom.

Helen warned us that James's fourth example using the prostitute, Rahab, was particularly controversial.[8] Rahab was a prostitute who lived in Jericho where she operated an inn. She didn't know anything about the God of Abraham. Her community worshiped the moon.[9] All she knew were the stories she had heard about the Hebrews conquering other larger nations in miraculous ways. She'd heard the story of the Red Sea parting when they came out of Egypt. She knew about their victories over their enemies as they made their way to the promised land. When the two Jewish spies walked into her establishment, she knew why they were in town. The town was in trouble. The Jews planned to destroy her city. She was afraid of them and their God.

It didn't take her long before she confessed to these men that she believed their God was the real God and she wanted to make a deal with them. She would get them out of the city safely if they would save her family. She was not only saved from the destruction of her city, but she married into the Jewish nation and became a great, great . . . great grandmother of Jesus.[10] She was a servant to these men because she believed in their God. A life of worship has faith that takes personal risks in order to serve God.

8. Josh 2:1–21; 6:17, 23–25.

9. McConville and Williams, *Joshua*, 189.

10. Matt 1:5.

In addition to telling the story, Helen noted something of real importance here—something that made James's use of this example controversial. Rahab's faith was not counted as righteousness because she begged forgiveness for her prostitution. Prostitution was wrong, of that there was no doubt. It was obviously not God's call upon anyone's life. However, it was not overcoming prostitution that saved Rahab; it was the risk she took to serve God's people.

Helen broke down again, but the tears this time came with a glowing smile. "For me," she said, "in this story I see an imperfect woman who risked everything to become a child of God. I want to risk my own comfort in order to become a servant." She punched Rodney's arm saying, "That may sound easy to Rodney who gave up lots of money being a doctor to go be a missionary. But it is really hard for me and I have trouble knowing how to do that and take care of my twins at the same time."

I asked Helen, "Do you know who can answer these questions of how you should serve God?"

"The Holy Spirit," she whispered.

She was right. The Holy Spirit had already started transforming her desires. I suspected it wouldn't be long until Helen became more and more aware of how God was calling her to live out God's claim on her life. Helen asked us to pray for her, so we did. We all gathered around her chair and put our hands on her shoulders. Liz sat beside her and held one hand while Helen held a Kleenex and wiped away her tears with the other. Out loud, we prayed for Helen. This was a prayer of pure and undefiled worship—asking for someone's servanthood to become a reality.

A life of pure and undefiled worship has faith, which produces good works. Yet, a life of worship is not produced by keeping a set of rules, believing a particular theology, or even by doing a random set of good deeds. A life of worship is produced by listening to the wisdom of the Holy Spirit and then letting the Holy Spirit empower one to serve God and others. This is faith. It is an action word. It is this kind of faith, one that is lived out at real cost to its owner—financial, social, and emotional cost—that is relevant to the suburbs, in fact, to the world.[11]

11. Dunn, *Theology*, 58–60.

19

A Life of Worship Speaks Words That Bless Others—James 3:1–12

Not many of you should become teachers, my brothers and sisters, for you know that we who teach will be judged with greater strictness. For all of us make many mistakes. Anyone who makes no mistakes in speaking is perfect, able to keep the whole body in check with a bridle. If we put bits into the mouths of horses to make them obey us, we guide their whole bodies. Alternatively, look at ships: though they are so large that it takes strong winds to drive them, yet they are guided by a very small rudder wherever the will of the pilot directs. So also, the tongue is a small member, yet it boasts of great exploits. How great a forest is set ablaze by a small fire! In addition, the tongue is a fire. The tongue is placed among our members as a world of iniquity; it stains the whole body, sets on fire the cycle of nature, and is itself set on fire by hell. For every species of beast and bird, of reptile and sea creature, can be tamed and has been tamed by the human species, but no one can tame the tongue—a restless evil, full of deadly poison. With it, we bless the Lord and Father, and with it, we curse those who are made in the likeness of God. From the same mouth, come blessing and cursing. My brothers and sisters, this ought not to be so. Does a spring pour forth from the same opening both fresh and brackish water? Can a fig tree, my brothers and sisters, yield olives, or grapevine figs? No more can salt water yield fresh.

—JAMES 3:1–12

Despite staying composed in the face of humiliation, I knew Olivia must have been going through a tough time. Being new in town, she couldn't have had a very big support network, so I invited her to meet me for dinner one night after work. It would be a girls' night out. Olivia and I sat outside the restaurant in my Prius. It was raining and we were waiting for the downpour to stop so we could make a dash for it. While we waited, Olivia handed me her iPhone and said, "Read this note from Joe. Someone who works for me had emailed him a question and this was his answer."

The person initiating the email had asked Joe, at Olivia's direction, a question clarifying some marketing work that he was doing directly for Joe. Joe's response was a truly ugly attack on Olivia. I wondered if Joe was getting sloppy. On the other hand, maybe he had wanted Olivia to see the email.

In the verses we were to study this month, James warned teachers that they were going to be judged with greater strictness than those who were just followers. He was especially talking to people like Joe who have stepped up to the position of elder. Joe was very proud that he had been elected an elder at The Church in the Suburbs decades ago and he let it be known professionally. In fact, every chance he got, every interview he did, he talked about being an elder in his church. An elder is a leader and teacher responsible for making both spiritual and practical decisions for the church.[1] James wanted people in Joe's position to take their responsibility very seriously and to be above reproach. James's concern was somewhat different from what was found in other parts of Scripture about elders that focused on false teaching.[2] James was more concerned with arrogance that leads to insulting those in one's care.[3] Yet, Joe's note about Olivia was insulting and reprehensible and an unacceptable way for any follower of Christ to act. It was a terrible attack upon her. This wasn't the first time I had heard about Joe's less-than-stellar example of Christian leadership, but it was the first time I had witnessed it this up close and personal.

On one hand, Joe encouraged his employees to go to church and discouraged them from behavior he felt was un-Christlike. Needless to say, not everyone would agree that he had the full scope of right and wrong well thought out. He had a reputation for picking and choosing what he felt was Christian behavior. He didn't like his employees to drink, swear, or be promiscuous, but he seemed just fine with his own manipulation of the truth, backbiting, and destroying those he didn't like. He had a horrid temper and

1. Moo, *James*, 123, states that teacher was one of the three authoritative positions in the early church along with the apostle and prophet. They interpreted Scripture for—among other things—church policy and practice.

2. 1 John 4:1–3; 2 John 1:7–11; 2 Pet 2:1–2; 2 Tim 4:3.

3. Chester and Martin, *Theology of the Letters*, 28–30.

he defined right and wrong based on established cultural norms—not necessarily with Jesus's teachings in mind.

It may have appeared to Joe that because Olivia's subordinate was writing directly to him, the subordinate was going over Olivia's head, making some kind of subversive career move. Therefore, Joe had wrongly identified the man as an ally. Joe's answer back to the man harshly criticized Olivia, blaming her for problems existing long before her arrival. He even gave "facts" about her career history that weren't accurate. "Facts" Joe knew were lies. There Joe was, the head of the company, the self-professed church elder and follower of Christ, and he was obviously trying to build a case—the same one he had tried to build with Rodney against Olivia—that Olivia was disloyal and incompetent. The same one he had built with the last couple of executive women he had run off. The email was very reckless, especially in the business world, where such things might end up in litigation. Olivia's subordinate had emailed her the note from Joe—an act that would probably get him fired if Joe were aware.

I asked Olivia what she was going to do.

"Well, it is obvious that my time at the company is very limited. I probably should be looking for another job, but I am still praying about what to do next. I don't feel it is the right thing to do to try and keep the job by fighting Joe, nor do I feel the right thing to do is to become his doormat and kowtow to gain his respect."

"To be honest, from his comments at our study group, it doesn't sound like either approach would work," I said sadly.

"I agree. From the women I talked to—thank you for giving me their names—I understand that he is practiced at ousting women who take either approach. My concern is not so much how do I keep this job, or even how do I get another job, but what does God want me to do next."

"Do you feel stressed out about this?" I asked.

"Not really. I have been setting aside thirty minutes a day to pray. I read Scripture for five minutes, lay out the issue before God, and then listen. This is so new to me, but asking the question of what God wants feels right instead of thinking about the next rung on the ladder."

Olivia and I went on to talk about all kinds of things that night that had nothing to do with Joe. Amazingly, she was less stressed out over Joe than I was. He made me angry at the arrogance with which he ran his business, repeatedly mistreating the women who worked for him. I also knew several of the board members and executives who worked with Joe. They made me angry, too. How could they sit by and let Joe harass yet another woman this way? Did the leadership at Joe's company really sit dumbfounded that they could have hired another bad apple while Joe gained more and more confidence at how easily they were duped? I had a hard time believing that the board bought into another set of manipulated facts. They must have been gaining something from going along with Joe's behavior.

Olivia and I had a good time that night despite what was looming. Even so, preparing for the next lesson in the days that followed only served to increase my anger at Joe. It seemed as though James had written this section in response to Joe's email.

James connects "the tongue" to the major mistakes that teacher-leaders make. Teacher-leaders can do both a lot of harm *and* a lot of good with their communication. As can everyone. I like how James narrows communication down to the most primitive type of communication: the tongue. The first century had few ways of communicating beyond the spoken and written word. Though access to the written word was more widespread than once believed, by today's standards communication was limited.[4] Today we talk to one another by email, voice mail, text messages, instant messages, and even blogs. The written word is abundant in newspapers and magazines. We tweet and post statuses on Facebook, too. Maybe, occasionally, we even use our tongues to speak to one another. Nevertheless, what James has to say applies to all forms of communication—not just oral communication. Before James gets to the real meat of how pure worship and the tongue relate, he sets the stage by giving us four examples of communication: the bridle, the rudder, fire, and the beast.

First, James gives the example of the horse's bridle. The bridle communicates to the horse which direction to go and when to start and stop. James would have liked his congregants to keep themselves in check with an imaginary bridle that controls their communication. They might even picture God in control of their bridle, guiding them in what they were to say. Interestingly, with this example, James teaches that when God controls their communication, their actions will be under God's control, as well.

Second, James gives the example of the ship's rudder—a relatively small piece of equipment, which harnesses the power of the waves in order to control the direction of a large boat. He teaches that even though his congregants may feel small and insignificant, what they communicate can influence the direction of much larger entities.

Third, James gives the example of a small, seemingly unimportant, even unintentional, fire, which could set things on a course for destruction. He teaches that insignificant, but poor, communication can have the consequence of destroying significant things.

4. Millard, *Reading and Writing in the Time of Jesus*.

Finally, James says it is easier to tame an animal than our tongues. He teaches us that no human is disciplined enough to succeed in controlling their tongue. This initially offers us little hope when we realize that by our own power we cannot be perfect in our communication. However, we know that God has promised that the Holy Spirit will give us wisdom and power to guide and enable our communications. A life of pure worship relies on the Holy Spirit for both wisdom and power in our communications.

The group gathered in November as usual and walked through the Scripture together. The days were crisp, cool, and getting shorter. Nothing significant really happened during the meeting other than a few random confessions of gossip addiction and stirring up trouble by not containing one's opinions. Joe ignored Olivia for the most part, although Rodney, ever since the evening Joe went on his diatribe against women, made every effort to befriend Olivia. It was working. She had found a loyal friend in Rodney who no longer seemed to expect perfection from her.

The most important part of the lesson, in my opinion, was the last thing James says about the tongue. James summarizes the difference between communication that flows from pure worship and communication that doesn't. A person who is worshiping God with their life offers blessings and not curses to others. They seek to build up those who hear them speak and not tear them down. Their communication has the full force of God's love behind it. There is no middle way. We cannot bless God while cursing others. A life of worship demands not just a right relationship with God, but a right relationship with others, too.

There was a current example that I wanted to use at the meeting. The speaker of the Kansas House of Representatives had conveniently sent out an email that week to a few friends and constituents that had gone viral.[5] It was not well penned or well thought out. He wrote that he was praying Psalm 109 for the president. Those verses the speaker quoted wished death for the president. He was cursing the president, with whom he disagreed, instead of blessing him. James directs Jesus's followers to use their communications to bless and not curse. There was nothing wrong with the speaker stating why he disagreed with policies of the president. In fact, it was his duty. On the other hand, James said we are not able to worship God and at the same time curse others. We can't cloak our curses as prayers.

Just as God spoke the universe into being and sent the word of God in human form to earth, our words have great powers, too.[6] We can create understanding, misunderstandings, goodwill, or chaos with them. We

5. Kuo, "Kansas House Speaker," para. 4.
6. Gen 1:3, 6, 9, 11, 14, 18; John 1:1.

can teach others great lessons or lead them astray. As Jesus was headed to Jerusalem for the last time to die on the cross, he was met with resistance in a city where he had stopped to prepare. The disciples asked permission to curse the people of the village—to bring fire down upon them and destroy them. Jesus responded, "You do not know what manner of Spirit you are of. For the Son of Man did not come to destroy men's lives but to save them."[7] It is important to know what kind of Spirit we have within us. The Holy Spirit does not put curses into our mouths, but words that bless others.

When I was done with the lesson, Liz looked over at Pastor Eddie, her sparkling blue eyes ablaze, "Speaking of using our communication unwisely . . . Pastor Eddie?" She stared at him until he realized that she was not happy with him.

"Yeah?" Even Eddie could tell he was about to get lectured in a way that only Liz could get away with.

"I have stopped checking Facebook on Mondays because of you," Liz said in a cute old lady tone that while coated in "nice," also meant business. "And I think this lesson is a good time to bring it up."

Eddie had this little game he played every Monday on Facebook. The police department posted mug shots on their website every Monday morning of anyone who had been arrested the previous week. Eddie would go to the website and get the most revolting mug shot he could find. Then Eddie would post it on his Facebook page and his friends would take turns commenting with wisecracks. The comments were generally extremely demeaning. Truly, the mug shots were of the most unfortunate people. These were not pictures of people who had had happy childhoods. Their faces gave no indication that they had ever experienced love or compassion—only pain and sadness. I doubt seriously that they had had proper educations or someone to fight for their well-being when things went wrong. Now Eddie was entertaining himself and his friends at their expense.

Eddie squirmed in his seat, "Oh come on Liz. It isn't as if these people are going to know we are making fun of them. And you have to admit they look pretty funny." Then he laughed—cackled really.

The wrinkles around Liz's usual pleasant face became sterner. She was not going to be shaken off so easily. "Eddie, you are just heaping curses upon people already broken. God created each and every one of those people in his likeness. You should be praying for them. And quite frankly, I agree with James. I don't think you can make fun of them like that and then turn around and say that you love God."

---

7. Luke 9:55–56 KJV. The Greek manuscript used by the NRSV translators does not contain these words, therefore the NRSV translation simply says that Jesus "turned and rebuked them."

The room was deadly quiet.

"Geez, Liz. I love God."

There was a long pause while Liz and Eddie were locked in a stare. Eddie was thinking about what he would say. He didn't want to give up this hobby, but he couldn't think of a way to justify it either.

After a moment, he complied, "Alright, Liz, you have made your point. I won't post them anymore." Eddie let his head drop to his chest and he let out a deep audible sigh. While his head was down the rest of us looked at each other and laughed.

"Stop laughing," mumbled Eddie. Then he looked up and started to try and justify himself again, only to catch the look on Liz's face. It was then that he gave up for good.

A life of pure and undefiled worship communicates blessings and not curses. Whether Eddie knew it or not, Liz had just blessed him.

Olivia lingered after the meeting waiting to get me alone. "I am going to address the email with Joe tomorrow at work. The subordinate who sent it resigned to take another job in an entirely different field so I won't be affecting his career."

"Well maybe today's lesson will encourage Joe to apologize?"

"I doubt it."

"Me, too."

"Will you pray for me right now?"

"Yes!" We prayed that Olivia's words to Joe would be a blessing and not a curse. Moreover, that Joe would be predisposed to listen and that the bond of the Holy Spirit, who reconciles us not just to God but also to each other, would be strong.

I got a call from Olivia the next day after her meeting with Joe. His bald head had turned bright red and yelling ensued after she showed him the email. He accused her of knowing the man was going to resign and setting this whole thing up. He turned it right around on her. No apology. He berated her competence, stood up, walked to his door, and told her to get out of his office—an action that could be seen through the glass walls by numerous employees. He told her that she was through at the company. As Olivia and I were talking, an incoming call from Joe showed up on Olivia's phone. She told me that she would take the call and call me back after they talked. Meanwhile I prayed.

Joe had apologized profusely to Olivia, offering to authorize the funds for her redesign of the marketing organization and promising to make sure engineering would get on board, too. He told Olivia how much he liked her and wanted her on the team. He overflowed with compliments for her and apologized for his earlier behavior.

Olivia called me back immediately. As she told me what had happened, my first reaction was that Joe was coming around. I felt our prayers had been answered and the power of God had done a wonderful thing! I thought our study of James could take credit. However, as soon as I expressed those sentiments, Olivia straightened me out. She was so much smarter than I was. She told me that Joe was only buying time to find a reason to fire her. He needed to get others on board; otherwise, it would make him look bad. This was the kind of game Joe played and he played it very well.

Olivia was right. I trusted her instincts. In addition, she wasn't the first woman to whom this had happened either. Joe was highly intelligent. He could read people extremely well and was attempting to play upon her emotions by acting helpless and needy. His erratic behavior was highly calculated. He had no empathy for Olivia. What a miserable existence Joe had. How had my good friend, his wife, Annie, stood it? Had he been able somehow to compartmentalize Annie from the women he worked with? I had no idea what went on in Joe's mind, but whatever it was, it wasn't right.

20

A Life of Worship Sows Seeds of Peace—James 3:13—4:10

Who is wise and understanding among you? Show by your good life that your works are done with gentleness born of wisdom. But if you have bitter envy and selfish ambition in your hearts, do not be boastful and false to the truth. Such wisdom does not come down from above, but is earthly, unspiritual, devilish. For where there is envy and selfish ambition, there will also be disorder and wickedness of every kind. But the wisdom from above is first pure, then peaceable, gentle, willing to yield, full of mercy and good fruits, without a trace of partiality or hypocrisy. And a harvest of righteousness is sown in peace for those who make peace. Those conflicts and disputes among you, where do they come from? Do they not come from your cravings that are at war within you? You want something and do not have it; so you commit murder. And you covet something and cannot obtain it; so you engage in disputes and conflicts. You do not have, because you do not ask. You ask and do not receive, because you ask wrongly, in order to spend what you get on your pleasures. Adulterers! Do you not know that friendship with the world is enmity with God? Therefore whoever wishes to be a friend of the world becomes an enemy of God. Or do you suppose that it is for nothing that the scripture says, "God yearns jealously for the spirit that he has made to dwell in us"? But he gives all the more grace; therefore it says, "God opposes the proud, but gives grace to the humble." Submit yourselves therefore to God. Resist the devil, and he will flee from you. Draw near to God, and he will draw near to you. Cleanse your hands, you sinners, and purify your hearts, you double-minded. Lament and mourn and weep. Let your laughter be turned into mourning and your joy into dejection. Humble yourselves before the Lord, and he will exalt you.

—JAMES 3:13—4:10

In lieu of the December meeting, the guys went golfing together, while the girls got together for lunch one day at a charming tearoom located in a 1920s Victorian house located just off of Main Street. The tearoom had been designed for just such feminine gatherings. It was a place where few men would be caught dining. The plan was that the guys would meet and discuss the verses for this week at the clubhouse and we would discuss them in the tearoom. Before we talked about the verses, Helen had questions for Liz about how she had discovered her ministry to the homeless. So over organic chicken curry and wild blueberry black tea, Liz, with her typical down-to-earth frankness, shared her experience as more of a warning than an inspiration.

Liz's father was a minister whom she adored. He had had a heart for the poor that he instilled in her at a very young age. With the exception of a year or two lapse after her divorce, most of her adult life had been spent volunteering for every charitable cause that came her way. Then to her surprise, in more recent years, she had come down with a severe bout of shingles that had put her in the hospital for several weeks. She had no doubt this was due to pushing herself too hard. Even though she knew that she had been over-volunteering, she wasn't about to give it up. Yet, she needed a way to get it all balanced out.

Liz had gotten caught in the trap of performing good works so she would feel good about herself, not because God wanted her to do them. However, it wasn't until we were studying James together that she realized that she had been doing random acts of kindness instead of intentional good works that were born of the Spirit's leading.[1] Liz was determined from now on that she would only do the works God had called her to do—ones that made a real difference to the world and matched the talents God had given her—no more random acts of kindness that had previously consumed and tired her out.

In fact, since she had joined the Modern Mystics, Liz had taken to setting a time aside every month to ask God about her opportunities to serve God during the coming month. She sat quietly meditating on which opportunities were hers to take on and which ones God had planned for someone

---

1. See chapter 15 for the discussion on random acts versus intentional good works.

else to do. Liz made it clear that it was not a matter of choosing what she wanted to do the most, but of listening to what God wanted. However, most of the time, she and God synced up pretty well.

Liz ended by saying, "My granny, rest her soul, used to tell me anybody could get married, but it took skill to marry the right person. She was right—and I won't elaborate on how I picked the wrong boy." For a moment none of us could figure out how that related to anything we had been talking about in the tearoom. Liz saw the looks on our faces and added, "Likewise, I think it also makes sense that anyone can find a ministry to do, but it takes skill to find the ministry that God wants you to do."

"Ooooh!" we each uttered the one syllable agreement, laughed, and nodded our heads that now we understood.

"So start praying, Helen! And don't you settle," finished Liz by patting Helen's hand.

Liz's advice was great. Her comments led right into the verses we were going to discuss. James challenges us by writing that our works should be "done with gentleness born of wisdom." The Apostle Paul puts it this way: we are "created in Christ Jesus for good works, which God prepared beforehand to be our way of life."[2] God had indeed prepared intentional works for Helen to do—works that fulfilled God's mission in the world. These works were planned before we were even created. Then in God's timing, the wisdom of the Holy Spirit would gently give birth to these works.

James also wanted to give his congregants some tools for distinguishing between "wisdom from above" (from the Holy Spirit) and "earthly wisdom." Earthly wisdom is not gentle and leads to "disorder and wickedness," whereas wisdom from above leads to peace. James pointed out that the Holy Spirit is not at work in the heart of a person who relies on earthly wisdom. Instead, their heart is powered by "bitter envy and selfish ambition" and they create disorder and wickedness of every kind. A person with this kind of wisdom wants something for themselves—not for God and others. Contrast that with the hearts of those powered by wisdom from above. Their hearts are "pure, then peaceable, gentle, willing to yield, full of mercy and good fruits, without a trace of partiality or hypocrisy." Earthly wisdom generates only temporary peace—if even that. Wisdom from above brings about true and lasting peace. James encourages his readers to become true peacemakers.[3]

The Old Testament calls this kind of peace *shalom*—a peace that is wholeness in every part of our being and extends into everything and

2. Eph 2:10.

3. Perkins, *First and Second Peter*, 122.

everyone around us.[4] It isn't a compromise or placation. It isn't a partial solution. It is complete wholeness for the entire community. This is what God wants for us. *Shalom* was what Jesus described in the Sermon on the Mount.[5] And it is what James reiterates here.[6]

This was a very serious conversation for the pink and white tearoom, which was far more familiar with gossip and mimosas than serious discussion over sweet tea. With a laugh, the waitress pointed this out to us as she took our order. Even so, we had things on our minds and were not to be deterred by her nudging us to lighten up.

Helen shared a story from her childhood growing up in a coastal town in South Georgia. The story of her next-door neighbor was an excellent example of earthly wisdom and false peacekeeping that only harms. She described the narrow tree-lined street where she grew up. It dead-ended at a dock where one could sit and watch the Atlantic splash its way onto the marshy beach. Spanish moss hung from old southern oaks. Hot humid summers and days were spent at the nearby beach.

Her best friend and next-door neighbor was Marsha Rayburn. Mr. Rayburn was the county judge and Mrs. Rayburn was what people used to call a housewife and mom of six kids. By all accounts, the kids were good children. They did well in school, took pride in being honest and kind, and minded their parents. Yet, Marsha was not quite as smart or as attractive as the others in the family were. Her intelligence and looks were average, but Mr. Rayburn had no tolerance for her lack of exceptionalism. He could not see that Marsha was sweet or that she had a beautiful desire to be kind to others. What he called "the child's lack of common sense" was a punishable offense in his mind. He showed little mercy to Marsha, picking on her frequently.

If he had a bad day at work, he would single Marsha out and speak abusively to her of the disabilities he perceived. If he gave Marsha a task to do and she didn't do it perfectly, he would force Marsha to stay in her room alone for days at a time. At first Mrs. Rayburn would stand up for the child, but that only made the father angry with Mrs. Rayburn. Then he would verbally abuse his wife, as well. The father accused Mrs. Rayburn of not disciplining Marsha enough, so he decided that he must make up for it by becoming harsher and harsher with her. Mrs. Rayburn decided that to keep the peace, she must treat Marsha harshly at least when the father was at home. When that didn't work and the father would mistreat Marsha

4. Samson and Samson, *Justice in the Burbs*, 178–79.

5. Matt 5:9.

6. Yarbrough and Stein, *James*, 203.

anyway, Mrs. Rayburn would look the other way. Sadly, what Mrs. Rayburn was doing was not real peacemaking. It was not the *shalom* that God desired for the Rayburns and especially not for Marsha.

Eventually Marsha became a teenager. Before long, she was asking to go to high school dances and parties, but her father would not let her go. Nor would he let her date or take part in afterschool activities. Marsha became more and more depressed. Eventually, at eighteen, Marsha ran away one night after her father had sent her to her room for the weekend—a punishment for coming home late from school Friday afternoon. Mrs. Rayburn had confided in Helen's mom that she was relieved that Marsha was gone and she prayed that Marsha would find a better life.

No one heard from Marsha for more than five years. Then the year after Mr. Rayburn died of a heart attack, Marsha returned, homeless and battered. Marsha had lived a horrid existence in the years she was absent. She had tried to hold down jobs, but she developed an eating disorder that kept her malnourished and ill most of the time. She turned to drugs, which led to HIV, and then AIDS.

That afternoon, Marsha made her way onto the family porch, but instead of ringing the doorbell, sat down on the porch swing. The swing had a squeak, which brought Mrs. Rayburn to the front door. When Mrs. Rayburn saw Marsha, she became overwhelmed and wept. Helen's mother had been walking the dog and had witnessed Marsha's return. She quickly put the dog inside the fence and hurried over to see Marsha, who was frail and obviously ill.

Mrs. Rayburn's attempts at peacemaking while her husband was alive were not attempts at true peace at all, but selfishness on her part. Mrs. Rayburn, in those years that Marsha was gone, had recognized this. She begged Marsha for forgiveness. Marsha moved home that day and died three months later from complications due to AIDS. Wisdom from above results in good works that create *shalom*—the wholeness that fills all of creation and envelops everyone in its path. When shalom is created, we experience a "harvest of righteousness." Earthly wisdom hurts and cripples those in its path. It creates the conflicts and disputes that James describes as "cravings that are at war within."[7]

Fortunately, James offered a cure to false peacemaking—to keep us from living the way the Rayburns had lived. James's way would have created *shalom* for their entire family:

> Submit yourselves therefore to God. Resist the devil, and he
> will flee from you. Draw near to God, and he will draw near to

7. Yarbourgh and Stein, *James*, 207–9.

you. Cleanse your hands, you sinners, and purify your hearts,
you double-minded. Lament and mourn and weep. Let your
laughter be turned into mourning and your joy into dejection.
Humble yourselves before the Lord, and he will exalt you. (Jas
4:7–10)

James would have told the Rayburns that their double mindedness—
acting on their own desires as if they were God's desires—needed to stop.
God hadn't made Marsha to be who her father wanted her to be. If the Rayburns had drawn near to God, putting aside their own desires for Marsha,
this would have no doubt become clear. They might have found themselves
asking God to show them how to help Marsha become who God created her
to be instead of demanding that she conform. They certainly would have
given up their selfish concerns and freed her to be herself. Instead, James
said, "You want something and do not have it; so you commit murder." Awfully strong words. Yet, in a sense, Marsha's parents triggered Marsha's death
long before she ever left home.

In doing so, the Rayburns chose "enmity with God." James was using
the word "enmity" as a first-century Jew who was influenced by how the Old
Testament used the words "love" and "hate." In the Old Testament, these
words are not emotions. They are an alignment. If you hate someone, it
means you are not aligned with him or her. Therefore, when James said that
we have enmity against God, he meant that we are not aligned with God.[8]
Marsha's parents would never have said that they hated God, but they certainly were not aligned with God's wishes for Marsha. They had selfish plans
for her and their family. They were out of alignment with God and instead
aligned with their own selfish desires.

Being out of alignment with God and in alignment with the world
were common afflictions. I had once seen a bumper sticker that summed
it up by saying, "We buy things we don't need with money we don't have to
impress people who don't like us." One who does this has chosen "friendship
with the world" and "enmity with God."

In the end, James ties this whole section of verses together by sum-
marizing what a life looks like that produces good works born of the Holy
Spirit's wisdom and sown in peace. Shockingly, James says it looks like grief:
"Lament and mourn and weep." This word translated "lament" was used
elsewhere in first-century literature to describe an army whose food was
gone and who had no shelter from the bad weather.[9] In telling his congregants to lament, James was telling them to get rid of their luxuries and to

8. Stott, *Message*, 146–47.

9. Smith, *Practical Faith*, CD 5.

substitute a life of humble existence. He also told them to mourn and to weep—something we, too, will do when we become aware of the brokenness in the world and its needs.[10]

Looking at Liz across the table from me, I saw a woman who could have spent her life chasing things for herself, but instead she chose to advocate for the homeless. She even gave up the luxury of sitting in the pew with her friends and instead went to church with the homeless. Liz's behavior demonstrated the meaning of "lament" in the first century. Moreover, as she sat with the homeless, she mourned and wept as she became aware of their needs and of the world's brokenness that kept them from having shelter.

Lament, mourn, and weep are shocking commands. They seem disconnected from producing works born of wisdom and sown in peace, but in the Sermon on the Mount, Jesus taught, "Blessed are the poor in spirit, for theirs is the kingdom of heaven. Blessed are those who mourn, for they will be comforted."[11] James was just repeating Christ's teachings. We grieve because as the Holy Spirit guides us into good works, we come to an awareness of the great degree to which the world is broken.[12] Even though this awareness causes our hearts to break, it also prompts us to work for *shalom* for all of creation and all of its creatures. James taught that in working for *shalom*, we experience God's grace and are exalted.

Somewhere over a dessert of lavender *crème brulee*, the girls began to brainstorm over ways that they could bring *shalom* to the suburbs. The ideas were varied. They ranged from monumental to simple. They had a great desire to do something as a team. They had no idea what that something was, but the idea was conceived that God had something going on that they were to participate in together. The lunch ended too soon and back to work I went.

10. Barclay, *Letters of James*, 108–9.
11. Matt 5:3–4.
12. Carson, *Jesus' Sermon on the Mount*, 19–20.

21

A Life of Worship Does Not Judge
Others—James 4:11–12

*Do not speak evil against one another, brothers and sisters. Whoever speaks
evil against another or judges another, speaks evil against the law and
judges the law; but if you judge the law, you are not a doer of the law but a
judge. There is one lawgiver and judge who is able to save and to destroy. So
who, then, are you to judge your neighbor?*

—JAMES 4:11–12

In January, as a sort of pre-meeting mental appetizer, I passed around an
email that had come out just that week to our subdivision's homeowners.
It was from a homeowner who reported witnessing a black man changing
his shirt behind the sign at the entrance to our neighborhood. In the email
he typed, "I think that the man is homeless. Please make sure your doors
are locked and belongings secure." Then I read the Scripture and asked the
group what James would have to say about this email.

"Well . . . that email judges not only that one man, but all homeless
people as thieves."

"I bet if the man was white no one would have thought twice about it."

"What an overreaction—I have never seen a homeless person any-
where around this neighborhood."

"Better safe than sorry."

It turns out the man was one of my neighbors, the father of a brave
African American family who had moved into our all-white neighborhood.

143

He had been out jogging and ducked behind the sign to get out of the direct sun while he paused for a drink of water and to put his shirt back on. The "better safe than sorry" response had come from Eddie. He started to defend it, but Liz stared him down until he was afraid to say more.

With Eddie subdued by Liz's supernatural powers, I reminded the group of another example from reformed history that I had brought up briefly in an earlier meeting. John Calvin wrote an extensive (and really quite tedious) systematic theology.[1] I read more than a thousand pages of it in seminary. My problem with John Calvin was not his theology (although I wasn't in complete agreement with every detail), but his life. Like James, I have a hard time getting excited about someone's theology when he or she doesn't live out the teachings of Jesus—especially the teaching on loving others:

> "Teacher, which commandment in the law is the greatest?" Jesus said to him, "'You shall love the Lord your God with all your heart, and with all your soul, and with all your mind.' This is the greatest and first commandment. And a second is like it: 'You shall love your neighbor as yourself.' On these two commandments hang all the law and the prophets." (Matt 22:36–40)

John Calvin had some terrible lapses in compassion for others. He also held the belief that he had not only the authority, but also the duty to judge others.[2] He believed, in his own words, that he was doing "combat for God's glory."[3]

One incident stands out above all the others. John Calvin had an acquaintance with whom he corresponded named Michael Servetus. He was an accomplished Spanish physician with an interest in theology. The two of them had disagreements over many points of theology, but their differing views of the Trinity seemed to be the most egregious to Calvin. Calvin believed that God was three distinct persons all from the same substance. Servetus believed this was against Scripture's teachings, saying that God was not three distinct persons, but assumed different dispositions as needed. They called each other names. Their conversation concluded with Calvin declaring Servetus to be a heretic. He warned Servetus to stay away from Geneva—where Calvin was living—or he would make sure Servetus did not leave Geneva alive. Servetus would not be deterred. For some reason he came to Geneva to hear Calvin preach anyway and Calvin had him arrested.

1. Calvin, *Institutes of the Christian Religion*.

2. Zahnd, *Radical Forgiveness*, 143–45.

3. Calvin, *Defensio Orthodoxae Fidei* (1554), 46–47, cited in Zahnd, *Radical Forgiveness*, 144.

He was tried and sentenced to die as a heretic. Servetus suffered the most painful death allowable by religious court, which meant being burned alive at the stake. Calvin and the other religious leaders had judged Servetus.[4]

James tells us that those who live a life of pure and undefiled worship do not judge others. There was nothing wrong with Calvin and Servetus having disagreements over discussions about theology, but Calvin had no right to judge Servetus's relationship with God. Only God can know our hearts. Furthermore, the truth of the matter is that we can only pretend to understand the Trinity completely. It is a mystery. The Bible never uses the word "Trinity" nor does it give us an explanation as to the details of how the Trinity works. I believe that Calvin was right in what he believed about the Trinity, but it goes against all we know of Christ to kill another human being over a difference of theology.

I also think what Calvin had forgotten (and what we often forget) was a scene in the Gospel of Mark where Jesus was confronted by some scribes who claimed the work that Jesus was doing was empowered by the ruler of demons, Beelzebub.[5] Jesus said these scribes were blaspheming the Holy Spirit with this claim—claiming that the work of the Holy Spirit was actually the work of Satan. Next Jesus said something really harsh to them. He said that there is no forgiveness for this sin. Jesus said that anyone who claims the work of God is the work of Satan has committed an eternal sin. Now I don't claim to understand all the theological ins and outs of these verses, but I do know that Jesus was strongly cautioning us against judging someone to be under the control of evil when they were actually doing God's work.[6]

Could Calvin really know that Servetus was a heretic? Perhaps he was a follower of Jesus who was just mistaken about this one point of theology. What if Servetus was right and Calvin was wrong? Do Christians have to agree theologically to be doing God's work together? James has already taught us that we are to speak in a way that blesses others—not curses them. To read Servetus's writings, it seems to me that he had a passionate reverence for Scripture and a love for Christ.[7]

The meeting that month was simple, but not insignificant. Rodney was still struggling with being a prophet without offending everyone who didn't see things as he did. He told a story of his latest opportunity. The Church in the Suburbs had a "Dinner Out" program every quarter where members would get together in groups of six or so at people's houses. People were

4. Stanford, *Murder*.

5. Mark 3.

6. Wright, *Mark*, 38.

7. Serveto, *On the Errors of the Trinity*.

chosen at random to have dinner together and get to know one another. Rodney, his wife, and Olivia ended up with four others at one of the long-time member's houses. Rodney's wife had been as enthusiastic as Rodney was at adopting Olivia into their family so they had a great evening.

However, the longtime church member, whose house hosted the dinner, dominated the discussion. She and her husband were quite wealthy. They lived in the most expensive house in the most expensive neighborhood within a ten-mile radius of the church, and that was saying something. It was a magnificent neoclassical Italian home and was more than large enough for their family of four. In fact, several families could have easily been accommodated in the house and still have had plenty of legroom. They had recently spent a small fortune on updating the kitchen, but it wasn't enough. They wanted a bigger house and made plans to add on a significant master bedroom. The hostess spoke with great drama as she asked the group to pray for her during the construction, which she boasted would cost more than $300 thousand, but was going to be "oh so very, very, very stressful."

Rodney said that the hostess's prayer request completely hit him the wrong way. For him and his wife, a luxury was having a washing machine on the mission field—not a dryer—just a washing machine. They hated doing the laundry by hand. One could only imagine how much laundry their three biological and five adopted children could produce. It was time consuming and hard on the hands. Nevertheless, they had gone without a washing machine for several years, while they put money toward things needed in the hospital.

Rodney began to tell the story, "Olivia and I don't want to be judgmental, but we are bringing this up to the group, because . . ."

"Olivia is not bringing this up!" chirped in Olivia as she leaned in smiling at Rodney in a way that said she had grown to like and appreciate him despite his rough edges. "However, I did appreciate the restraint you showed at dinner, considering how you once beat me up for my Jaguar which—I must point out—was only a third of the cost of their bedroom addition! I thought you did a good job of staying calm."

Smiling sheepishly, starting over, and this time emphasizing "I," Rodney continued, "Okay, I am bringing this up because it doesn't feel right to show restraint. Three hundred thousand dollars for a better master bedroom? That would build four clinics in Africa—it could save thousands of lives. My silence felt like I was supporting her. Doesn't someone need to tell her that it is pure evil to be indulging in that kind of luxury when there are sick and starving people in the world?"

"Tell us how you really feel," teased Olivia.

Rodney laughed, but quickly shook his head and then pondered out loud, "How can Christians so easily delude themselves into thinking that they are doing the will of God? When in actuality their faith is nothing other than belief about God with no real concern for doing the work of God?"

Exasperated with himself and disgusted that he didn't know how to handle these situations, Rodney added, "But what concerns me even more right now is whether I should speak up or not. I need you guys to give me advice."

Rodney had a tendency, as Olivia had experienced firsthand, to judge and attack. Neither judging nor attacking was appropriate. But what was appropriate? How do we speak truth and sow seeds of peace at the same time? The woman was guilty of many things, but wasn't Rodney guilty of what James had just warned us against—"speaking evil against another or judging another?"

If we translate the Greek literally, what James says is that we should not "speak against one another." The word "evil" is not technically there. The word translated "speak against" refers to any form of speaking against another person. Not only should we not slander or make false charges, but we should also not speak against another in a way that is true in content, but hurtful or manipulative in presentation.[8]

Was Rodney, on one hand, by saying nothing, allowing the hostess to head down the wrong path, thinking all the while that he supported her? Do friends let friends take the wrong path without warning them? On the other hand, how could Rodney say anything and not be acting as the woman's judge? To judge your neighbor is to violate an important aspect of our faith. It places us in a position that James tells us only God can hold. This is one of those times when thinking about "what would Jesus do" simply doesn't cut it, because we are not Jesus.

The group didn't have all the answers, but we came to three conclusions meant to help Rodney. Helen jotted them down in her journal twice, then pulled out one copy and handed it to Rodney. He read them back to us:

1. Since each situation will be different, ask God for wisdom in every situation and do not speak up until you feel God is leading you to speak.

2. Never speak up when you aren't doing it out of love for the person you are confronting.

3. Speaking up in a public place and in front of others isn't usually a good idea. Honor the person you are speaking to with respect and privacy.

8. McCarthy, *James*, 220–21.

Rodney felt okay with the second and third pieces of advice we had given him. He admitted that instead of always acting out of love and for the person's well-being, sometimes he was just angry. Still, the first piece of advice troubled Rodney. He asked, "Under what circumstances would God ever tell me not to speak up?"

Eddie told Rodney that Jesus encouraged his disciples to use a bit of common sense when they approached people with the gospel—and not to approach people who weren't open to it. The Scripture Eddie quoted was terribly harsh, but it did seemed to apply. "Do not give what is holy to dogs; and do not throw your pearls before swine, or they will trample them under foot and turn and maul you."[9]

It dawned on me that this was a teaching that Eddie had set as a primary directive in his life. A teaching he had been trying to instill within me the morning that he met me in the parking lot telling me to ease up on what Joe didn't want to hear. It was following this teaching that kept Eddie out of trouble with the congregants. Yet, there did come a time when Jesus spoke up knowing he would be abused for the sake of the gospel. I think the key was that Jesus knew when that time had come because he prayed and asked God—just as we are to do. Rodney would need to learn to ask in every situation.

Because Rodney had wanted our advice, we gave it to him. We all agreed unanimously that in Rodney's case, if he didn't perceive that the hostess could see his good intentions, then perhaps it was wise not to approach her. Then Eddie added another verse—just in case Rodney approached her and she became upset. "If any place will not welcome you and they refuse to hear you, as you leave, shake off the dust that is on your feet as a testimony against them."[10] In other words, if you speak up and the person won't listen, then don't keep bothering them—you are done. Go on your way.

Rodney listened intently. He had built up a lot of righteous indignation against the consumerism of American Christianity. As he traveled around the United States during his year of furlough, seeking funding for his work in Africa, he constantly struggled against speaking the harsh truth to many of his best financial supporters. In each town, they would generously provide housing for him, usually in their own homes. Yet, when he visited their homes and saw that what they contributed to the care of his patients in Africa was nothing compared to the waste they produced with their extravagant lifestyles, he wanted to let them have it. Rodney often worried that

9. Matt 7:6.

10. Mark 6:11.

taking their money, without speaking truth to them about how he thought the servants of Christ should be living, was immoral.

However, in a way, James was giving Rodney a break. He didn't have to be the judge and he didn't have to feel responsible for converting into servanthood every one of the people funding his medical clinic. He could seek God's direction and only speak out when God wanted him to speak.

Eddie closed the meeting with an example from an experience he had had at The Church in the Suburbs. A few years back, the previous senior pastor had resigned, and Eddie and Liz had served on the committee to find the new pastor. There was another congregant on the committee who had worn the rest of them out by asking every candidate they interviewed if he or she would be willing to tell certain people that they could not join the church. Eddie remarked that the thought of turning anyone away was ridiculous.

Liz jumped into the middle of the story and said that one pastoral candidate finally asked that congregant who it was that she thought wasn't good enough to be a member. The answer was the used car lot owner who had been visiting their church. The woman claimed that everyone in town knew he was a thief. She wanted assurances that the new senior pastor would get rid of the man.

Eddie said he had been so proud of Liz for speaking up that night. He said Liz's words would have made James proud.

Liz replied, "I can't remember exactly what I said that night. But God has told me that I am not to be a judge. I am to be a lover. I will love anyone who comes to our church. I will never judge them or send them away." Those who live lives of pure and undefiled worship don't judge others. Instead, they are to free to love one another unconditionally, leaving the judging up to Jesus.

22

A Life of Worship Knows God Is in Control—James 4:13–17

Yet you do not even know what tomorrow will bring. What is your life? For you are a mist that appears for a little while and then vanishes. Instead you ought to say, "If the Lord wishes, we will live and do this or that." As it is, you boast in your arrogance; all such boasting is evil. Anyone, then, who knows the right thing to do and fails to do it, commits sin.

—JAMES 4:13–17

Olivia and I both served on a committee at church that helped define and guide the women's programs. She had left me a message earlier in the week regarding the next meeting of this committee. Friday was often the time I returned calls that I just couldn't get to any sooner. My callback caught her in the middle of planning her work schedule with Joe for the next week. I could hear both of them gathered around the speakerphone at Olivia's conference table. I asked them if their day was going smoothly. How Olivia kept so even keeled knowing Joe was against her was something that continued to amaze me. I would have given him a piece of my mind by then and quit, but good for her!

Joe and Olivia answered in unison, telling me that they were headed to Dallas to begin the process of setting up a sales office that would go live within the next three months. They were going to be interviewing some candidates to run it. Dallas was an open market and they believed that they would make a lot of money there.

It sounded good to me. Yet, suddenly what I had been preparing for in the next lesson hit me. Neither of them sounded in a hurry—so I asked, "Have either of you read the next set of verses in James?"

Both of them had.

"Well then, I guess what you needed to complete your plans was for me to call you and warn you that James might say your plans are arrogant and boastful! In fact, James might even go so far as to also call them evil."

They both laughed.

Joe said, "Oh come on!" I knew he was shaking his head on the other end of the line, thinking once again that I had gone off the deep end. "Okay, we are going to open an office in Dallas 'if the Lord wishes' and the *crik* don't rise. Are you satisfied now?"

"If the *crik* don't rise?" mused Olivia.

"It must be a Southern saying," Joe explained. "If the creek rises, it washes out the bridge and you can't get across it to do whatever you had planned to do."

"I see!" she joked. Then to me she added, "I can't wait to hear more at the study!"

Is James really serious? Does James really want Joe and Olivia to tack the words "God willing" onto their every plan? Probably not.[1] However, James did want Joe and Olivia to make their plans with the knowledge that God was in control. Since we know that God is in control of our well-being and our resources, we have no reason to fear whatever may come. We can also trust God to care for us so that we can care for others with our resources instead of hoarding them. Once again, James seems simply to be teaching what Jesus had already taught.

> Then Jesus told them a parable: "The land of a rich man produced abundantly. And he thought to himself, 'What should I do, for I have no place to store my crops?' Then he said, 'I will do this: I will pull down my barns and build larger ones, and there I will store all my grain and my goods. And I will say to my soul, Soul, you have ample goods laid up for many years; relax, eat, drink, be merry.' But God said to him, 'You fool! This very night your life is being demanded of you. And the things you have prepared, whose will they be?' So it is with those who store up treasures for themselves but are not rich toward God." (Luke 12:16–21)

Jesus wanted the man to think beyond his own needs—beyond saving for his own well-being—and to think about God's call on his life. The

1. Moo, *James*, 162.

implication was that others may have immediate need for the man's resources and God would have preferred he share rather than hoard them. The followers of Jesus were to think differently. They knew God was in control so they prioritized sharing resources over planning for future resources.[2]

I would have to say that this was a very interesting challenge at The Church in the Suburbs. A lot of accomplished people went to church there. Clarence Jordan described us well when he interpreted James for the Cotton Patch Gospel, "Hold on a minute now, you who talk so big . . . you don't know one blessed thing about tomorrow . . . all such strutting is downright wicked."[3] We were accomplished in a lot of things the world considered very valuable. It was easy for us to make the world's goals our goals—to get rich, to have nice things, to have lots of money put away for retirement, to be powerful and successful. It was easier to hoard one's resources than to look for a way to use them to bless others.

In Joe's and Olivia's situation, they were assuming without really giving it any thought that if all logical signs pointed to a successful business in Dallas, then they certainly ought to be headed to Dallas to open a sales office. They believed, like the rest of us, that being successful in our endeavors was our right—as if our choice to be successful was the only deciding factor—that in business decisions God didn't matter.[4] Furthermore, the board of directors would have thought Joe and Olivia had gone nuts if they started putting "God's will" as a bullet point on their strategic plans.

Given these hurdles, what did God want from them? Everything. God wanted to be involved in all of their plans—even their business plans. James reiterates Jesus's teaching in the Lord's Prayer, "Your will be done, on earth as it is in heaven."[5] He wants us to enter completely into a relationship with God, seeking God's priorities, plans, and timing. The ability to do this starts with the knowledge that God is in control and we are not. In essence, James, like Jesus, is teaching us to pray, "Not my will, but yours be done," with our entire lives.[6]

At the next study meeting, we boiled all of this down to "those who worship God live knowing that God is in control." We didn't believe that James was telling us not to plan, but to plan knowing we (and our resources) belonged to God. Because of this knowledge, our plans should start by accepting that the circumstances of our lives may change tomorrow. James

---

2. Wright, *Luke*, 150–54.

3. Jordan, *Practical Religion*, 10.

4. Motyer, *Message*, 160.

5. Matt 6:10.

6. Luke 22:42.

says, "You do not even know what tomorrow will bring." In addition, since God often only gives us enough wisdom for today (Jesus taught the disciples to pray for their *daily* bread), we might have to wait until tomorrow to get further wisdom, to see the whole plan, or even just the next part of the plan.[7] Besides, servants don't make their own plans. They are aware that many times, they must wait patiently on the master until God is ready to give them an itinerary. Rushing ahead is fraught with all kinds of problems. Yet, there is no need to worry about tomorrow. We can rest in that knowledge—secure in a future that is unknown. Knowing God is in control frees us for service.

Next James asks the question, "What is your life? For you are a mist that appears for a little while and then vanishes." The word *mist* is probably better translated as "a puff of smoke."[8] It doesn't last long. When we know that God is in control, we know that our biggest plans are small compared to God's eternal picture. We have a choice to limit our lives to following our own small plans or living as part of God's eternal plans. Each of us can have a purpose that is bigger than our immediate reality. We need to think beyond our own lives when we are discerning God's plans and think about God's mission on a larger scale than our immediate circumstances.

Finally, James teaches, "You ought to say, 'If the Lord wishes, we will live and do this or that.' As it is, you boast in your arrogance; all such boasting is evil. Anyone, then, who knows the right thing to do and fails to do it, commits sin." The word that is translated *arrogance* was a characteristic associated with the first-century equivalent of a snake oil salesman.[9] This arrogant person offered cures for things that couldn't be cured. When we make plans believing that we can make them happen, we sin. Only God can bring our plans into being.

We want to tone James down. We can't possibly lump our selfish plans in with the really evil stuff—say, murder or adultery. However, when we make plans that are not God's plans, it is the same as saying to God, "I am independent of you." It is, according to James, not just passively corrupt; it is aggressively evil. Moreover, it is not the reality of what it means to be a servant of God. It is arrogant—proud confidence in one's own wisdom. James calls us out on it. Those who worship God recognize that God is in control of everything and they willingly yield to God's control.

Joe complained that I was not putting enough emphasis on the fact that God gave *some* of us good minds to make plans with and that we should use them. I think he felt the entire lesson was ridiculous. He was a man

7. Matt 6:11.

8. Moo, *James*, 160.

9. Barclay, *Letters of James*, 114.

who had led a business to very respectable heights. In addition, although he didn't deny that God was somehow in control, I don't think Joe wanted to give accolades to God that were due to him. He wanted credit for the plans he had made. Since he'd never sought direction from God in his business, he took offense at James—and hence, me. But I was getting used to it and barely noticed it.

Olivia had called me back later in the evening the day that I had caught her and Joe in her office making plans for Dallas. She confided that she was going to resign. I was surprised—and yet not so surprised. A stranger would have thought things were going great from hearing them over the phone.

"What has pushed you over the edge?" I asked.

"I took an afternoon off work last week. Rodney and his wife took me to the women's shelter. It was their regular volunteer day and I tagged along. I have been back twice since."

Olivia went on to tell me that seeing such great need made her job seem meaningless. She told me that she and her husband had lots of resources that they could use to help others. She didn't need to have an income, nor did she feel morally right continuing in a job where she was subject to blatant abuse from her boss.

I asked her if there had been more problems between her and Joe. She said he had not spoken directly to her in weeks, canceling all of their one-on-one meetings until he had come to her office to plan the trip to Dallas. It was unusual that he would be part of the trip—normally the opening of the branch would be her organization's independent work. It was odd that Joe had chosen to get involved. It was likely an indication that he was planning her departure and wanted to have a hand in picking the branch manager so that the transition would be smooth.

She imagined that had she not become a follower of Christ in the last few months, she would have just laid low in this job until she had found another one. However, her taste for the corporate world had disappeared. She felt God calling her to a different life entirely and she wanted to resign in order to figure that out. Her resignation was not out of frustration with Joe or out of fear of being fired, but so that she could spend some time discovering the specifics of what God wanted her to do next. She highly expected God was calling her to work with underprivileged women in some way, but she had no idea how.

"How do you feel about all of this?" I asked her.

"Good. Not looking forward to telling Joe, but good."

"Have you told your husband?"

"Yes. He is happy about it. He has been trying to break the daily ties with his firm in Chicago and move down here with us."

"Will you move back to Chicago instead now?"

"No. He wants to put the reigns of the company into his partner's hands and move down here. He needs to get out of Chicago for a while so he can separate from the firm and let them get used to the caseload without him. We may end up back in Chicago at some point, but we will stay here at least until the kids are out of school this year and probably much longer."

"What does he think of your newfound faith?"

"Well . . . he really likes the idea of the two of us getting involved in charitable work together. He has always been a philanthropist and talked about retiring and doing volunteer work. He even says he will go to church with us, but he is more than a little suspicious of organized religion."

"You can tell him we aren't all that well organized!" We both grimaced at my joke. Then I added, "Olivia, it all sounds wonderful."

If it was possible to hear someone smile over a phone line, I believe that I could hear Olivia smiling. I hung up and sat silently for a few minutes praying for her. I felt thankful that I had been witness to this transformation in her life. It seemed surreal, mystical, and right.

That conversation had taken place several days before the study. After the study, Olivia stayed while everyone headed home. She was dressed in a white button down shirt with her jeans tucked into her boots. She looked more relaxed than I had ever seen her.

"I just have one thing to tell you," she said. "I know it must be close to your bedtime—but this lesson kind of seals the deal for me. Knowing God is in control means that I don't have to worry about the next steps. For someone who is a natural planner and organizer that means something. I am so excited to move forward 'secure in an unknown future.' And my husband will be down here for good this weekend!"

With that, Olivia seemed to bounce out the door and up to the curb where her Jaguar was parked. It seemed like I could always evaluate Olivia's spiritual disposition as she walked away. The stress that had made her so awkward and laughable at times was gone. Almost. Then she tripped again. Talk about *deja vu*! Well, some things just don't change! Nevertheless, something—no, someone—had set her free to be completely who she had been created to be!

23

The Meeting That Never Happened

A few weeks flew past and I heard from no one, but as the old saying goes, "When it rains, it pours." So when Rodney called the church that morning, the drizzle that would soon become a downpour started.

Rodney didn't waste time with the traditional hello greeting. He started right in, "Did you know that Olivia resigned from Joe's company?"

"Rodney, I can't really answer that question due to confidentiality issues."

"Right." Pause. "Well, she resigned."

Rodney had been on another hunting trip with Joe. Just a few hours before Joe had picked up Rodney, Olivia had told Joe that she was resigning. Joe had poured out all that had transpired as he drove. Apparently, she had not minced words, telling Joe that his behavior had been out of line. She had listed out specific occasions dating back to her arrival at the Atlanta headquarters months before. Joe presented each of these situations to Rodney as if Olivia was unreasonable and overly dramatic. Stuck in Joe's mind was that she had promised him that her comments would stay between the two of them. Joe questioned the sincerity of her promise and wholeheartedly believed that she was setting him up for a lawsuit. At first, Rodney couldn't understand why this was bothering Joe. Until Joe confided that he had ended up settling out of court with the last female who had invaded his executive team. She had sued him personally. He hated having women in the work force. They didn't play by the rules and had no loyalty to him. All Rodney could do was listen. Joe wasn't looking for advice.

Olivia had also told Joe that his behavior was not the reason she was resigning—she wanted to take some time off to do some nonprofit work.

She offered to stay until he could replace her, but Joe had told her to collect her stuff from her office and get out immediately. He didn't even want her to say good-bye to her staff. Joe was proud that he had thrown her out.

Rodney said Joe drove fast and furious, ranting about Olivia the whole way to the hunting lodge. Then with just as much passion, about an hour after getting to the lodge, Joe was frantically trying to find a phone to call Olivia. There was no cell coverage at the lodge. He eventually found a land-line in the kitchen office. Rodney could hear Joe begging her to stay. Joe tried flattery and when that didn't work, Joe actually cried pathetically, still trying to convince her to stay. It was clear to Rodney that Joe's behavior was not only very manipulative, but also completely unstable.

Olivia didn't budge. Olivia firmly told Joe that she had already cleaned out her desk and would not be returning to the office. Rodney said Joe moped for the rest of the evening and then after about an hour of hunting the next day wanted to cut the trip short and return home, which they did.

I pointed out to Rodney that we probably didn't want to get caught up in their drama, in order to let Joe and Olivia work out whatever was going to happen. He agreed. No sooner had we hung up than in walked Joe to my office. Even the top of his head was red. To say that he was angry with me was an understatement. I stood up from my desk partly out of some kind of primal reaction to fear and partly in order to seem welcoming.

"Did you know that Olivia resigned?" he said, standing eye to eye with me.

"Did Olivia resign?"

"Yes, to go pursue some kind of dang charity work."

"I see."

"You put this idea into her head!" and with that he slapped my desk with his hand.

"Joe, Olivia makes her own decisions." I kept my tone very calm and respectful. Yet, I felt I was looking a psychopath in the eyes. No. Psychopath sounded too strong. Maybe I meant sociopath. I wasn't afraid he was going to harm me. Yet, his level of anger was very high. All of his emotions were out of proportion to the situation at hand.

Joe didn't care about Olivia's career. Her departure was not going to affect his company any more than the other female departures had affected his company. He was simply angry that this time he didn't get to dump her first. Humiliating the women he fired was fun for him. Duping others into believing the women were unfit was fun for him, too. But this time, he felt dumped and humiliated instead. This was the first time that I understood Joe's game. He got off on two things: making these professional women feel worthless and duping others into supporting him. Somehow, it made him feel good about himself. He didn't know what to do now that she had beat him to it.

I offered Joe a seat and said that I would get us some coffee. He sat down, rejecting the coffee. I went to get my coffee anyway, taking my time, hoping he would have a chance to calm down. Honestly, I didn't really expect him to be there when I returned.

However, he stayed. When I came back, before I was even inside the door, he announced that he was done with the study group. I asked him to think about it some more. He had made a commitment to stay engaged even if we had conflict, and I asked him to keep that commitment. I encouraged him either way to come to the next meeting so that he could tell the group that he was leaving it. I reminded him of how much the group admired him and would be disappointed if he left. He growled at me for a few more minutes and left my office.

The rain had grown heavier and heavier. The office was rather small to begin with and now the darkness from the afternoon clouds filled it. A long time ago, I had learned to pray at times like this. I switched on my desk lamp and began to pray. I started by asking the Holy Spirit to open my eyes to its wisdom and to give me power to act on that wisdom. I laid out the situation before God, telling God all the details. Then I stopped talking and listened. Into my free flowing thoughts God spoke. God said to wait. Simply to do nothing except prepare for the next study group meeting.

When the night of the meeting arrived, everyone showed up, including Joe and Olivia. Even the air felt heavy. I started the group off saying I wondered if we might do something different and take a few minutes to pray for each other. I wondered if anyone had concerns that he or she would like to share. Joe spoke up first. He stood as he went on a rant directed at me. Everyone was looking at him with eyes wide. I was hoping I would handle this dressing down as well as Olivia had handled the beatings she had received. I certainly hoped, as the pastor of the group, that I would come out looking godly and not silly and emotional. The truth of the matter was that I felt like crumbling. Determined not to speak until he was done, I waited.

Before Joe could really get into it, Liz spoke up, "Joe, I need to say something before you go any further."

If it had been anyone else, Joe would have spoken right over her. He was on a roll. However, Liz had a way about her. She was spunky, but gracious all the time in a way that said you didn't mess with her.

Joe stopped and sat down.

"I don't know how to say this," started Liz. Her gorgeous bright blue eyes filled with tears, but didn't overflow. Everyone was quiet.

Helen reached out her hand and held Liz's hand. She was the first to speak, "Liz, just tell us."

"I am dying."

A gasp went through the room. It was such a shock that no one really believed her. She went on to tell us that she had found out just yesterday that she had advanced pancreatic cancer. It was inoperable and she only had a few months.

Helen cried. Olivia got on her knees in front of Liz and held onto both of Liz's knees. Rodney put his face in his hands. Joe stood up, walked to the window, and just stared out. After a bit, Pastor Eddie asked if he could read something to us. No one answered, so he opened his Bible. Who knew what he would read. I just hoped it would be semi-appropriate.

"From Isaiah 41," said Eddie. "Fear not, for I am with you; be not dismayed, for I am your God; I will strengthen you, I will help you, I will uphold you with my righteous right hand."

Amen. No Scripture could have been more appropriate. The news had cut us dead in our tracks. There was nothing to say or do except to lean into God.

Liz turned to Joe and said, "Joe, I am asking you this. I want you to stay in this group. I want the group to keep meeting. I want us to get along and love each other. I may not live long enough to finish the study, but if I don't, I want you to finish it together. All of you."

Joe didn't turn around. He was still facing the window looking out. His head rocked backward with his nose toward the ceiling. He took in a long deep breath and afterward quietly said, "Okay."

Helen asked the details of the prognosis and if she was in any pain. Liz said the only way she knew anything was wrong was that her back hurt from time to time. The doctors were just as surprised to find it as she was.

We prayed for Liz. We even asked God to heal her. But Liz said, "I don't think healing me is in God's plan."

"Liz, why wouldn't God heal you?" Rodney was adamant that she should be fighting for a miracle!

Liz said, "It is my time to go. I am old. I have had a great life. And I am ready. The lesson last month is what I have been holding onto. 'Those who worship God live—*and die*—knowing God is in control.' I do not doubt that God is in control even of this."

More tears. The study never happened that night. It was important to Liz that we not get distracted, so she proposed we meet the following week instead of waiting a month. We all agreed. As we were leaving, Joe walked over to Olivia and told her he owed her many apologies. He seemed very genuine. However, I now realize Joe was a genius at manipulation. In addition, I suspect he was using this emotional evening to manipulate Olivia in some way that was unknown to me. Olivia waved her hand, smiled genuinely at Joe, and said, "Forget about it, Joe. I am glad we will still be in this study group together."

As the last person left for home, I closed my front door and cried. And cried.

24

A Life of Worship Gives Resources to Others—James 5:1–6

Come now, you rich people, weep and wail for the miseries that are coming to you. Your riches have rotted, and your clothes are moth-eaten. Your gold and silver have rusted, and their rust will be evidence against you, and it will eat your flesh like fire. You have laid up treasure for the last days. Listen! The wages of the laborers who mowed your fields, which you kept back by fraud, cry out, and the cries of the harvesters have reached the ears of the Lord of hosts. You have lived on the earth in luxury and in pleasure; you have fattened your hearts in a day of slaughter. You have condemned and murdered the righteous one, who does not resist you.

—JAMES 5:1–6

As Liz requested, we met the following week. Liz was happy and engaged as if she had not dropped her devastating bombshell on us. The rest of us tried to act normal, too, taking our cues from her, but we were all much more thoughtful and quiet than usual. The last meeting seemed surreal. I think we were in denial. Liz looked fine. It was impossible to believe that she would be leaving us. In addition, the night's Scripture seemed so completely off topic from our immediate needs and concerns. Yet, it was probably the lesson from James's epistle that spoke the most to The Church in the Suburbs. I might have been worried that Joe would be angry at my interpretation of these verses, but given Liz's request at the last meeting that we all get along,

I was sure he would not express his frustration with me—at least not in front of Liz.

James and Jesus were both very consistent in defining the rich as anyone who has more than they need. Most of us in the suburbs fell into this category.[1] Once again, James did not mince words. However, neither did Jesus when it came to wealth. I passed out a summary of several passages where Jesus talked about wealth in the gospels:

- Do not save up treasures on earth. (Matt 6:19–21)

- One cannot serve wealth and God. (Matt 6:24)

- To be perfect, you must sell your possessions and give to the poor. (Matt 19:21)

- With resources comes great responsibility. (Matt 25:14–30)

- When the poor give a little, it is better than when the rich give a lot. (Mark 12:41–44)

- The rich have already received their reward. (Luke 6:24)

- It is difficult for a rich person to enter the kingdom of heaven. (Luke 18:25)

- Do not hoard resources. (Luke 12:15–23)

- Sell your possessions and give to the needy. (Luke 12:33)

- Don't invite the wealthy to your feasts. (Luke 14:12–14)

- It is difficult for the wealthy to see the need to repent. (Luke 16:19–31)

After reading these passages, I posed a question to the group: "Based on these Scriptures, can someone living as a servant of Christ get rich and stay rich?" I got blank stares, which was exactly what I had expected. I didn't know the answer either. On the other hand, maybe I did know the answer, but it was too hard to accept. James offered no possibility for the existence of a rich person who did not oppress the poor. He wasn't trying to teach the rich how to be rich and godly at the same time. He was trying to open the eyes of the rich so that they could see how they were oppressing the poor.[2]

They all sat considering the question until I broke into their thoughts. I asked them to consider Andrew Carnegie. He wasn't a religious person, but he was noted by his contemporaries to be the world's richest man. History records that he built his fortune on the backs of steel workers who weren't always treated and paid fairly. Then in later years, he was quoted as saying,

1. Motyer, *Message of James*, 163–65.
2. Laws, *Epistle of James*, 197.

"The man who dies rich dies disgraced."[3] He claimed that he spent the first third of his life getting an education, the second third amassing a fortune, and the last third giving his fortune away. I wondered out loud if he had given his fortune away to make up for his earlier years in the business world where he had supposedly disregarded his employees' well-being.

That got Joe's attention. He spoke in a reserved tone, but there was a hint of anger, "I know where you are going with this. You want all of us to be hippies—sell our stuff and move in together. Nevertheless, riches are a sign of God's blessings—that a person has pleased God. I suspect there is a more biblical answer to having wealth if we dig deeper."

Rodney quickly followed up, "I guess I disagree with you, Joe. Someone once said, 'If you have two coats, you've stolen one from the poor.'"[4]

Joe growled a bit. Then went silent.

Olivia spoke quietly, "I am coming to the same conclusion Rodney, but I am still not living the way James promotes." Helen, Liz, and I shook our heads in agreement. We, too, believed Rodney was right, but we hadn't done anything about it. The truth was that we didn't know what to do.

Olivia went on, "Off-loading wealth is not easy if you do it in a responsible way. It takes some genuine thought and planning. Perhaps the only way you can know for sure that your money is being used productively is if you are involved in the organizations and with the people taking your donation."

Rodney, more than the rest of us, had a right to speak on this subject. He had given up a life of guaranteed wealth and prestige to take care of an impoverished people, so when Rodney began to speak, we listened. "Like Olivia is saying, you really can't address needs unless you walk with the people who have needs. The suburbs just serve to close you off from those in need. When you never see another person in need, much less never get to know them, then you become calloused, indifferent, and insulated." Rodney felt the suburbs, especially The Church in the Suburbs, needed to wake up and take a good look outside the walls they had constructed that keep them insulated from the pain and suffering in the world. It was past time, in his opinion, for the church to realign its priorities with Jesus's priorities.

Olivia told us of her visit with Rodney and his wife to the women's shelter. In just a few visits, she had come to realize that these women were not what the stereotypes promoted. Each woman had her own story and heartbreak. Some were very intelligent, but had had health issues that had caused them to fall on hard times. Others were mentally handicapped and

---

3. Nasaw, *Andrew Carnegie*, 350.

4. The quote is attributed to Dorothy Day, in Claiborne, *Irresistible Revolution*, 166.

had no family to offer them food or shelter. There was no one solution for all of them.

Before Olivia could finish, Helen asked if she could tag along next time Olivia went. The answer was an enthusiastic, "Yes!"

Then Olivia finished by saying, "The suburbs make it very hard for us to understand the needs of others and help. Trying to solve the problem of poverty, while being isolated from it, just makes rich people—even if they really are compassionate—more likely to come up with non-solutions and hurt the people they are trying to help rather than offer real solutions."

This conversation was a great introduction to James's teaching on four crimes that the rich are guilty of:

- Hoarding things that others need
- Benefiting from treating others unjustly
- Wasting resources on themselves
- Destroying the righteous

HOARDING THINGS THAT OTHERS NEED

Your riches have rotted, and your clothes are moth-eaten. Your gold and silver have rusted, and their rust will be evidence against you, and it will eat your flesh like fire. You have laid up treasure for the last days.

—JAS 5:2–3

Once again, these verses were almost directly taken from Jesus's Sermon on the Mount.[5] James and Jesus were in complete agreement. Yet, the verses brought up so many practical questions for the group. How do we distinguish between what we need and what is luxury? Do we take just enough resources to exist? Or can we have a few comforts, too? How many articles of clothing are enough?

Personally, I wondered about my collection of folk-art wrought-iron reindeer. To me, they were beautiful, but they had no practical function and they were known to rust. Conversely, doesn't art glorify God and doesn't someone have to buy beautiful things so that the artist can make a living? Wouldn't the world be a dim place without artists?

More questions flowed. What size houses should we live in? Is it okay to have rooms that are never or only rarely used? What kind of car is

---

5. Matt 6:19–24.

appropriate? None of us had the answers. Without answers, we risked inaction. We knew by now that inaction was equal to dead faith.

In my experience, the rich were usually sitting around trying to figure out the minimum poor people really need, but this conversation was so different. We were trying to figure out what we really needed and what we could give away. That was a start!

It became obvious to the group that the answers to these questions would vary with each person, because the Holy Spirit would work differently in each of our lives. It was no mistake that James had most recently taught that we should take care not to judge.[6] In addition, we remembered that James was not teaching us to set up a list of rules to follow, but giving us examples of a life of worship.

Helen had been giving this some very practical thought. "I saw a good sale on high-quality hiking boots and I ordered some even though I have a cheaper pair that already works well enough. When they arrived in the mail, I felt so guilty that I returned them and gave the money I would have spent to a charitable cause. I decided right then that I will not buy anything until I have considered whether the return on investment was higher if I invest in myself by buying the item or if I invest my money in someone who is in need." Letting go of the idea that we deserve luxuries while others have nothing is not easy. Our culture thrives on telling us we need more of everything and that we deserve it.[7]

Helen continued, "I had another thought about hoarding wealth. When we keep the riches we don't need, I think they make us fat and lazy—just like overeating." After the twins were born, Helen had found she was heavier than was healthy for her. However, she worked hard and lost the weight. She had kept it off until recently when some of the pounds were creeping back. She said that she realized that having a healthy weight was about "not eating the excess." In that regard, she said that giving up one's resources was a lot like losing weight. You needed to come to grips with what you really needed to be healthy and then you needed to let go of the rest.

Next, she questioned her own savings account, wondering if she was storing up treasures that would rot. "The world teaches you to save, save, save. But is it hoarding to save for the twins' college education or for a rainy day—when meanwhile there are people who are in need now?"

Difficult questions! Of course, to the way the world thinks, these are absurd questions. The wisdom of the world says to pay yourself first.

6. See chapter 21.
7. Nystrom, *James*, 278–83.

Helen elaborated that she and her husband had decided to determine an amount that would provide the girls a solid education and make her and her husband secure in retirement without the excess she had referred to earlier. They wanted to stop trying to accumulate wealth just for the sake of doing it and put their money where it could make an impact in the world now. "Otherwise, we are going to miss out on watching God work!"

I had planned to tell the group the legend of a long ago professor at my seminary. He was a bachelor who, upon landing the job at the seminary in his early thirties, determined how much money he needed to live on at the time and in his retirement. He talked it over with God and came to believe that God was telling him to live on a fairly frugal amount, save a certain amount for his later years, and give the rest away to those in need. He did this for years. Whenever the seminary gave him a raise, he gave the extra money away. Nevertheless, as times changed and inflation took hold, he found he was no longer able to live on the original amount he had set aside. Even though he was now giving far more away than he had originally been able to give, he felt terrible about taking more for himself. He actually struggled about giving himself a living wage! I am told that he prayed about it for some time before he realized giving himself a raise was what the Holy Spirit wanted him to do. What an example of servanthood!

Joe sat looking deflated. He was obviously determined not to create any waves. All the same, it showed all over his face that he was disgusted with all of us. We simply didn't understand that the pursuit of wealth is what keeps our society healthy. In his mind, we were all ignorant of how the world works. Ignorance was not something he could respect.

BENEFITING FROM TREATING OTHERS UNJUSTLY

Listen! The wages of the laborers who mowed your fields, which you kept back by fraud, cry out, and the cries of the harvesters have reached the ears of the Lord of hosts.

—JAS 5:4

These verses generated a whole new set of questions. Did we know if the person who made our clothes was paid and treated fairly? Was the person who harvested our food able to provide shelter, clothing, and food for themselves and their children? Did we care that in this country it is legal to pay someone less than a living wage? Servants of Jesus are to make it their business to know where their money is going and to take action so that justice is done. James knows the rich aren't prone to compassion just because they have excess. He accuses them of holding back laborers' wages while basking in luxury.[8] I wondered out loud if we didn't need to ask ourselves every time we made a purchase if what we were buying was a product of just labor. James adds a lot of effort to being a Christian. This is not work most suburban Christians recognize belongs to them. When was the last time we had stood up to an injustice? Not just talked about it, but also did something proactive to right it? Christians have had two thousand years to improve the plight of the poor, but the majority of us throughout the centuries have looked the other way.

WASTING RESOURCES ON THEMSELVES

You have lived on the earth in luxury and in pleasure; you have fattened your hearts in a day of slaughter.

—JAS 5:5

Since James had just addressed the abuse of and lack of concern for fellow human beings in verse 4, I had come to believe that in verse 5 James was talking about the earth's resources. While studying for the lesson, I couldn't find a single scholar who agreed with me, but I still thought I was on to something. I asked the group what they thought.

Liz said, "Preach it, girl!" Therefore, I did.

How many of us are misusing creation so that we can have luxuries? Have we hurt the earth without even giving it a second thought? Do we drive luxurious gas hogs? Do we know if our appliances are energy efficient? Are the products we buy produced and packaged with care for creation in mind? James expects us to take this seriously, because to act as if it does not matter is like an animal filling itself up without realizing that as soon as it is fat, it will be slaughtered. If we waste what the earth provides, soon we will have set up a system that will no longer support us. Our caring for creation is important to God. In fact, it was our first responsibility back in the garden of Eden.[9]

We all admitted that we were pretty uneducated on what it meant to live faithfully on the earth. We realized we would have to get educated on living a sustainable lifestyle. Once again, we'd have to ask the Holy Spirit to guide us. Being sustainable would look different depending on where we lived, what resources were available to us, and which natural resources needed protection.

8. Paying the worker fairly was first mentioned in the Old Testament in Deut 24:14–15.

9. Gen 2:15.

DESTROYING THE RIGHTEOUS

You have condemned and murdered the righteous one, who does not resist you.

—JAS 5:6

The rich have a habit of destroying the righteous. How many times have we witnessed it? The righteous speak truth to the rich, calling them to a new way of being—a way where they do not profit from the poor, where they accept their responsibility to care for those in need, where they do not waste the earth's resources. Being called into accountability angers the rich and powerful. The righteous are often punished for speaking out. History is filled with martyrs who have experienced this—even modern martyrs such as Martin Luther King Jr. and Jonathan Daniels.[10]

We had finished a rather lengthy, but good discussion. Somehow, the subject had taken over and we had almost forgotten Liz's illness until she closed the meeting for us by telling us one of Jesus's parables. Liz had always had worthwhile things to say, but now whatever she said, we tried all the more to listen carefully to her. We knew she had just a little while on the earth and she was choosing her words carefully.

"There was a rich man who had the nicest clothes and food that money could buy. Outside of the rich man's house lay a poor hungry man covered with sores. The rich man did not offer him food or medicine and the poor man died. The poor man's soul went to a place of comfort. Later when the rich man died, his soul went to a place of evil. The dead rich man asked to go back to his family to tell them that not caring for the poor would land them in an unpleasant afterlife. However, the rich man was told that his family had not listened to the prophets who warned them and that they would not listen now even to a dead person." Liz's story was from Luke 16:19–31.

Most of the group was feeling challenged—except for Joe, who had checked out of the conversation long ago. Pastor Eddie had the same look he had had on his face when he told me that I needed to tone down James or I would get in political trouble. It felt to me that he wasn't about to add to the conversation for fear of gaining Joe's wrath.

Then, to my surprise, Eddie spoke up, "While there might not be many physical needs in the suburbs, we shouldn't overlook that there are plenty of spiritual needs. What if . . . when the rich address the physical needs of the poor, that in that very action, the spiritual needs of the rich are met?"

10. Johnathan Daniels was a twenty-six-year-old white Episcopal seminary student who, during civil rights protests, dived in front of a bullet meant for Ruby Sales, a seventeen-year-old African American girl. His story is told in Merrill, *Decency and Nobility*.

I hated to admit it! Eddie's insight was where my year-and-half-long thoughts on the subject suddenly came firmly together. They solidified within me that the spiritual needs of the rich are addressed when the rich reach out to those in physical need.

I tried to sum up what had just been said as if it were my own idea, "Only God could set in motion an ecosystem of giving and getting and giving away again that benefits everyone. The rich serve the physical needs of the poor, but the poor serve the spiritual needs of the rich. And if all goes well, sooner or later, the world would be a far better place without the class distinctions that exist today."

In a moment that showed my vulnerability, I asked, "Do you think I could tell this to a rich congregant who comes to me suffering from a spiritual need? I mean seriously, could I tell them frankly, but gently, that they are suffering spiritually because they are focused on themselves instead of serving those in need?"

"Dear, that is exactly what you just said to all of us," said Liz, confused.

"I didn't mean to!" I laughed.

Liz shook her head and said with a firm seriousness that meant she wanted me to hear her clearly, "You must stop being afraid of us, dear. We love you!"

As usual, Helen recorded the meeting in her journal, outlining four questions we came up with that servants of Christ might ask themselves about their money:

- What resources do I have that others could use?

- Are my personal purchases a better investment than using those resources for someone else?

- Is whatever I purchase made justly (protecting both the human resources and the earth's resources)?

- How can I enter into relationship with those in need?

Then in true Liz fashion, she said, "I suddenly want to put my PJs on and go to bed, folks!" She circled the room hugging each of us. We said goodbye to her and then everyone else stayed a little longer to talk about how we were dealing with Liz's devastating news. Rodney shared that Liz had given him access to her medical records and he was talking to a friend from medical school who was doing pancreatic research in Atlanta. He had sent the man Liz's records. There was a chance she might be a candidate for a new cancer treatment.

25

A Life of Worship Endures until Christ Returns—James 5:7–11

Be patient, therefore, beloved, until the coming of the Lord. The farmer waits for the precious crop from the earth, being patient with it until it receives the early and the late rains. You also must be patient. Strengthen your hearts, for the coming of the Lord is near. Beloved, do not grumble against one another, so that you may not be judged. See, the Judge is standing at the doors! As an example of suffering and patience, beloved, take the prophets who spoke in the name of the Lord. Indeed we call blessed those who showed endurance. You have heard of the endurance of Job, and you have seen the purpose of the Lord, how the Lord is compassionate and merciful.

—JAMES 5:7–11

As it turned out, Liz was a candidate for experimental surgery for pancreatic cancer, and Rodney got her worked into his doctor friend's schedule. The surgery would be extensive and traumatic to the body. The statistics for success were low. It took some convincing to get Liz on board, but after Rodney spent an afternoon in the doctor's office explaining and pleading with Liz, she finally consented.

Therefore, between the May and June meetings, Liz packed her bag and headed to the hospital. The news that her cancer might be treatable was wonderful for all of us to hear and some of us were convinced beyond doubt that she would be okay after all. We all prayed for Liz's healing and took a deep sigh of relief. She had to check into the hospital several days before the actual surgery. They were to do some tests and preparation. This period of time overlapped with our June meeting. I was pondering over whether to go ahead with the meeting or cancel it this month and wait for Liz. When I stopped by to see her at the hospital that morning, she asked if I thought we could bring the meeting to her and have it at the hospital in the chapel. I talked to the chaplain and he made the arrangements.

So we all gathered at the hospital for the lesson. Liz was in a disturbingly good mood even though she told us outright that her heart was not into the surgery. She told us that she was having the surgery for the sake of Rodney and her son. She surmised that they would never rest well unless they felt she had done all that she could. Nevertheless, she was still convinced that it was her time to go. Her words brought a lot of sighs from the group and a lecture from Pastor Eddie. He scolded her about the importance of having a positive attitude. Joe joined in with Eddie, but Liz wasn't going to pretend things were going to be okay. Nor was she the least bit sad about it.

I started the lesson with an Old Testament story. Isaiah was a prophet who God had told right up front that he would be a terrible failure by all human standards.[1] Simply put, the people were not going to listen to Isaiah's prophesies and he was going to endure great suffering as he tried to minister to them. God was straightforward with Isaiah and he accepted—actually begged for—the assignment anyway. Therefore, as instructed by God, Isaiah began to warn the people that because they worshiped false gods, mistreated the needy, and did not take care of God's creation, God was going to withdraw his protective shield from around them. With a broken heart, Isaiah watched on as the destruction happened. However, God was not done with Isaiah. God had yet another job for him! Unfortunately, this one was going to be no more successful. His second job was probably harder than his first. It was to offer the same people, who had mocked him and refused to listen to him, the hope of the coming Messiah.[2] As expected, the people did not listen. This went on for years.

All those years of doing what was right and begging the people to reform took their toll on Isaiah. By chapter sixty-four of the book bearing his name, Isaiah cried out to God, "Tear open the heavens and come down!"[3] Enough already! He wanted the Messiah to come immediately. He had grown impatient with God. He begged God to surprise them "with

1. Isa 6:8–13.
2. Isa 53.
3. Isa 64:1.

awesome deeds that we did not expect!"[4] Little did Isaiah know that it would be several hundred years before the Messiah was born. No sooner did Isaiah get this tantrum out of his system than he remembered that God knew what God was doing, "Yet, O LORD, you are our Father; we are the clay, and you are our potter; we are all the work of your hand."[5] Our hope is misplaced if we think that God will always take away all of our problems with a quick fix. However, God will use our problems and disappointments—like the potter uses mud—and will form us into functional vessels for use in God's work.[6]

I had told this story, because, like the people to whom Isaiah was prophesying, we, too, were waiting for Christ's return. James's congregants had been waiting, too. We all needed assurance that there was purpose in both our present lives and our long wait. The very mention of the day when Jesus will return tells us that the world is not purposeless, but approaching a divine event to which all of creation is moving.[7] James uses the word *parousia*, the word commonly used throughout the New Testament to describe the day when Jesus returns to earth as judge.[8] The word, as used in other first-century Greek literature, meant the arrival of royalty, often in order to demand allegiance.[9] The arrival of a royal judge would be threatening, but James tempers it by reminding us of how "the Lord is compassionate and merciful."

James also seems to be saying, on one hand, that the return of Christ is going to happen quickly, since he is standing at the door. On the other hand, James seems to be warning the church that they are going to need patience and endurance—indicating that it might be a while. Perhaps James is saying that Christ's return *could* transpire within a very short period—not that it *had to* happen immediately.[10]

Interestingly, James tells us to face the job of waiting with the patience of a farmer. James is not describing a passive patience.[11] Taking James's example further I described to the group something breathtaking that I once witnessed at my son's college in the Western North Carolina Mountains one

---

4. Isa 64:3.

5. Isa 64:8.

6. Gardner, *Work of the Potter's Hands*, 2–4, 56.

7. Barclay, *Letters of James*, 24.

8. Jesus describes his return in Matt 24 and specifically uses the word *parousia* in Matt 24:27, 37, 39.

9. McCartney, *James*, 240–41.

10. Moo, *James*, 174.

11. Barclay, *Letters of James*, 125.

fall.[12] Farmers from all over the area descended on the college with their horses and old-fashioned plows. They gathered to help the students plow the fields that made up the student-run organic farm. It gave me goose bumps to stand in the hills, look down on the valley, and see the farmers and the aspiring student-farmers on the horse-powered plows. There was so much laughter and fun going on. The school owned a couple of horses and plows of their own, but with the help from local farmers, many of whom were alumni, the work became a weekend-long party.

Even after the plowing was done, the aspiring farmers had much work to do before the exciting days of harvest arrived. Being patient while they waited didn't mean they sat by idly. They were always busy. They prepared the ground, planted the seed, weeded, watered, fertilized, and kept pests away from the plants. They had to keep their tools and machinery in good shape, too. Yet, no matter how hard a famer works or how good they do their job, much is out of the control of the farmer. An attack by pests, disease, heat, and cold, or the timing of the rain can thwart their hard work. A farmer cannot be easily frustrated, nor can a farmer do all the work alone. The farmer needs the community of other farmers. They come together to do the work, find innovations, learn sustainable methods that preserve the earth and our health, and even share experiences. They must get along and respect one another to be effective—perhaps, even to survive. As James points out, grumbling among themselves would be counterproductive. To James, even being critical of another is to cast judgment on them.[13] Farming isn't for the undisciplined. Neither is waiting for the coming of Christ.

To illustrate his point further, James mentions the guy named Job who lost everything (family, home, and health) because God allowed Satan to attack him.[14] Throughout the whole tragedy, Job endured. He stayed strong knowing God was not punishing him nor had God left him. Job didn't try to end his own life even though his best friends encouraged him to do so. Instead, Job persevered declaring, "For I know that my Redeemer lives, and that at the last he will stand upon the earth; and after my skin has been thus destroyed, then in my flesh I shall see God!"[15] Job waited for God's purpose, compassion, and mercy to be revealed. We, too, must persevere despite hardship, having faith that the purpose, compassion, and mercy of God is about to be revealed.

12. Warren Wilson College in Asheville, NC.

13. Moo, *James*, 175.

14. Please see chapters 11 and 14.

15. Job 19:25–26.

When I was done, Liz spoke first. She was sitting in the middle of the front pew in the kitschy chapel that had almost certainly been designed by the same interior designers who create the ambiance in airport bars. She was surrounded with Helen on one side and Pastor Eddie on the other. The rest of the group sat in the pew behind her. I had pulled up a couple of chairs facing the front pew, but no one had joined me. They were too afraid to look Liz in the eyes. The emotion was more than anyone could handle. From the look on Liz's face, these verses had obviously meant a lot to her.

I thought she was going to tell us that the story of Job had encouraged her to endure. Perhaps now she knew she was to fight this cancer with all the strength she had. Surely, she was going to claim victory and we would all sit back and watch our prayers being answered. For a second, I truly thought we were going to see a miracle. Sadly, that was not where she was going.

"I can see the coming of Christ for me—it is closer for me than it is for any of you. I feel like an old farmer who has been tending the fields for a long time." Oh Liz. No one knew what to say.

She was very much like an old farmer, minus the sunbaked skin and overalls. She had overcome adversity—the humiliation of a prominent husband who had left her for another woman. She had turned her sorrow into a focus on raising her son and helping others. She had worked tirelessly for the homeless for decades. She had not only spoken out for them, but with her own hands and feet, she had brought comfort to them. She had hugged them, held them, fed them, and made sure they had shelter when it was cold. She had been their voice into a society and a church who just wanted them to disappear.

She went on to tell us that James spoke to her, because even in these weeks—or maybe months—before her death, she would still be farming—still be doing God's work. It was true. Even now, she was teaching us, caring for us, preparing us for her death. She was even teaching us how to die with dignity and grace. She was not sad. As James put it, she was "blessed" because she had endured.[16]

Liz had the surgery the next day. The doctors saw what they could not see before, metastasized cancer. The surgery, which was supposed to last many hours, lasted all of fifteen minutes. They closed her up and sent her home to die. Rodney, Joe, Liz's son, and I were waiting in the waiting room when Rodney's surgeon friend came to tell us the bad news. We hugged and cried—openly wept, really. All but Joe. He stood up, walked out of the waiting room without a word to anyone, and went home.

16. Nystrom, *James*, 287.

26

A Life of Worship Speaks Truth—James 5:12

Above all, my beloved, do not swear, either by heaven or by earth or by any other oath, but let your "Yes" be yes and your "No" be no, so that you may not fall under condemnation.

—JAMES 5:12

One day, shortly after Liz's surgery, I was sitting in my office. It was almost May and the weather was fabulous: a bit windy, but sunny with highs in the low eighties. I was gathering up some of my things to go down into the courtyard and work at a picnic table where the pastors and staff often gathered to eat homemade lunches or had small committee meetings when the weather cooperated. As I was headed down there, Olivia and a man twenty years her senior arrived. The man was obviously Olivia's husband. He was a good-looking man in great shape in his mid-fifties—old enough to be her father, but young enough to be very attractive. I could see immediately what she saw in him. He somehow put a person at ease without becoming less of himself. He was someone who had obviously made his mark in the world, but who didn't see himself as better than others. I immediately liked him.

Olivia introduced him and we walked out to the picnic table together to chat. Olivia looked truly happy and so did he. It was hard to imagine that this man was retiring from the daily management of his firm at such a young age.

We chatted about the logistics of his move to Atlanta until finally he said to me, "Olivia has found God here. And a family."

Then he told me something that I had not known about Olivia. Her parents had been killed in a car accident the summer of her senior year in high school. She had gone to live with an elderly spinster aunt, finished her senior year of high school in a new town, and then gone on to college. Though her parents had left her a lot of money, she had no real family of her own.

"This church is the family Olivia had always wanted."

I looked over at Olivia. She smiled, her eyes glazed with tears, and then she looked away and laughed. It was a sweet laugh. It was the kind of laugh where you've settled matters deep in your heart—a feeling that bubbles over when all things are right in the world.

Olivia's husband explained that neither of them had been religious, but he was not opposed to learning more about God. He was excited about Olivia's quest to get involved with the Atlanta in-town women's shelter and looked forward to volunteering with her. In talking about the women's shelter, he mentioned something else of which I had not been aware. Helen and Olivia were now working together three days a week at the shelter. They were even dreaming of ways they might do something that would impact vulnerable women in the suburbs.

I looked at Olivia in anticipation to see if she would explain a little bit more about her and Helen's dreams, but she only smiled mischievously— glowing like an expectant mother—and said, "Don't worry, we will be coming to you for help when we get a little more organized."

I couldn't wait! This was really big stuff. Two women, experienced and capable in the business world, had been brought together to accomplish something for the kingdom of God. Olivia knew everything about marketing and sales. Helen knew about operations. Together they were quite a team. It sent goose bumps all over my arms. My dreams that the Epistle of James would somehow transform us were coming true. It made me feel a little dizzy.

Olivia's husband went on to talk about how much their children were enjoying the church, too. They had shared some Bible stories with him over breakfast—one, in his words, about a "man-eating whale." Then he asked if he could join the church. It was a beautiful conversation to go along with a beautiful day!

Olivia's phone rang and she moved away from the table to take the call. While she was gone, Olivia's husband confided that he was relieved that Olivia was no longer working for Joe. He expressed his disappointment in Joe, telling me that some days over a matter of hours Olivia had witnessed him lose his temper, cry pathetically looking for sympathy, and be outgoing and gracious. Then he told me something I didn't know. Years ago, long before I knew Joe, Joe had confessed in a public interview with a technology magazine that he had a drinking problem. Many of his friends suspected that he had never gotten the help he needed. In fact, there were rumors that he had turned to prescription drugs now instead of alcohol. Olivia's husband surmised that all of this played into his erratic behavior.

Though I didn't voice this out loud, what continued to sadden me the most was that Joe's board, many of whom I knew from church, continued to enable Joe instead of getting him the help he needed. They helped neither Joe nor the women that he abused. At least one of the women had sued Joe personally for defamation of character and won a settlement. You would think—at the very least—that they would have done something at that point. But no, even then, it was all kept very secret.

Coincidentally, it turned out that Olivia's subordinate, the one who had forwarded Joe's disgraceful email to Olivia just before he had resigned, was my neighbor. When I put two and two together about his identity, I took a chance and caught him outside one evening walking his dog.

He willingly relayed Olivia's story to me as soon as I mentioned her name. Then I asked him why the board never put an end to Joe's bad behavior. The man had been with the company a long time and knew where the skeletons were hiding. He blamed it on a culture of secrecy. Joe would manipulate the woman's credibility by starting a rumor that the woman had done something worthy of being fired. There would be no details given as to what she had done or who had made the allegations. Everything was kept very hush-hush.

Personnel, worried over keeping their own jobs, would present to the board that an allegation against the woman had been made, stating that details had to be kept secret for the sake of the company and to protect the woman involved. Joe wouldn't ask that she be terminated; he just wanted to begin a process of investigating, even acting as though he was on her side. Since no information was given to the board as to what she had done or who had reported her doing it, there was little the board could do to check out the story. It would be left in the hands of personnel to investigate the supposed allegations and report back. Personnel was either corrupt or incompetent or both. Nevertheless, they did whatever Joe told them.

Still confused that such nonsense could actually go on in a big public company, I asked the same question again. He repeated that the board was told that to protect the woman's dignity, the person's reputation who had reported her, and the company from a lawsuit that the entire situation must be kept secret—not only from the board, but from the rest of the company.

The board was made to promise that they would not to talk to each other or anyone else inside or outside of the company about the allegations. In fact, they didn't even know what the allegations were or who had made them. Therefore, there could be no independent investigation.

My neighbor explained that in every case he had ever witnessed, Joe was the only one who did not keep the secret of what was being alleged. Joe would spread rumors about the woman through somewhat pathetic, but innocent and unsuspecting people, who were delighted that such an important man was confiding in them. The rumors were always along the lines of her being mentally unstable or incompetent. He pointed, as an example, to the email Joe had sent him about Olivia. The rumors spread rampantly and reached the board quickly. At that point, the board really had no choice but to agree that the woman needed to leave. Joe was a brilliant manipulator who had no compassion for others. He called Joe a classic white-collar psychopath. The culture of secrecy that permeated the company and allowed a person like Joe to thrive while destroying the careers of others was sickening.

In the verses we were studying this month, James had taught that those whose worship was pure and undefiled sought truth—not secrecy. A culture of secrecy is what transpires when power is needed over those not in the know. Rarely does it produce a just outcome. James had set an example of truth telling in this epistle by speaking frankly and daring to say exactly what he intended without a smoke screen, double meanings, manipulation, or religious platitudes.[1]

When it was time for the July meeting, Liz had been convalescing at home for a few weeks. I called her to see if she wanted me to pick her up and bring her to the meeting, knowing that the answer would be no. However, this time Liz asked if we would move the meeting to her house. I made all of the calls and everyone showed up.

Her house was a modest Sears and Roebuck house—it was purchased from page twenty-two of the Sears and Roebuck catalogue back in the early 1900s, long before Liz owned it. Painted in a perky bright light blue with white trim, it suited Liz to a tee. Though Liz had begun experiencing debilitating pain in her back earlier in the week, most people would not have known anything was wrong. Hospice had been brought in and she was now very comfortable although unable to go out.

As had become our habit, I started the evening by reading the text we were to study that night and then gave some background. In first-century Jewish culture, the Jews had developed a whole list of rules around telling

---

1. Palmer, *Book That James Wrote*, 81–82.

the truth.[2] You could swear an oath by your head, the earth, heaven, or Jerusalem. Breaking your word carried higher consequences depending on whatever you swore by. Once again, James was just reiterating what Jesus had taught at the Sermon on the Mount. There, Jesus went so far as to attribute this practice of oath taking to "the evil one," since everything his followers said should be truth.[3] Swearing was not necessary if the truth was always spoken. Followers of Jesus should be known to have a character of truth speaking and promise keeping.

Though our culture isn't as formal in our truth telling versus lying protocols, we have remarkably similar issues. For instance, we talk about white lies versus black lies. Santa Claus is a white lie told apparently to entertain kids and maybe even to control their behavior. We promise them gifts from Santa if they are nice and a bag of coal if they are naughty. A white lie is usually something seemingly insignificant or maybe told to protect someone's feelings. A black lie, on the other hand, is something we tell that has bigger consequences—often told with bad intentions. Our culture accepts white lies while frowning on black lies.

The problem is that there is no way we can accurately determine when our lying will be hurtful. How do we know that telling a child a white lie about Santa Claus on Christmas Eve, but the truth about Jesus on Christmas morning, won't affect the child so that they question anything told to them?

This was driven home to me after I visited an Alzheimer's patient. He was having a spell for a few days where he did not recognize his wife. She was just leaving his room when I came for a visit. After she left, he told me that woman had pretended to be his wife, but that she was not his wife. I went along with the story thinking that pretending with this man was the kindest thing to do. It seemed to calm him down. I thought it was just a white lie. However, later that day, I got a call from his wife. She wasn't upset, but she did ask what I had told her husband. I told her that I had "pretended" with him that she was not his wife. Just hearing the words come out of my mouth made me sick to my stomach. It had suddenly dawned on me that I had lied to this man. Well, it turned out that he was now telling everyone that the pastor had been by and that the pastor had indeed confirmed that this woman was an imposter. He was agitated and frustrated when people corrected him. I had made things worse with my white lie. How horrible. Why had I thought lying was a good idea?

The next day, Rodney phoned me. I was out running some errands. He diverted me to a coffee shop where he and Eddie had something they said I

2. McCartney, *James*, 247.

3. Matt 5:34–37.

needed to see. I entered the shop to see Rodney and Eddie with coffee mugs in hand standing below the giant flat screen TV watching the local morning news. Joe's picture was on the screen. It was a photograph grabbed from his company's website. He looked younger and in better shape than he really was, wearing a grey suit, red tie, and finely striped blue shirt.

"My gosh guys, what is going on?"

"Breaking news. Joe has been caught doing some dirty dealing," exclaimed Rodney, looking me in the eyes and shaking his head sideways as if to say that it had been coming.

"No!" I was stunned. Even with all the nonsense, I didn't think Joe was capable of criminal activity.

Just then, another photo flashed up on the screen. It was of a fiftyish-year-old man, overweight, and kind of sloppy looking. "That is my old college roommate," said Eddie, obviously in shock. No. It wasn't shock. Eddie was scared.

"What?" I half shouted, remembering that Joe had been paying Eddie to be a courier between the two men. "Eddie? Did you know about this?"

"Hell no!" Eddie was shaking.

I thought he was going to faint. I took the coffee out of his hand so he wouldn't spill it. "Let's sit down."

Rodney was the only one of them calm enough to talk. He explained what was being reported on cable news that morning. Joe had been getting insider information from Eddie's old roommate on large, key government contracts. He used the information to outbid the competition. Charges had been filed against Joe, Eddie's old roommate, and a couple of Washington bureaucrats who Joe had been caught bribing.

"Rodney, do you think it is true?" I asked.

"Absolutely." Rodney looked away from the screen to get my reaction. "Don't you?"

"It just seems so stupid. Joe has everything—success, notoriety, money. Why would he risk it?"

Eddie interjected, "Oh, it's true. It all makes sense now. And I am going to go to jail, too."

"No, you aren't," Rodney and I said in unison.

I put my arm around Eddie and pulled him toward me. "Eddie, I know that you haven't done anything wrong—at least intentionally. You can't let yourself get worked up over this."

"They have an audio tape of Joe sealing the deal with an undercover FBI operative," Eddie pointed out, watching the transcript run across the bottom of the screen. We watched for a moment, then Eddie asked, "Is Joe in jail?"

"Nah. With his money? He's out on bond," declared Rodney. "But you better get a lawyer, Eddie."

Eddie closed his eyes and put his head on the table.

Rodney tried to call Joe. He left a message saying he'd like to come by and see him. Joe never called back. The story played nationally for a few days and then died down. Joe was staying out of the public eye while his lawyer handled the press. We would only see Joe one more time and that would be at Liz's funeral.

27

A Life of Worship Prays—James 5:13–20

Are any among you suffering? They should pray. Are any cheerful? They should sing songs of praise. Are any among you sick? They should call for the elders of the church and have them pray over them, anointing them with oil in the name of the Lord. The prayer of faith will save the sick, and the Lord will raise them up; and anyone who has committed sins will be forgiven. Therefore confess your sins to one another, and pray for one another, so that you may be healed. The prayer of the righteous is powerful and effective. Elijah was a human being like us, and he prayed fervently that it might not rain, and for three years and six months it did not rain on the earth. Then he prayed again, and the heaven gave rain and the earth yielded its harvest. My brothers and sisters, if anyone among you wanders from the truth and is brought back by another, you should know that whoever brings back a sinner from wandering will save the sinner's soul from death and will cover a multitude of sins.

—JAMES 5:13–20

Preparing for the last lesson in James in between visits to see Liz was over-whelming. Liz had been close to passing from this world into God's arms for more than a week. Her tiny body was so thin now. Gone was the sparkle in her eyes. She was almost unrecognizable. Most of the time, she was in a sleep-like coma. However, sometimes she would be awake long enough to utter a few labored sentences that were usually encouragement for whomever was in the room with her.

As I read the last verses in James, I was jarred back to the days before I started this study group. I had felt hopeless because I did not know how to offer *spiritual* healing to the congregants who came to me seeking comfort. Now here I sat, beside Liz's bed, wishing I could heal her *body*. Her spirit didn't need healing. Not only had Christ done that two thousand years ago in the resurrection, but she had been a good and faithful servant rising above the problems in her life to serve God.

I had gotten in touch with all the members of our group the morning of the study. Liz was too sick for us to meet at her house so we would meet at my house. Joe did not answer my phone call, but had his secretary return it saying he would not be there. She gave no reason why.

About noon, Liz's son called to say that Liz had died.

I called everyone again, leaving a message for Joe's secretary. The rest of us decided to gather at my house that night as usual—though nothing was "as usual." Yet, we had become a family and needed to be together in our grief. In addition, Liz had insisted that we finish the study and we were determined to honor that request, so as soon as everyone arrived, Helen suggested that we get the last lesson out of the way before our emotions got the best of us.

Therefore, I immediately started in on the lesson. James closes his epistle by teaching that those whose worship is pure and undefiled pray. I believe that James addresses prayer last not as a nice-to-have add-on, but as something he wants to emphasize. It is essentially his last words to the church. In addition, I have no doubt that lack of prayer is the number one reason why so many who have sought to follow Christ have came up short. I just bet James would have agreed. Without prayer, we'd be trying to follow someone to whom we never talked directly, and more importantly, someone to whom we never listened.

Paul tells the church in Thessalonica to pray without ceasing—to be in continuous relationship with God.[1] James asks no less. He says that when we have troubles, we should pray.[2] When we are happy, we should pray. We should sing songs of praise. Because of what all of us were feeling for Liz, I choked on my words as I added that crying out tears of grief before God was no less prayerful than joyful singing.

---

1. 1 Thess 5:17.

2. Nystrom, *James*, 304, points out that the word for *troubles* actually means "to suffer misfortune."

The point was that prayer is a never-ending part of a life lived in pure and undefiled worship. Yet, prayer also needs to extend beyond a quick "help me," "forgive me," and "give me." If a hurried prayer life is the only type of prayer life we have, then we are unlikely to grow in the spiritual maturity we need to serve God. We must set aside time to intentionally talk and listen to God. Jesus did. He set an example of getting alone in the early hours of the morning to pray.[3] In addition, he would get alone to pray when he was under stress.[4] An example of this was on the night of his arrest.[5] Jesus took his disciples with him to pray that night. They were to pray together, while he prayed alone. Unfortunately, they fell asleep and, disappointed, Jesus prayed without them. He laid out his situation before God and listened as God spoke. Jesus told God his desires. He even asked God, if possible, not to send him to the cross. God said no. Therefore, Jesus, in obedience, asked for the power to do God's will, and the angels ministered to him.

These times alone with God were times when I believe that Jesus mostly listened. Likewise, I believe our most effective prayers are also when we sit still in the presence of God and listen. God has no trouble speaking into our free-flowing thoughts.[6] Even when God does not speak to us in the moments where we are quiet and intentionally listening, intentional prayer sets our mind on a course to be open to hear God speaking at other times and places, too.

In the first few verses of this section, James focuses on individual one-on-one conversation with God. Then in the next few verses, he focuses on ways the community should pray together specifically over sickness and sin. In our individual prayers, it is appropriate and important to bring our problems and joys to God—to lay them out before God and seek to see them as God sees them. However, many of us, rather than talking directly to God, make the mistake of first bringing our problems to prayer groups or putting them on prayer lists asking others to pray for us—neglecting our direct relationship with God.

I was grateful when Rodney spoke up. I was tired and wanted the lesson to be over even though I knew it was important. Rodney told a story of a man named Jelani in his church in Africa. Rodney took Tuesday mornings off from the clinic to lead a men's Bible study. About a hundred African men gathered in the dark before work for teaching and then met in small groups for discussion and prayer afterward. Jelani would often monopolize much

---

3. Mark 1:35; Matt 14:23; Luke 6:12.
4. Luke 22:41–44; John 12:27–28; Heb 5:7.
5. Matt 26:36–46.
6. Ps 46:10.

of his small group time telling about his marriage problems. Jelani and his wife did not see eye to eye on any matter before them. For a year, the men's small group listened to Jelani sympathetically and non-judgmentally. Week after week, they watched him tell the events of his marriage from the past week and often cry. Then finally, the small group leaders came to Rodney asking for his help. The men said they had prayed for Jelani for more than a year now and there was no improvement. They wanted Rodney to tell them what to do both to help Jelani, but also to stop him from monopolizing the small group so that other people's concerns could be heard.

Little did these men know that Rodney had also been meeting with Jelani for one-on-one counseling and more prayer. Rodney had been disappointed at Jelani's progress, too. This was when they finally realized what was going on with Jelani. Jelani was substituting others praying for him rather than talking to God himself. Rodney asked Jelani at their next one-on-one meeting how often he got alone and listened to God. Jelani thought about it for a while embarrassed to tell Rodney the truth. Jelani's final answer after some prodding and coaching was "never." Rodney told Jelani that he needed go to God directly for wisdom before going to others. Jelani's small group reinforced this idea. Over the next few months, Jelani seemed to become a different person. He became a person who relied on God rather than others to help him. It also freed Jelani and his small group to listen to other's concerns.

Jelani was under the same misconception as most of us. We think whenever we have a problem that the spiritual thing to do is to call up all our friends, call the prayer hotline at church, or make a list and bring up the concern the next time prayer requests are made. However, this is not what a mature Christian does. The first thing a mature Christian does is to seek God directly, asking for wisdom and power. Then, if after doing that things seem to be awry, James indicates that the next thing to do is to ask for intercession. However, authentic intercession may be a little different from what most people have grown to expect.

The men in Jelani's small group thought during that long year of listening to Jelani's problems that they were interceding on Jelani's behalf when they would pray for him. However, intercessory prayer is far more than just telling God that someone else has a problem. Intercessory prayer is seeking God's direction for that person when the person cannot make headway in his or her own prayers. Perhaps they are too physically sick, the spiritual warfare is overwhelming, the sin in their life is consuming them, etc. When this happens, James instructs his congregants to call the leaders of the church and ask them to intercede with prayer and oil. In other words, God will give wisdom and power to the elders on behalf of that person and the person requesting the intercession should heed the wisdom and accept the power as if God had spoken directly to them.[7]

Jelani didn't really qualify for this kind of intercessory prayer. Jelani had been able to seek God on his own, but hadn't even tried. If Jelani really wanted these men to intercede for him, then he needed to be aware that intercession meant that they would be seeking God's wisdom for him to act on afterward.

For many people, including Jelani, when you explain intercessory prayer as a way for more mature Christians to seek God's wisdom on their behalf, it is a game changer. Most feel that kind of prayer infringes on their privacy. Perhaps they just wanted you to use your relationship with God to get a blessing for them. Perhaps they had hoped that the more people who prayed for them, the better chance God would give them what they wanted. In other words, they weren't really asking for discernment and God's wisdom on their behalf. What they really wanted was prayers to make God behave as they desired. This is not intercessory prayer. Intercessory prayer is when a third party seeks wisdom and power on behalf of the person needing it.

I told the group that James gives two examples of intercessory prayer in these verses. One is where the person is sick. The other is where the person is struggling with sin. The moment the words were out of my mouth, Eddie blurted out, "We had a person who was sick. And we have a person who is struggling with sin." The irony of this hadn't escaped me either, though I didn't comment. I paused, let what Eddie had said sink in, and then went on.

The sick person in James's example isn't experiencing the common cold. A person with a common cold can still lift up their concerns directly to God. James is talking about the kind of sickness that is so debilitating that the sick person can't come to the elders. The elders have to go to them. The sick person is likely in a state of mind or body where they are unable to pray themselves. He or she is asking for true intercession, "Pray, as if you are me! Ask God for wisdom for dealing with this illness. Ask, as if you are me. Listen, as if you are me. And I will follow whatever God reveals to you." The elders are to pray and anoint him or her with oil.[8]

Pastor Eddie shook his head, deeply upset, "Liz wouldn't let us intercede for her. I asked her to let me call the elders and pray over her. She said no." Eddie put his head in his hands and openly wept. Sophie arose from where she always sat at the base of Eddie's chair and licked Eddie's hands

---

7. Smith, *Practical Faith*, CD 6.

8. Mark 6:13 and Luke 10:34 describe times when Jesus anointed the sick with oil.

until he put them down and then she licked the tears on his face. Eddie moaned the words, "Liz was like a mother to me."

Helen, stroking Sophie's back, because she couldn't reach Eddie's hands, said, "Eddie, Liz didn't need our intercessory prayer. She had already prayed and knew God's answer. She knew this was her time. She was ready to go."

"I know," he replied. More silence followed until I picked up the lesson again.

In James's second example, he uses Elijah's story to teach about intercessory prayer for those needing to overcome sin. God had appointed the prophet Elijah to intercede for Israel because Israel had not been faithful to God nor had they been practicing justice.[9] Worse yet, the people of Israel had wandered so far from the truth that they were unable to pray for themselves. They had no desire to do God's will, but God sent Elijah to intercede. First God told Elijah to pray for drought so that the people would see they had wandered from God. God answered his prayers, and the drought lasted for three years and six months. Then God told him to pray for rain. Elijah interceded for the people again and prayed for rain. The message James was sending to his congregation was that those who worship God are to pray on behalf of those who have fallen into sin. It was not that Elijah was perfect himself; he was just the intercessor who had a great desire for his nation to be reconciled to God.[10]

Then we sat in silence again, each praying in our own way. We waited for the peace that passes understanding to fall upon us.[11] The sky outside grew dark as evening came. Eddie broke the silence in an intercessory prayer for Joe. He thanked God for God's eternal forgiveness, prayed for Joe's protection, and asked God to let Joe know we loved him. James had taught that "the prayer of the righteous is powerful and effective." Never in a million years would I have thought that I would see Eddie as a righteous person, but he was.[12] Not perfect, but his heart was pure gold.

The lesson was over. The study was over.

Olivia nodded toward Rodney, "As you all know, Rodney and his family are headed back to Africa in September. With Rodney's approval, I have reserved a room at the church on the morning that Rodney is leaving. I

9. 1 Kgs 17–18.

10. Moo, *James*, 193.

11. Phil 4:7.

12. Nystrom, *James*, 317, describes the righteous person as one who is in touch with the heart of God.

thought it would be nice for us to see the family off. They are going to come by on their way to the airport. Can all of you come?"

Unanimously and in unison, we all said yes. Then everyone sat again in silence for a while longer. I think we were in shock, really. No one spoke. Yet, once again, we were okay with the silence. Two empty chairs were among us—one for Joe and one for Liz. Our hearts ached. Eddie told us that he had gotten a lawyer from the church to represent him, but it didn't look like he was under any kind of suspicion. However, at some point he would have to give a deposition.

Then Helen began to sing what we all knew was Liz's favorite hymn. It was a simple prayer of praise. We all joined in and sang the best we could.

28

Goodbyes

Liz's graveside service took place three days later. At Liz's request, the senior pastor, Pastor Eddie, myself, Liz's son, and his wife were the only ones in attendance. It was elegant, somber, and quiet. Afterward we returned to the church where a standing-room-only crowd had gathered for a memorial service. The service, in stark contrast to the rite at the graveside, was upbeat and full of hope. Sitting behind the pulpit, I thought I was handling the emotions I felt just fine, until the doors of the narthex opened about five minutes into the service and in came a vanload of homeless from one of the shelters where, for twenty-five years, Liz had befriended and cared for the guests who stayed there. Liz had requested seats be reserved for them in the front of the sanctuary, so they were brought right down front. James would have approved. Their active participation in the service made the celebration of Liz's life even more joyful.

Joe was in the balcony sitting alone. He spoke to no one and slipped out before the congregation was dismissed. It was the last time I ever saw him. Although Pastor Eddie and I both phoned him several times over the next few months, he never responded. He resigned from his company and the committees he served on at church. He simply disappeared. The case had not gone to court, the last I heard, although the press said both Joe and Eddie's college roommate faced possible prison time and millions of dollars in fines. Even so, we felt a loss at his disappearance.

Olivia reserved the meeting room at church for the day Rodney and his family would head back to Africa. It was a hot, sweltering Deep South kind of day. Rodney was excited to be going home to Malawi where he had what he called "meaningful" work to do. His wife and kids were happy, too.

We shared a late breakfast and listened to stories about Africa told mostly through the eyes of Rodney's kids. We laughed and giggled with them. Liz's son had arranged to show up toward the end of our meal. He had a letter from Liz to read to us. In it were a few sentences to each of us:

> *Dear Friends,*
>
> *I have nothing of any monetary value to leave you so don't get your hopes up. You are my dear friends and so I will leave you some God-given wisdom.*
>
> *To Olivia, you are a new creation on a brand new journey. Worship God purely on this journey and do not be stained by the world. Care for the vulnerable people who make your heart break. God's heart also breaks for these people. You will know how to help them, because you will walk alongside them. Go do something big, Olivia—something that changes the world.*
>
> *To Helen, the ministry you have been seeking is forming right now. I suspect it is a lot bigger than you expected. God sent Olivia to you so you will have someone to walk with on those trips outside of your comfort zone. There will be many. You and Olivia are going to make a difference right in your own backyard. Take those steps that God has called you to take to get things in order. Keep challenging consumerism and all matter of things unjust. See the suffering of this world as something you should be repulsed by, but also as something to which you should bring the light of Christ.*
>
> *To Rodney, never stop speaking the truth—just learn to balance it with love—and you will be fine. You are my hero. I am forever grateful to you for trying to save the life of an old woman. Now go save the lives of those who need you in Malawi.*
>
> *To Pastor Eddie . . .*

Before Liz's son could read Eddie's part, Eddie stopped him. With tears flowing, Eddie covered his face and managed to mumble, "Please. Just make a copy for me and I will read it later." Liz's son touched Eddie on the shoulder, complied with Eddie's request to stop, and jumped to the next person.

Liz's son must not have realized Joe was absent, because next he read what Liz had written to Joe.

> *To Joe, God has given you great resources that are not yours to keep. Help fund the charitable work Rodney will do in Africa and the work that Olivia and Helen will be doing here. Use your wealth and your contacts to raise money for them so that they have no financial worries.*

I was glad that Liz had died not knowing what had become of Joe. It would have hurt her very deeply. Who knows, though, our God is an awfully big God, full of love and mercy. Perhaps someday Joe would return.

Then Liz's son turned to me, "Pastor, she didn't have much to say to you. And I am not really sure I understand what she did say."

I said, "Okay." I was a little disappointed until he read her words.

Pastor, the Holy Spirit wants to speak through you. Let her.

It made me laugh and cry all at the same time. I loved Liz!

The Spirit had taught me much in the last months. I had learned that in the suburbs, more often than not, we fall short of being the slaves of Christ. I think this is, in major part, a result of having removed ourselves from the vulnerable and needy. In the suburbs, we show favoritism by putting up walls to keep out those who are not like us economically and socially. The work that James points us toward is out of sight and out of mind. Our hearts do not break for those in need, because we are not living near them, not in relationship with them, not aware of the injustices that need to be righted, and not mindful of the resources that we could contribute to their good.

Those of us in the suburbs have a distorted view of faith and worship and that distortion is making us sick. We think that faith is to believe hard enough and that worship stops during the last praise song on Sunday mornings. Being a servant of God has lost all meaning as we strive to believe a right theology and keep a right set of rules. Then, when we think we have it just right, we use our theology and rules to judge who is in and who is out of the kingdom of God. However, James has taught us that faith is not what we believe. Faith is an action word and worship is what we do with our lives.

We have lost this in the suburbs, but we do not even know it. We become spiritually sick when trials and problems hit us. We become confused and bitter, thinking that our master is here to serve us by fixing all of our problems and by showering blessing upon us. We do not see the wisdom and power that God has provided us to deal with our troubles and to get on with the business of being the servants of God. We do not see it, because we never signed up for servanthood in the first place. We came to God for the ticket to heaven—to be served, not to serve. Therefore, when problems hit, we get stuck within ourselves without purpose and without joy. This is the epidemic that has torn through our tall-steeple churches, gated communities, and luxurious clubhouses.

However, in James's epistle, he offers us hope. He tells us that faith is an action word, which the servants of God live out. He tells us that those who worship God purely and undefiled live differently. They accept the outcast. They do the good works God has created for them to do. They speak with words that bless others. They strive for true and lasting peace. They do not judge. They live knowing God is in control. They share their resources generously with those in need. They do God's work waiting for the kingdom of God to break through into the harsh realities of life. They speak truth. And they enter in to a deep relationship with God.

Therefore, this chapter is not the end. It is only the beginning of the journey. In case chapter 1 has been forgotten by now, I suggest you reread it. To this day, Olivia and Helen are the beautiful hands and feet of God to an ever-growing number of *Latina* girls. Rodney is still in Africa bringing needed medical care to the impoverished, and Eddie—well—Eddie is still Eddie. He didn't change, but I did. I grew to see the goodness in him. Isn't that just how God works?

PART 3

Putting Servanthood into Action

The Parable of the Good Samaritan—Dissecting the Samaritan

One morning, I ran into a stranger of a different denomination. Because of our theological and political disagreements, just being near him made me uncomfortable. Yet, he insisted on talking to me anyway. He said, "There was a man who was going down from the city to the suburbs, and fell into the hands of robbers, who stripped him, beat him, and went away, leaving him half dead. While traveling, I came near him; and when I saw him, I was moved with compassion. I went to him and bandaged his wounds. I put medicine on them. Then I put him in my car, brought him to a hospital, and took care of him. The next day I took out my wallet, gave it to the hospital, and said, 'Take care of him; and when I come back, I will repay you whatever more you spend.'"

I asked, "Why did you help this man? Don't you have problems of your own?"

The stranger replied, "I do. But if I do not care for him, what will happen to him?"

Jesus said, "The stranger showed the man mercy. Go and do likewise."

—ADAPTED FROM LUKE 10:30–37

29

Study Guide

This study guide can be used by individuals or groups. The study has twelve sessions. It can be done in twelve weeks or as a monthly, yearlong study. For group study, everyone will need their own copy of *James in the Suburbs* and a journal to record notes on the readings, reflections, and answers to study questions. Have poster-sized sheets of paper and markers available for meetings. Always start and end every study with prayer. The starting prayer should include asking for the Holy Spirit's guidance and wisdom. The closing prayer should be for the Holy Spirit's power in putting what was learned into action. Each study is divided into three sections: Reading, Journal Work, and Group Work. The Reading and Journal Work are to be done at home. The Group Work is done together when the group meets.

STUDY 1.0: INTRODUCTION TO THE STUDY GROUP

Read chapters 1–4.

Journal Work

1.1 Chapters 2 and 3 describe The Church in the Suburbs. Use your journal to record both a physical and spiritual description of your church or spiritual community.

1.2 Likewise, chapter 4 describes the men and women who joined the pastor's study group and why they joined. Use your journal to record a physical and spiritual description of yourself and include why you are doing this study. Did you immediately relate to any of the characters in the book—if so, why?

Group Work

1.3 Summarize and discuss chapters 1–4.

1.4 Use the poster-sized sheets of paper to make two collective lists—one of the positive attributes of your church and one of the negative attributes of your church. Save these lists to be used in later studies.

1.5 Allow time for each person to share the description of himself or herself.

STUDY 2.0:
INTRODUCTION TO THE EPISTLE OF JAMES

Read chapters 5–7.

Journal Work

2.1 Read the Epistle of James in one sitting as if it were a letter written by your pastor to your church. Use your journal to record your first impressions of the Epistle of James.

2.2 Read the Sermon on the Mount in the Gospel of Matthew chapters 5, 6, and 7. Use your journal to record where the Epistle of James and the Sermon on the Mount have similarities.

2.3 Record what it means to you to be "a slave of God and the Lord Jesus Christ." Where are you a servant already? Where are you resisting servanthood?

Group Work

2.4 Summarize and discuss chapters 5–7.

2.5 Use the poster sized paper to outline the similarities between the Sermon on the Mount and the Epistle of James.

2.6　Allow each person time to discuss how they are doing as a servant.

STUDY 3.0: JAMES'S STRATEGY

Read chapters 8–10.

Journal Work

3.1　Meditate on James 1:1–5. Use your journal to record your first impressions.

3.2　Use your journal to record any problems that are you going through right now. How long have you been dealing with these problems? How are they affecting you and others? Are you letting them hold you back from serving God and others?

3.3　Apply James's strategy in chapter 9 to your problems. What is your plan for moving forward as a servant of God and others?

Group Work

3.4　Summarize and discuss chapters 8–10.

3.5　Discuss the process of meditating upon the Scripture verses. Share tips on getting the most out of this time.

3.6　Allow each person time to share one problem they are going through. What has God revealed to them about how to deal with it? Pray for each person and their situation after they have shared. Do not ask God for a specific outcome, but for the Holy Spirit's wisdom and power to deal with the problem.

STUDY 4.0: WISDOM AND DOUBTS

Read chapters 11–12.

Journal Work

4.1　Meditate on James 1:5–7. Use your journal to record your first impressions.

4.2   Use your journal to make a list of what wisdom is and of what wisdom is not.

4.3   Ask for wisdom by laying out your problems before God. Don't ask for a specific outcome. Just tell God about the problem. Then spend time listening for an answer. God may work immediately through your free flowing thoughts or God may reveal the wisdom in another way at another time. Be open to hearing God speak whenever and in whatever way God chooses. Record what happens in your journal.

4.4   Has God given you wisdom in the past? Do you have faith that God will give you wisdom now and in the future? Record your thoughts in your journal.

Group Work

4.5   Summarize and discuss chapters 11–12.

4.6   Make two lists. Make one of what wisdom is and is not. Make another of why we ask for wisdom and don't get it.

4.7   Allow time for everyone to share what it was like to ask for wisdom this week.

STUDY 5.0: TURNING TOWARD SERVANTHOOD

Read chapters 13–15.

Journal Work

5.1   Meditate on James 1:9–25. Use your journal to record your first impressions.

5.2   Record your experience with the trial of having too little and the trial of having too much.

5.3   Describe a problem that you have dealt with in your life. What was this problem's potential? What did it teach you? Did you learn the right lessons from it? How can you use the lessons from this problem to serve God and others?

5.4   Look at a problem you are dealing with now. Journal this problem's potential.

5.5 Ask God to show you areas of your life where you are a hearer of the word and areas of your life where you are a doer of the word. Record what God reveals.

Group Work

5.6 Summarize and discuss chapters 13–15.

5.7 Discuss areas where your church community hears the word of God, but does not act. It could be helpful to bring back the list the group made in study 1.0.

5.8 Allow time for everyone to share a problem and that problem's potential.

STUDY 6.0: PURE AND UNDEFILED WORSHIP

Read chapter 16.

Journal Work

6.1 Meditate on James 1:26–27. Use your journal to record your first impressions.

6.2 Read 1 Corinthians 8. Use your journal to record how Christians should handle theological differences. Have you or your church ever had a theological conflict? How did you handle it?

6.3 What do you believe is the minimum one must do to call himself or herself a servant of Christ? Record when (or if) you intentionally became a servant of Christ. What good works stand as proof that you are a servant of Christ?

Group Work

6.4 Summarize and discuss chapter 16.

6.5 Discuss how Christians with different views should behave toward one another. Does your church practice this? Do you?

6.6 Discuss the minimum one must do to be a servant of Christ and the minimum one must do to go to heaven. Read Ephesians 2:8–10.

6.7 Discuss whether there is a difference between religion, worship, and service. What does having a relationship with God have to do with these things?

STUDY 7.0: IMPARTIALITY AND GOOD WORKS

Read chapters 17–18.

Journal Work

7.1 Meditate on James 2:1–26. Use your journal to record your first impressions.

7.2 Write about a time when you or someone you knew experienced favoritism. How was that situation against the good news of the gospel?

7.3 Ask God how you and your church can become the hands and feet of Jesus in your neighborhood, in the community around your church, and in the world. Make a list of the possibilities.

Group Work

7.4 Summarize and discuss chapters 17–18.

7.5 Discuss the ways that Christians practice favoritism. How does this practice destroy the community of God? Share personal experiences.

7.6 Discuss the last paragraph in chapter 17.

7.7 Make a list of ways you can be the hands and feet of Jesus in your neighborhoods and in the community around your church. How can your study group make this happen?

STUDY 8.0: WORDS AND SEEDS

Read chapters 19–20.

Journal Work

8.1 Meditate on James 3:1—4:10. Use your journal to record your first impressions.

8.2 Write about your style of communication. Have you worn a bridle, been a rudder, behaved like a fire, or acted like an uncontrollable wild beast? Do your words bless others or harm them?

8.3 Make a list of the good works you have done in the last week. Were they random acts of kindness or intentional good works born of the Spirit and sown in peace?

8.4 Write about a time when your good works seemed unsuccessful. Were they unsuccessful because they were random and not guided by the Spirit? On the other hand, were they unsuccessful simply because serving God doesn't always look like success?

8.5 Has someone ever given you a blessing or a curse? What effect did that have on you?

Group Work

8.6 Summarize and discuss chapters 19–20.

8.7 Discuss what it means to offer an authentic blessing to someone.

8.8 Share the effect that blessings or curses have had on your life.

8.9 Discuss what it means when James calls us to lament, mourn, and weep. How should we do this as individuals and as a whole church?

STUDY 9.0: JUDGING OTHERS AND GOD IN CONTROL

Read chapters 21–22.

Journal Work

9.1 Meditate on James 4:11–17. Use your journal to record your first impressions.

9.2 Write about the three people (or three types of people) that you tend to criticize the most. How do you judge them (openly or covertly)? James poses the question, "Who are you to judge them?" Answer James.

9.3   Why is it wrong to make even common sense, every day kinds of plans without engaging God in your plans? What harm does it do? What is your strategy for engaging God in your plans?

Group Work

9.4   Summarize and discuss chapters 21–22.

9.5   Make a list of ways people judge others (both openly and covertly). In each case, what motivates us to judge others? How can we encourage each other to overcome a judgmental spirit?

9.6   Allow everyone time to share their strategies to include God in their futures.

STUDY 10.0: GIVING RESOURCES TO OTHERS

Read chapters 23–24.

Journal Work

10.1 Meditate on James 5:1–6. Use your journal to record your first impressions.

10.2 Write about a crisis in your life. How did it change the trajectory of your life?

10.3 Make a rough inventory of your resources (belongings, money, talents). Can you put any of these things to better use?

Group Work

10.4 Summarize and discuss chapters 23–24.

10.5 Allow time for everyone to share about a crisis he or she has experienced that changed the trajectory of his or her life.

10.6 Make a list of the needs of vulnerable populations in your community. Brainstorm on how you might collectively address these needs. Don't assume you need to start a new organization.

STUDY 11.0: ENDURING AND SPEAKING TRUTH

Read chapters 25–26.

Journal Work

11.1 Meditate on James 5:7–12. Use your journal to record your first impressions.

11.2 Write about a situation where God called you to endure. How did you do?

11.3 Make a list of ways that people avoid speaking the truth. What would James have to say about these avoidance methods? How should Christians behave toward and relate to others?

Group Work

11.4 Summarize and discuss chapters 25–26.

11.5 Discuss how we can help each other endure. What is helpful and what is not?

11.6 Make a group list of ways people get around speaking the truth. How should Christians behave and relate to others?

STUDY 12.0: PRAYING AND GOODBYE

Read chapters 27–28.

Journal Work

12.1 Meditate on James 5:13–20. Use your journal to record your first impressions.

12.2 Decide on a time that you will set aside to pray every day going forward.

12.3 What good works has God created you to do? If you do not know, why is that? Is it because you have not been praying and listening to God speak? How can the members of your small group work together to support each other in serving God?

12.4 If you have done this study with a group, write an individual note of encouragement to everyone in your group to be given to them at the next session—concentrate on what you see them doing as a servant of God. If you have done this study guide as an individual, write a note to yourself encouraging yourself to continue in the way that James taught.

Group Work

12.5 Summarize and discuss chapters 27–28.

12.6 Allow everyone to answer the questions: What works has God created you to do? How can your church work together to support each other in serving God? Bring back the lists from studies 7.0 and 10.0.

12.7 Exchange the individual notes of encouragement and pray for the servanthood of each member.

Bibliography

Andersen, Francis I. *Job: An Introduction and Commentary*. Tyndale Old Testament Commentaries 14. Downers Grove: InterVarsity, 2008.

Bamberger, David. *My People: Abba Eban's History of the Jews*. Vol. 1. Springfield, NJ: Behrman, 1978.

Barclay, William. *The Letters of James and Peter*. Daily Study Bible Series. Philadelphia: Westminster, 1976.

Beavis, Mary Ann. "Ancient Slavery as an Interpretive Context for the New Testament Servant Parables with Special Reference to the Unjust Steward (Luke 16:1–8)." *Journal of Biblical Literature* 111 (1992) 37–54.

Beck, Melinda. "City vs. Country: Who Is Healthier?" *Wall Street Journal*, July 12, 2011. http://online.wsj.com/news/articles/SB10001424052702304793504576434442652581806.

Bock, Darrell L. *Luke*. Baker Exegetical Commentary on the New Testament 2. Ada, MI: Baker Academic, 1996.

The Book of Common Prayer. New York: Seabury, 1979.

Brown, Steve. *A Scandalous Freedom*. New York: Howard, 2009.

Calvin, John. *Commentary on James*. Translated by John Pringle. Kindle ed. Waikato, New Zealand: Titus, 2013.

———. *Institutes of the Christian Religion*. 2 vols. Translated by Ford Lewis Battles. Louisville: Westminster, 1960.

Carson, D. A. *Jesus' Sermon on the Mount and His Confrontation with the World: An Exposition of Matthew 5–10*. Bloomington, MN: Baker, 2004.

Chester, Andrew, and Ralph P. Martin. *The Theology of the Letters of James, Peter, and Jude*. Cambridge: Cambridge University Press, 1994.

Claiborne, Shane. *The Irresistible Revolution: Living as an Ordinary Radical*. Grand Rapids: Zondervan, 2008.

Clancy, Tomas. *Republic of Malawi*. Countries of the World. Charleston, SC: CreateSpace, 2012.

Clifford, Richard J. *The Wisdom Literature*. Interpreting Biblical Texts. Nashville: Abingdon, 1998.

Cohen, Shaye J. D. *From the Maccabees to the Mishnah*. Louisville: Westminster, 2006.

Durantine, Peter. "Penn State Aide Tells Court What He Saw." *New York Times*, NY ed., December 17, 2011, D1.

Elliott, Karen M. *Women in Ministry and the Writings of Paul*. Winona, MN: Anselm Academic, 2010.

Eusebius. *Eusebius: The Church History*. Translated by Paul L. Maier. Grand Rapids: Kregel Academic & Professional, 2007.

Gardner, Leonard. *The Work of the Potter's Hands*. Charleston, SC: BookSurge, 2007.

Glancy, Jennifer A. *Slavery in Early Christianity*. Minneapolis: Fortress, 2006.

Goetz, Dave L. *Death by Suburb: How to Keep the Suburbs from Killing Your Soul*. San Francisco: HarperOne, 2006.

Guthrie, Nancy. *Hearing Jesus Speak into Your Sorrow*. Carol Stream, IL: Tyndale, 2009.

Hartin, Patrick J. *A Spirituality of Perfection: Faith in Action in the Letter of James*. Collegeville: Liturgical, 1999.

Hsu, Albert Y. *The Suburban Christian: Finding Spiritual Vitality in the Land of Plenty*. Downers Grove: InterVarsity, 2006.

Jordan, Clarence L. *Practical Religion; or, The Sermon on the Mount and the Epistle of James*. Koinonia "Cotton Patch" Version. Americus, GA: Koinonia, 1964.

Kroesbergen, Hermen. *In Search of Health and Wealth: The Prosperity Gospel in African, Reformed Perspective*. Eugene, OR: Wipf & Stock, 2014.

Kuo, Lilly. "Kansas House Speaker Apologizes for Email." *Reuters*, January 19, 2012. http://www.reuters.com/article/2012/01/20/us-usa-campaign-obama-psalm-idUSTRE80J0A720120120.

Ladd, George Eldon. *The Gospel of the Kingdom: Scriptural Studies in the Kingdom of God*. Grand Rapids: Eerdmans, 1959.

Laws, Sophie. *The Epistle of James*. Black's New Testament Commentary. Ada, MI: Baker, 1993.

Longman, Tremper, and David E. Garland, eds. *Daniel—Malachi*. Rev. ed. Expositor's Bible Commentary 8. Grand Rapids: Zondervan, 2008.

Love-Fordham, April L. "Using Biblical Storytelling in Pastoral Care to Initiate Spiritual Transformation." DMin diss., Gordon-Conwell Theological Seminary, 2011.

Luther, Martin. "Against the Robbing and Murdering Hordes of Peasants." In *Martin Luther*, edited by E. G. Rupp and Benjamin Drewery, 121–25. London: Arnold, 1970.

———. *On the Jews and Their Lies*. Translated by Martin H. Bertram. Sebeka, MN: Coleman Rydie, 2008.

Mason, Steve. *Josephus, Judea, and Christian Origins*. Peabody, MA: Hendrickson, 2009.

Maynard-Reid, Perdrito U. *James: True Religion in Suffering*. Abundant Life Bible Amplifier. Nampa, ID: Pacific, 1996.

———. *Poverty and Wealth in James*. Eugene, OR: Wipf & Stock, 2004.

McCartney, Dan G. *James*. Baker Exegetical Commentary. Grand Rapids: Baker Academic, 2009.

McConville, J. Gordon, and Stephen N. Williams. *Joshua*. Two Horizons Old Testament Commentary. Grand Rapids: Eerdmans, 2010.

McGee, J. Vernon. *First Corinthians—Revelation*. Thru the Bible with J. Vernon McGee 5. Nashville: Nelson, 1983.

Merrill, Ivy. *Decency and Nobility: The Life of Jonathan Myrick Daniels*. Bloomington, IN: AuthorHouse, 2005.

Millard, Alan R. *Reading and Writing in the Time of Jesus*. New York: New York University Press, 2000.

Moo, Douglas J. *James*. Tyndale New Testament Commentaries 16. Downers Grove: InterVarsity, 1985.

Motyer, J. Alec. *The Message of James*. The Bible Speaks Today. Downers Grove: InterVarsity, 1985.

Murphy, Frederick J. *Early Judaism: The Exile to the Time of Jesus*. Ada, MI: Baker Academic, 2006.

Nasaw, David. *Andrew Carnegie*. New York: Penguin, 2007.

Nystrom, David P. *James*. NIV Application Commentary. Grand Rapids: Zondervan, 1997.

Palmer, Earl F. *The Book That James Wrote*. Grand Rapids: Eerdmans, 1997.

Perkins, Pheme. *First and Second Peter, James, and Jude*. Interpretation. Louisville: John Knox, 1995.

Piburn, Sidney. *The Dalai Lama: Policy of Kindness*. Boston: Snow Lion, 1990.

Plantinga, Cornelius. *Not the Way It's Supposed to Be: A Breviary of Sin*. Grand Rapids: Eerdmans, 1995.

Rice, Howard L. *Reformed Spirituality: An Introduction for Believers*. Louisville: Westminster, 1991.

Rives, Stanford. *Did Calvin Murder Servetus?* Charleston, SC: BookSurge, 2008.

Samson, Will, and Lisa Samson. *Justice in the Burbs: Being the Hands of Jesus Wherever You Live*. Ada, MI: Baker, 2007.

Scharfstein, Sol. *Torah and Commentary: The Five Books of Moses; Translation, Rabbinic and Contemporary Commentary*. Brooklyn, NY: KTAV, 2008.

Selvaggio, Anthony. "Hearing the Voice of Jesus in the Epistle of James." *Reformation 21*, June 2009. http://www.reformation21.org/articles/hearing-the-voice-of-jesus-in-the-epistle-of-james.php.

Serveto, Michael. *The Two Treatises of Servetus on the Trinity: On the Errors of the Trinity*. Harvard Theological Studies 16. Eugene, OR: Wipf & Stock, 2013.

Smith, Malcolm. *Indwelling Spirit*. Lecture series. 4 CDs. New Carlisle, OH: Unconditional Love International, 2009.

———. *Power of the Blood Covenant: Uncover the Secret Strength of God's Eternal Oath*. Tulsa: Harrison, 2010.

———. *Practical Faith (James)*. Lecture series. 6 CDs. Bandera, TX: Unconditional Love International, no date.

Smith-Christopher, Daniel L. *Biblical Theology of Exile*. Overtures to Biblical Theology. Kitchener, Ontario: Augsburg, 2002.

Stevenson, John. *The Epistle of James: A Faith That Works*. Charleston: Createspace, 2010.

Sudeshna, Ghosh B., and Elvira Morella. *Africa's Water and Sanitation Infrastructure*. Directions in Development. Washington, DC: World Bank, 2011.

Walton, John H. *Job*. NIV Application Commentary. Grand Rapids: Zondervan, 2012.

Webster, Tanner, et al. *The Oxford Handbook of Systematic Theology*. Oxford Handbooks in Religion and Theology. Oxford: Oxford University Press, 2009.

Winston, David. *The Wisdom of Solomon: A New Translation with Introduction and Commentary*. Anchor Bible 43. New York: Doubleday, 1979.

Wright, Tom. *Luke for Everyone*. New Testament for Everyone. London: SPCK, 2001.

———. *Mark for Everyone*. New Testament for Everyone. London: SPCK, 2004.

Zahnd, Brian. *Radical Forgiveness: God's Call to Unconditional Love*. Lake Mary, FL: Passio, 2013.